Lecture Notes in Compu 9

Edited by G. Goos, J. Hartmanis a

Springer
Berlin
Heidelberg
New York
Barcelona
Budapest
Hong Kong
London
Milan
Paris
Santa Clara
Singapore
Tokyo

Kurt Rothermel
Radu Popescu-Zeletin (Eds.)

Mobile Agents

First International Workshop, MA '97
Berlin, Germany, April 7-8, 1997
Proceedings

Springer

Series Editors

Gerhard Goos, Karlsruhe University, Germany

Juris Hartmanis, Cornell University, NY, USA

Jan van Leeuwen, Utrecht University, The Netherlands

Volume Editors

Kurt Rothermel
Institut für Parallele und Verteilte Höchstleistungsrechner (IPVR)
Breitwiesenstr. 20/22, D-70565 Stuttgart, Germany
E-mail: Kurt.Rothermel@informatik.uni-stuttgart.de

Radu Popescu-Zeletin
GMD Fokus, TU Berlin, DeTeBERKOM
Hardenbergplatz 2, D-10623 Berlin, Germany
E-mail: zeletin@fokus.gmd.de

Cataloging-in-Publication data applied for

Die Deutsche Bibliothek - CIP-Einheitsaufnahme

Mobile agents : first international workshop ; proceedings / MA '97, Berlin, Germany, April 7 - 8, 1997. Kurt Rothermel ; Radu Popescu-Zeletin (ed.). - Berlin ; Heidelberg ; New York ; Barcelona ; Budapest ; Hong Kong ; London ; Milan ; Paris ; Santa Clara ; Singapore ; Tokyo : Springer, 1997
(Lecture notes in computer science ; Vol. 1219)
ISBN 3-540-62803-7

NE: Rothermerl, Kurt [Hrsg.]; GT; MA <1, 1997, Berlin>

CR Subject Classification (1991): C.2, D.2, D.1.3, D.4.2-6

ISSN 0302-9743
ISBN 3-540-62803-7 Springer-Verlag Berlin Heidelberg New York

Typesetting: Camera-ready by author
SPIN 10549381 06/3142 – 5 4 3 2 1 0 Printed on acid-free paper

Preface

Mobile Agents offer unique opportunities for structuring and implementing distributed systems. A wide range of applications has been identified for mobile agent technonology, including electronic commerce, telecommunication services, network management, group work, and work flow management.

These proceedings contain the papers chosen for presentation at the 1st International Workshop on Mobile Agents, held in conjunction with ISADS '97 in Berlin, Germany, April 7-8, 1997. The workshop addresses various aspects of software agents, including agent models and languages, agent platforms, and applications of agent technology. The contributions primarily focus on aspects related with agent mobility — the ability of software entities to migrate from node to node in a computer network.

The Call for Papers attracted 34 submission from 12 countries. Of these submission the program committee accepted 18 papers to be presented at the workshop. Moreover, it was decided to organize a panel discussion on security in mobile agent systems. The 6 paper sessions of the workshop cover

- applications of mobile agent technology,
- system architectures and platforms,
- inter-agent communication,
- mobility issues and persistence
- control and management of mobile agent systems.

Many people have contributed to make MA'97 and these proceedings a reality. We express our thanks to all authors who submitted papers, and the members of the program committee who reviewed them on the basis of originality, relevance, presentation, and technical quality. We would also like to thank F. Hohl, S. Krause, and V. Tschammer, who did an excellent job in organizing the workshop.

April 1997 Kurt Rothermel, Radu Popescu-Zeletin

Organizations

Organized by:

Gesellschaft für Informatik (GI)

Informations und Kommunikationstechnologie Verbund e.V. (IKV)

In cooperation with:

DeTeBerkom

International Federation for Information Processing (IFIP)

GMD Fokus

Technische Universität Berlin

Universität Stuttgart

Committees

General Chair

Radu Popescu-Zeletin	DeTeBerkom, Germany

Chair

Kurt Rothermel	U. Stuttgart, Germany

Program Committee

Michel Banatre	IRISA, France
Paolo Ciancarini	U. Bologna, Italy
Stefan Covaci	GMD FOKUS, Germany
Oswald Drobnik	U. Frankfurt, Germany
Anastasius Gavras	TINA-C, USA
Günter Karjoth	IBM, Switzerland
Johannes Klein	Tandem Computers, USA
Winfried Lamersdorf	U. Hamburg, Germany
Thomas Magedanz	TU Berlin, Germany
Friedemann Mattern	TU Darmstadt, Germany
Manuel Mendes	Pont. U. Catolica, Brazil
Kinji Mori	Hitachi, Japan
Mike Rizzo	U. Malta, Malta
Otto Spaniol	RWTH Aachen, Germany
Peter Spies	TU Munich, Germany
Hugo Velthuijsen	KPN Research, Netherlands
Jan Vitek	U. Geneva, Switzerland

Organization Committee

Fritz Hohl	U. Stuttgart, Germany
Sven Krause	TU Berlin, Germany
Katja Schulz	IKV, Germany
Volker Tschammer	GMD FOKUS, Germany

Contents

An Agent-Based Approach for Quality of Service Negotiation and Management in Distributed Multimedia Systems

Luiz A. G. Oliveira*[1], Paulo C. Oliveira[2] and Eleri Cardozo[1]

[1] Faculty of Electrical and Computer Engineering
State University of Campinas
Campinas, SP - Brazil
affonso, eleri@dca.fee.unicamp.br

[2] National Center for Technological Research on Computing Applied to Agriculture - CNPTIA/EMBRAPA
Campinas, SP - Brazil
paulo@cnptia.embrapa.br

Abstract. Quality of service (QoS) is receiving strong attention due to its key role in distributed multimedia computing. QoS is not a new concept, being usually employed in the domain of computer networks to specify a set of parameters typically assigned to transport connections. As a rule, QoS is established through negotiation between service users and providers. The process of negotiation is simple if the resources are managed by a centralized entity (e.g. an operating system) or by a set of homogeneous entities such as a network protocol. Unfortunately, in distributed multimedia applications the negotiation and management of resources is a difficult task since resources are very diversified, dispersed and maintained by heterogeneous entities. To cope with diversity and distribution, an agent-based approach for QoS negotiation and management in open distributed environments is proposed in this paper.

1 Introduction

Multimedia systems are computing systems that employ several types of media such as text, graphics, audio, video and animation. A multimedia system is often a distributed system in the sense that its components are located in different processing nodes of a local or wide area network. Unfortunately, there are few experiences accumulated regarding a methodological design and implementation of distributed multimedia systems (DMS). Even the current standardization efforts being conducted in the field of distributed computing are still far from the effective incorporation of functions for multimedia processing in the proposed models and architectures. The lack of technology for developing DMS is explained by the difficulties concerning the manipulation of continuous media such as audio and video. These kind of media demand a continuous flow of information from a source to one or more sinks and impose certain timing constraints

* On leave from Federal University of Pará, Belém, Brazil

such as presentation rate, maximum delay, and synchronization level. In order to process continuous media, a DMS must implement a effective policy of resource management that dictates how resources are allocated, monitored, optimized and released. Since a DMS often runs across autonomous domains, resources management must be based on negotiation.

The issue of determining the best way to conduct negotiation and re-negotiation in DMS was not yet achieved. One possible approach is to centralize resource negotiation in a single entity - something like the Trader in ODP environments [1]. Other approaches based on brokerage [2] and client/server [3] [4] schemes were published recently. In the brokerage scheme a negotiation protocol links brokers (resource managers) located in each node of the network. A broker may act as a buyer when gathering resources or as a seller when offering available resources. In the client/server approach the application (client) interacts with a set of resource managers (servers) for resources negotiation and monitoring purposes.

The client/server and brokerage schemes need very complex interaction protocols if the following subjects are considered:

- asynchonous communication;
- global optimization in the allocation of resources;
- openness in terms of adding/removing resources;
- knowledge-based strategies for negotiation and management of resources;
- mechanisms for re-negotiation of resources.

We believe that these subjects demand more powerful schemes for negotiation and management of resources. One such scheme, agent-based system (ABS), is exploited in this paper. The paper is organized as follows. Section 2 identifies the main parameters related to QoS. Section 3 presents the phases of negotiation found in typical multimedia applications. Section 4 presents a brief introduction to agent-based systems. Section 5 contains our proposal for QoS negotiation and management. Section 6 describes the current research and development status, and section 7 addresses the concluding remarks.

2 The Concept of Quality of Service (QoS)

Intuitively, quality of service is a measure of how satisfied the user is with the media being presented. The quality of the media an application manipulates is a function of the resources available to the application. Resources include CPU and network bandwidth, storage capacity, types of peripherals and software systems. Continuous media are composed of a sequence of segments, each one consisting of the output of a sensing device (camera, microphone, etc.) sampled at a constant rate. These segments demand some processing before storage or transmission such as digitalization, filtering, compression, and so on. Segments are stored or transmitted in a predefined format. For instance, video segments (frames) consist of a grid of pixels each one encoded in a certain number of bits. For videoconferencing, 200x300 pixels of 8 bits each (256 colors) sampled at 20 frames per second and encoded according to the MPEG format is a common choice [5] [6].

In general, from the user's standpoint, QoS can be stated in terms of the following parameters (user's QoS parameters):

- resolution: how precise the digitalization process of a media segment is (a function of bits per segment, sampling rate, etc.);
- distortion: a measure of information loss per media segment due to transmission errors, lossy compression strategies, etc.;
- synchronization level: a measure of how stable is the presentation of media segments, either in the same flow (synchronization intra-media) or in different, but related media (synchronization inter-media or skew);
- interactiveness: how useful the media is for on-line cooperative work.

Usually the application works with a set of fixed QoS parameters or interacts with the user to choose them. In the latter case the user states quality in terms of subjective parameters such as "audio of CD quality", "video of poor quality", and so on.

From the system's standpoint, common QoS parameters are (system's QoS parameters):

- end-to-end delay: the elapsed time between the generation or access of a media segment and its presentation;
- delay jitter: the variation of the end-to-end delay;
- bit error rate (BER): the percentage of bits affected by transmission failures;
- package error rate (PER): the percentage of packets discarded due to transmission failures.

In general terms, end-to-end delay affects interactivity; jitter affects synchronization; and BER/PER affects distortion. Usual limits for these parameters in distributed multimedia applications are 100-250 milliseconds for end-to-end delay; 5-10 millisecond for jitter; 0.001-0.01% for PER and 0.01-0.1% for BER [5]. The lower these parameters are, the higher the quality of service is.

In order to provide QoS, an application must implement an effective policy of resource allocation and management. This paper proposes a protocol for QoS negotiation and management that relies on a combination of mobile and fixed agents. Although the protocol can not guarantee that the negotiated level of QoS is satisfied deterministically, we believe it provides a much better performance than the best-effort strategy adopted in current applications.

3 Quality of Service Negotiation and Management

QoS negotiation is the process of allocating resources in order to attend the application's demands. QoS management is the process where the allocated resources are monitored, renegotiated, accounted and released.

A typical multimedia session is divided into three phases [7]:

- Establishment: where the resources are allocated for the session;
- Management: where the resources are used and managed;
- Clearing: where the resources are released back to their managing entities.

The establishment phase is characterized by the following steps:

- QoS specification: where the user (or application) states the desired level of QoS;
- QoS mapping: where the QoS parameters stated above are mapped into system's parameters;
- resource negotiation and reservation: where the resources needed for the desired quality of service are negotiated (and reserved) with their respective resource managers;
- resource commitment: where the reserved resources are granted to the application;
- accounting: where the allocated resources are accounted for billing or statistical purposes.

The management phase is composed of the steps bellow:

- QoS monitoring: where the negotiated level of QoS is monitored;
- QoS re-negotiation: where resources are re-negotiated to cope with changes in application's needs or in the environment;
- QoS adaptation: where the negotiated QoS parameters are relaxed in order to circumvent adverse conditions such as network congestion.

Finally, the clearing phase contains one step:

- QoS termination: where the application closes a multimedia session, releasing all the resources allocated to the session.

The key point in QoS negotiation and management is how to implement these functions in such a way that the resources are optimized in a network-wide fashion. Next section introduces agent-based systems, a problem solving model that we claim may support effectively QoS negotiation and management in terms of flexibility, openness and resources optimization.

4 Agent-based Systems

The wide deployment of distributed systems has led to a strong demand for development paradigms which can meet requirements such as:

- rapid development and maintenance;
- platform independence: distributed systems must run on different hardware and operating system platforms; they must be developed once and deployed in the desired platforms transparently;

- interoperability: systems must adopt open standards in order to be able to easily interact with existing peers;
- ease of use: an increasing number of users, with different degrees of expertise, are using distributed systems and demand user friendly and personalizable interfaces;
- flexibility: system's components must assume a behavior compatible with the remaining components, with the environment, and with the user;
- efficiency: systems must use efficiently the available and probably scarce computer and network resources
- support to mobile computing: depending on the amount of information a distributed system handles, bringing code to where the information is located may be attractive.

Since the late 1980s, the client/server model has been widely adopted for distributed systems development. In that model, systems are partitioned into components (clients and servers) that assume fixed roles. This fixed roles assigned to the application's components, in addition to the synchronous nature of client/server communication (usually based on RPC), restricts the complexity of interaction protocols such as those supporting QoS negotiation and management in DMS.

The agent-based approach constitutes an alternative to distributed systems development, meeting the requirements mentioned earlier in a more comprehensive manner than the client/server model. Although the terms *agent* and *agent-based system* (ABS) are widely used by researchers in different areas such as distributed systems, software engineering and artificial intelligence, there is no consensus about their definition. In this paper, agents are considered as autonomous programs that act on behalf of their owners - users or other programs. In order to accomplish tasks assigned by their owners, agents may communicate as peers and cooperate to achieve common goals. The definition adopted focuses on the following fundamental characteristics of agenthood:

- delegation: users or other programs can delegate tasks to an agent and vest it with authority to act on their behalf;
- autonomy: an agent can make its own decisions, based on its owner's statement of goals, preferences and policies;
- communication: the ability agents have to interact with their peers, with the environment that hosts them, and with their owners;
- cooperation: agents can act in a collaborative manner in order to accomplish common goals (to do so they must be able to communicate employing high level semantics);
- equity: agents support the peer to peer model for distributed computing [8];
- flexibility: agents do not assume fixed roles; they may act like clients, servers, observers, etc., depending on their current needs.

Agent-based systems must support the fundamental characteristics of agenthood. Although not considered as fundamental, the characteristics described below are strongly related to agents:

- intelligence: the ability agents have to reason and learn from the interactions with other agents, their owners and the environment;
- mobility: agents can move across heterogeneous computer networks, aiming to progressively accomplish tasks that were assigned to them.

5 An Agent-based Approach for QoS Negotiation and Management

This section presents an architecture for QoS negotiation and management in distributed multimedia systems. The proposed architecture is based on an agency placed at each network node. The agency is a place where fixed agents exist and mobile agents are received, processed and dispatched to the next node. Agents are instantiated (created) by issuing requests to a Factory. The basic structure for inter-agent communication is a contract. A contract is composed of a structural part and a parametric part. The structural part is static and consists of a set of descriptors such as kind of resources (flows, buffers, etc.), negotiation constraints (acceptable margins, time-outs, etc.) and the targeted QoS. The parametric part is dynamic and shows the current values for the descriptors found in the structural part. Agents interact by processing contracts and contracts travel from agency to agency inside mobile agents. Figure 1 shows an agency for QoS negotiation and management.

Ten classes of agents are defined in the proposed architecture. They are presented as follows.

5.1 Fixed Agents

- *The Application's Agent* acts in behalf of an application being also a point of entry for the agency. It receives requests from the application, translates these requests into communication actions addressed to other agents and waits for results which are sent back to the application.
- *The QoS Mapper Agent* is responsible to map subjective user's QoS parameters into system's (quantified) QoS parameters. The mapping can be based on simple translation techniques such as tables, or sophisticated, knowledge-based schemes such those based on expert systems, fuzzy systems or neural nets.
- *The Resource Estimator Agent* has the mission of mapping between the system's QoS parameters and local resources. Like the QoS Mapper, this agent can employ a simple or a sophisticated mapping scheme.
- *The Resource Manager Agent* is responsible for the management of resources at its node. This agent interacts with the operating system and network infrastructure for resource reservation, allocation, de-allocation and reallocation.
- *The Local Negotiator Agent* is responsible for negotiating the part of the contract that involves local resources. This agent receives the resources needed

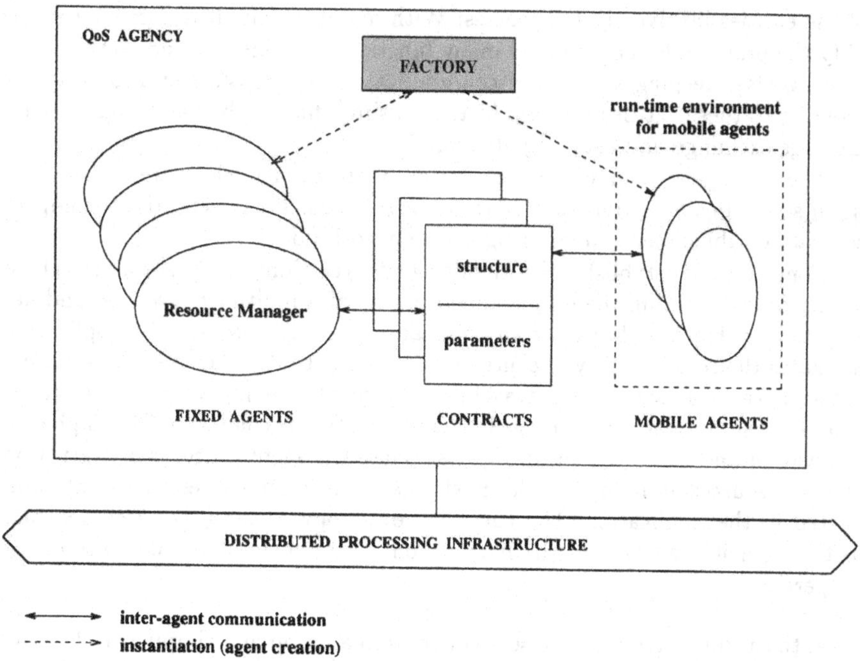

Fig. 1. Components of the QoS agency

from the Resource Estimator agent and interacts with the Resource Manager agent for resource reservation and allocation.
- *The QoS Monitor Agent* checks permanently if the QoS parameters stated in a contract are within their bounds. It interacts with the low-level resource management (operating system, network, etc.) in order to measure the quality of the flows received or generated by the application.
- *The QoS Adaptor Agent* is activated when some parameter in a contract goes out of bounds. If the parameter is managed locally it interacts with the Resource Manager in order to try to correct the problem locally. Otherwise, if the parameter relates to a remote resource this agent instructs the Application's Agent to start a contract re-negotiation activity. QoS Adaptors are knowledge-intensive programs better implemented with AI techniques.

Except for the Resource Manager, the agents listed above are instantiated when a session starts and last until the end of the session.

5.2 Mobile Agents

The chief motivation for employing mobile agents in QoS negotiation and management is protocol simplification. Achieving an efficient protocol for QoS negotiation and management is difficult because of the number, nature and complexity of the entities involved in the process. With mobile agents it is possible to simplify the protocol by partitioning many functionalities into autonomous entities (the agents), keeping simple the communication among such entities. Adding mobility to these entities is a step further in simplification by balancing between message exchange and code dispatching.

The QoS agency defines three classes of mobile agents, which are instantiated when some specific activities need to be carried out. These activities encompass contract establishment, monitoring and re-negotiation.

Contracts are established by mobile agents, the Contract Negotiators. These agents operate during the establishment phase of a multimedia session and negotiate a contract on behalf of an application - in other words, the application delegates the responsibility of contract negotiation to these agents. Contract negotiators carry a contract and travel from agency to agency where the resources stated in the contract are managed. The negotiation is conducted in two phases: reservation and commitment. In the first phase the agent proceeds a reservation of the resources it needs. In the next phase the reserved resources are committed to the application. The agent leaves a copy of the negotiated contract in the agencies involved in the negotiation. This scheme has some interesting properties:

- if the agent is not able to reserve or commit a resource it simply travels again releasing all the resources already reserved or committed;
- in the commitment phase the agent optimizes the resources (for example, if it has reserved resources for sampling 10 frames/sec at the source side but was able to reserve resources for displaying only 5 frames/sec at the sink side, it commits resources for 5 frames/sec on both sides);
- the scheme can be made deadlock-free by incorporating a deadlock avoidance algorithm in the resource managers or by imposing time-outs for committing the already reserved resources.

Contract Negotiators are instantiated when a multimedia session starts and are destroyed after a contract has being negotiated.

Contract monitoring is performed by mobile agents, the Contract Monitors. These agents are instantiated after the Contract Negotiator establishes a contract and are kept activated during all the management phase of a multimedia session. Contract Monitors travel from time to time in order to check if the parameters stated in the contract are being honored. In order to accomplish this task, an agent of this class travels to the agencies where the contract has acquired resources and inspects the parameters stated in the contract. The contract monitor interacts with the local QoS Monitors in order to get a picture of the quality of the flows using the resources. It also informs the agency the quality of the same flows measured at other nodes. When this agent comes back, a global picture of the parameters in the contract is evaluated, and the results of this evaluation are presented to the user (e.g. via asynchronous notification) or employed in decision-making. In the case of a persistent degradation of the parameters, two actions can be taken:

- the contract is re-negotiated in order to optimize the resources globally;
- the contract is terminated.

Contract re-negotiation is the process of changing the contract's components (structure and parameters). Typical situations where contract re-negotiation is necessary include:

- the application decides to change the QoS for a flow it manipulates;
- new resources must be added or removed to the contract (for instance, when participants join or leave a videoconference);
- a persistent degradation of QoS is detected during contract monitoring.

In the proposed architecture, contract re-negotiation is conducted by mobile agents, the Contract Re-negotiators. These agents travel to the agencies where resources must be re-negotiated. The agent is autonomous since it carries all the information it needs for contract re-negotiation. Contract termination is a special case of re-negotiation and is performed by this class of agents.

6 Current Research and Development Status

In the current research and development stage, the validation of the protocol for QoS negotiation and management has been concluded by formally specifying it in SDL [9] (Specification and Description Language). A state machine for each agent was defined in this language as well as the communication actions (signals in SDL) exchanged by each agent. For this task, a CASE tool from Verilog Inc., GEODE, was employed. GEODE can generate 100% of the code conforming with the specification. This feature may be useful for generating the fixed agents in the first prototype. Once the protocol is formally specified and validated through simulation, we will proceed with the implementation of our QoS agency.

The agency is shown in Fig. 2. An Object Request Broker (ORB) is employed for inter-agent communication in the agency. The ORB is a component of the Common Object Request Broker Architecture (CORBA) [10], the interoperability solution proposed by the Object Management Group (OMG). Orbix version 2.0.1 from Iona Technologies Inc. was adopted as a CORBA-compliant distributed processing tool.

The fixed agents are implemented as CORBA servers. A special server is implemented for contract storage and retrieving (the Contract Server). The Factory is an object attached to the ORB responsible for the instantiation of both fixed and mobile agents at run-time. The Factory receives requests through the ORB and interacts with the mobile agents run-time support (for instantiating mobile agents) or with the ORB (for instantiating fixed agents from the CORBA's Implementation Repository).

A run-time infrastructure to receive and dispatch mobile agents must have access to the broker since mobile agents, while executing, interact with the fixed agents through the ORB.

For mobile agents we are experimenting with three agent-based frameworks:

- *Tabriz 1.0* from General Magic, based on the Telescript [11] programming language. Tabriz is available for the following Unix platforms: HP UX, Solaris and SGI Irix.
- *Agent Tcl* alpha release 1.1 and *Agent Tk* [12] from Dartmouth College. These are extended versions of Tcl and Tk for supporting mobile agents, which are available for the following Unix platforms: Linux, Free BSD, IBM AIX, SGI Irix, DEC OSF/1, SunOs and Solaris.
- *Aglets Workbench* [13] alpha 4, from IBM's Tokyo Research Laboratory, is a visual environment for building mobile agent-based applications in Java. Aglets Workbench can be executed on Windows NT/95 and Solaris platforms.

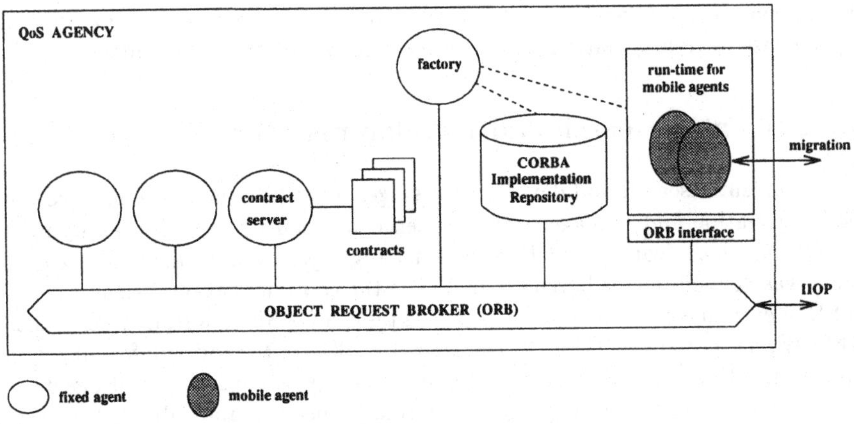

Fig. 2. QoS agency architecture

An important issue in this context is how these agent-based frameworks interact with the ORB. Tabriz allows C calls, thus a ORB interface may be easily implemented. Tcl-Dii [14] is a package for accessing Orbix through the Dynamic Invocation Interface which can be attached to Agent Tcl. Finally, since Aglets Workbench is based on Java, supported applications can use Iona's Orbix Web [15], a product that gives Java applets access to the broker.

7 Concluding Remarks

In this paper we proposed an architecture for QoS negotiation and monitoring. We believe that the proposed scheme is powerful when compared with more restricting approaches like trading and brokerage. We are convinced that many new requirements must be brought into QoS and our proposal which relies on agent-based systems is able to fulfill these requirements. Concerning the development status, we have finished the validation of the protocol for QoS negotiation and management through SDL. The implementation of the fixed agents was started and we are experimenting with the main frameworks for mobile agents. Since it is based on an open architecture, the implementation will serve as a testbed for QoS experiments. For example, a QoS Mapper agent-based on fuzzy logic can be compared with a mapper based on expert systems or neural nets.

Acknowledgments

This research is being supported by the following Brazilian funding agencies: FAPESP (grant 92/3507-0); CAPES and CNPq (grant 300723/93-8).

References

1. International Telecommunication Union (ITU), International Standard Organization (ISO): Reference Model of Open Distributed Processing (ODP) - Part 3: Prescriptive Model. Int. Standard 10746-3, ITU-T Recommendation X.903, Geneva, 1995.
2. K. Nahrstedt and J. Smith: The QoS Broker, IEEE Multimedia, Spring 1995, pp. 53-67.
3. A. Campbell, G. Coulson, and D. Hutchim: A Multimedia Enhanced Transport Service in a Quality of Service Architecture, Workshop on Network and Operating System Support for Audio and Video'93, Lancaster, England, Nov. 1993.
4. B. Kerhervé et al.: On Distributed Multimedia Presentational Applications: Functional and Computational Architecture and QoS Negotiation, Proc. 4th Int. Workshop on Protocols for High-Speed Networks, Chapman & Hall, London, 1994, pp. 1-17.
5. A. Vogel et al.: Distributed Multimedia and QoS: A Survey, IEEE Multimedia, Summer 1995, pp. 10-18.
6. B. Furht: Multimedia Systems: An Overview, IEEE Multimedia, Spring 1994, pp. 47-59.
7. A. Hafid and G. Bochann: An Approach to Quality of Service Management for Distributed Multimedia Applications, International Conference on Open Distributed Processing (ICODP95), Australia, Feb. 1995, pp. 319-340.
8. Coen, M. D.: SodaBot: A Software Agent Environment and Construction System, Proceedings of the CIKM Workshop on Inteligent Information Agents, CIKM 94, Gaithesburg, Maryland, 1994.
9. Belina, F. et al.: SDL with Applications from Protocol Specification, Prentice Hall International Ltd., 1991.
10. Object Management Group: Common Object Request Broker Architecture 2.0 Specification, OMG Technical Document PTC/96-03-04.
11. General Magic: Telescript Technology: Mobile Agents, WWW URL:http://www.genmagic.com/Telescript/Whitepapers/wp4/whitepaper-4.html.
12. Gray, R. S.: Agent Tcl: A Transportable Agent System, Proceedings of the CIKM Workshop on Intelligent Information Agents, CIKM 95, Baltimore, Maryland , 1995.

13. IBM Corporation - Tokyo Research Laboratory: Programming Mobile Agents in Java - A White Paper, WWW URL: http://www.trl.ibm.co.jp/aglets/.
14. G. Almasi et alli: TclDii: A TCL Interface to the Orbix Dynamic Invocation Interface, WWW URL: http://webstar.cerc.wvu.edu/dice/iss/TclDii/TclDii.html.
15. Iona Technologies Ltd.: OrbixWeb for Java. WWW URL: http://www.iona.com/Orbix/OrbixWeb/index.html.

Exploiting Code Mobility in Decentralized and Flexible Network Management

Mario Baldi, Silvano Gai, and Gian Pietro Picco

Dip. Automatica e Informatica, Politecnico di Torino
C.so Duca degli Abruzzi 24, 10129 Torino, Italy
[mbaldi | silvano | picco]@polito.it

Abstract. Network management is gaining increasing importance due to the pervasiveness of computer networks. Nevertheless, mainstream approaches to network management are presently limited by centralized management strategies and poor flexibility—a consequence of their rigid client-server architecture. In this paper we analyze how to overcome these problems by new design paradigms and technologies encompassing the capability to relocate dynamically the components of a distributed application. We evaluate the opportunities offered by this approach and provide feasibility considerations, also discussing a few interim architectural solutions adopted in our on-going implementation work.
Keywords: code mobility, mobile agents, network management.

1 Introduction

Computer networks are taking a pivotal role in present and future information systems. The increasing importance of computer networks has given rise to a high demand for adequate *network management*. The two main approaches proposed in the literature come from the Internet Engineering Task Force (IETF) and the International Organization for Standardization (ISO) and are characterized by centralization and a low degree of flexibility and reconfigurability. These problems are a consequence of the client-server (CS) paradigm adopted in the management architecture. *Management agents* co-located with network devices act like servers that communicate on request device data to a management station, where all the management computation actually takes place. This choice was aimed at keeping the agents as simple as possible, due to limitations on the resources available in the devices hosting them—a constraint being relaxed by technological achievements. Yet, it has been demonstrated [20] that this solution lacks scalability and generates congestion in the network area around the management station, thus heavily limiting the effectiveness of the approach.

The increased importance of computer networks has also stimulated research on large scale distributed systems. In this context, new approaches to application design and implementation have been developed that embody the notion of *code mobility*, i.e., the capability of moving dynamically the components of a distributed application among the nodes of a computer network [16]. The key idea behind code mobility is to provide a complementary solution (if not an alternative) to the traditional CS structure of distributed applications, thus enabling a better use of bandwidth resources and a higher degree of flexibility and reconfigurability. This idea benefits from the availability of new programming languages providing direct support for some form of code mobility. Nevertheless, the promises of this new research area are still to be verified by experimental evidence from the application in real world domains.

The synergy between research on network management and on code mobility is promising. Network management is looking for ways to overcome CS limitations and code mobility now provides technologies and design paradigms for this goal. On the other hand, network management provides a good test-bed for the mobile code approach. The goal of this work is to examine challenges and opportunities arising from the synergy of these two fields, investigating if and how code mobility can help in solving the problems of network management approaches. Application of code mobility to network management is not new [12,6], yet recent developments in code mobility [1,4] contributed ideas that subsume older approaches. In this paper, we propose neither a new full-fledged approach to network management nor precise modifications to current approaches. Our analysis and discussion is meant to provide suggestions for such activities and guidance for our on-going work on the implementation and assessment of a management application exploiting code mobility.

The paper is structured as follows. A brief overview on network management approaches is provided in Sect. 2, while Sect. 3 presents technologies and design paradigms based on code mobility. The core of the paper is Sect. 4, where benefits and drawbacks stemming from the application of code mobility to network management are evaluated together with some architectural solutions oriented to implementation. Finally, future directions for this work are discussed in Sect. 5.

2 Network Management Approaches

In this section, we present an overview of the approaches to network management found in literature, discussing how they do (or do not) provide support for decentralization and flexibility.

Mainstream Approaches The approach more widely applied comes from the IETF and is based on the *Simple Network Management Protocol* (SNMP) [2,3]. Of great relevance is also the one proposed by ISO for application within OSI networks, which is based on the *Common Management Information Protocol* (CMIP) [13]. The two approaches are very similar in the architecture they adopt though they differ slightly in the way they operate [10]. Both assume the presence of a *management station* (operated by the network manager) that interacts with *agents* running on network nodes, e.g., bridges, routers, and workstations. Agents are computational entities whose purpose is to provide a standardized interface for accessing information about the network device on which they reside. Each agent stores information in a local information base, named *management information base* (MIB) in the IETF approach, and *management information* *tree* (MIT) *database* in the ISO approach. The management station interacts with agents through a *management protocol* that specifies the packet format for a set of basic operations. Messages containing data and operation codes are transmitted using transport layer services.

Both SNMP and CMIP adopt a CS paradigm. The management station acts as a client that provides a user interface to the network manager and interacts with agents. Agents act as servers that manage remote access to their local information base. The management station fetches from agents small chunks of information (single data items or, in SNMPv2, a bulk of them), processes them, and requests further information or sends some data to agents by using very low-level commands. This fine grained CS interaction is called *micro management* and leads to the generation of high traffic and overload for the management station, that performs all the actual computation.

Drawbacks of Centralization in Network Management The IETF and ISO approaches are characterized by high centralization, since their architecture puts almost all the computational burden on the management station. Centralization has proven to seriously limit the scalability of network management [20]. As the dimension of the network grows, the management station has to communicate with a larger number of devices, and to store and process an ever increasing amount of data. This leads to the need for high cost hardware dedicated to the management station, to poor performance, or even to the impossibility to cope with the dimension of the network. In some cases, a separated network is employed to carry management data, but in most cases *in band management* is employed, that is, the very network that is being managed is used to carry management information. Consequently, the area of the network around the management station experiences heavy traffic due to the combination of messages sent around by the management station and those containing data from the devices. The worst shortcomings of the centralized in band approach show up during periods of heavy congestion, when management intervention is particularly important. In fact, during these periods: *i)* the management station increases its interactions with the devices and possibly downloads configuration changes, thus increasing congestion, *ii)* access to devices in the congested area becomes difficult and slow (sometimes even impossible), and *iii)* congestion, as an abnormal status, is likely to trigger notifications to the management station which worsen congestion. Similar problems affected routing table computation some years ago when it was centralized. A Routing Control Center (RCC) gathered information on network topology, calculated the routing table for each router in the network, and downloaded it into the proper device. The heavy traffic load in the area around the RCC and the difficulty of managing network areas far from the RCC led to the development of distributed routing, which is still being applied successfully. Analogously, in order to cope with problems that arise from centralization, the network management functionality must be decentralized, i.e., the complex diagnosing and information gathering activities must be moved from the management station station into the network. Both IETF and ISO have taken some steps in this direction by introducing some primitive form of decentralization in

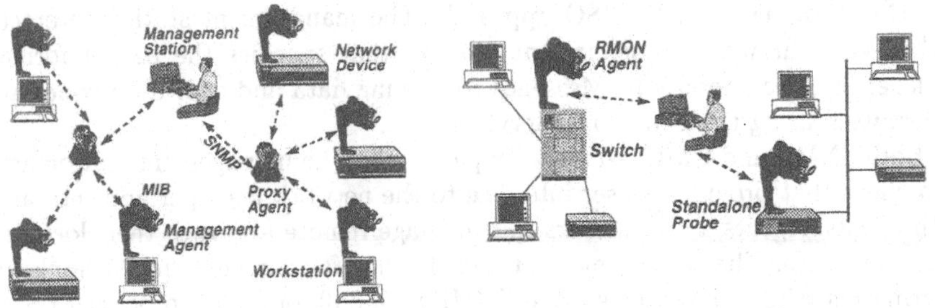

(a) SNMPv2 proxy agents. (b) RMON probes.

Fig. 1. Decentralization features in the IETF approach.

their approaches, as it will be described in the following section. In turn, the idea of decentralizing management functionality has been followed by the approach called management by delegation, that will be described later and will be taken even further by our solutions exploiting mobile code.

Decentralization Features Event notification is a first step in decentralization and aims at relieving the management station from some of its processing burden. SNMP agents are designed to notify upon the occurrence of a few significant events by issuing *traps*, i.e., messages sent without an explicit request from the management station. Since the IETF approach aims at keeping agents as simple as possible, they can notify only upon events that can be identified with a light computation. Typical examples are changes in the status of a link (from down to up, or vice-versa) or a device that has been reset. In turn, the ISO approach encompasses more complex agents, able to perform more processing on the data collected, thus increasing the number of significant situations (*events* or *alarms* in the OSI jargon) possibly dependent on several parameters that can be recognized and notified. Anyway, in both the approaches the agent is responsible only for the notification of an event and has no means of recovering from it. In other words, all the "management knowledge" resides on the management station.

According to the ISO approach, the management station can invoke actions on the objects stored in the MIT database, which is object-oriented. Execution of these actions, which can be fairly complex, reduces both the processing load on the management station and the management traffic. The IETF approach does not provide an explicit remote action invocation mechanism. Nevertheless, it can be implemented by forcing the agent to execute actions as a side effect of a change, operated by the management station, in predefined data items in the MIB. In other words, changes in the information base trigger actions performed remotely by the agent. SNMPv2 takes a step further towards decentralization by defining the *proxy agent* concept, i.e., a network management agent that acts as both a client and a server (Fig. 1a). On one side, a proxy agent sends commands to other agents and handles their responses; on the other side, it answers to commands received by a management station.

The IETF has proposed another approach, known as *Remote MONitoring* (RMON) [18], that introduces a higher degree of decentralization. RMON assumes the availability of network monitoring devices called *monitors* or *probes*. By monitoring packet traffic and analyzing the headers, probes provide information about links, connections among stations, traffic patterns, and status of network nodes. Hence, RMON can be regarded as a *traffic-oriented* approach because the status of the network is determined by direct inspection of the packets flowing in it, rather than inspection of the status of each device, like in the *device-oriented* approaches reviewed before. As shown in Fig. 1b, probe implementations can be stand alone devices dedicated to link monitoring or can be embedded into network devices. SNMP is used for communication between the management station(s) and the agent running on each probe. Some of the processing that in traditional approaches is performed by the powerful hardware of the management station, in RMON is performed by the agents on the probes *locally* and *independently* of the management station. A probe can detect failures, misbehaviors, and identify complex relevant events even when not in contact with the management station, which is likely to happen when the network is overloaded or in critical conditions—i.e., when network management is vital. The concept of *alarm* increases decentralization: the agent on the probe is configured to take periodic statistical samples of relevant parameters and, whenever a predefined threshold is crossed by any of them, to notify the management station. In addition, since the agent on the probe can perform semantic compression of data by pre-processing the information collected before sending it to the management station.

Management by Delegation Management by delegation [6] (MbD) represents a clear effort towards decentralization and increased flexibility of management functionality. The management architecture still includes a management protocol and agents, yet an *elastic process run-time support* is assumed on each device. Instead of exchanging bare CS messages, the management station can specify a task by packing into a program a set of commands to agents and sending it to the devices involved, thus *delegating* to them the actual execution of the task. Such execution is completely asynchronous, enabling the management station to perform other tasks in the meantime and introducing a higher degree of parallelism in the management architecture. In MbD, a portion of the functionality of the management station is actually decentralized and put directly onto the devices. Moreover, since the code fragments (which the authors claim can be written in any language) are not statically bound to devices, they can be changed and re-sent by the management station at any time. This enables more flexibility, because the management station can customize and enhance *dynamically* the services provided by the agents on the devices.

MbD can be considered a precursor of the ideas discussed here. Nevertheless, the paradigms described later cover different and broader aspects of mobility and can include MbD as a special case. Furthermore, they can be implemented by leveraging off of a number of languages providing abstraction expressly conceived for code mobility.

3 An Overview of Research on Code Mobility

Interest in code mobility has been raised mainly by a new family of programming languages, usually referred to as *mobile code languages* (MCLs), that recently mushroomed out on the Internet, coming both from industry and academia. The idea behind these languages is to overcome the limitations of CS using new paradigms embodying a notion of code mobility. Presently, CS is used as a design paradigm for distributed applications in a myriad of application domains. In this paradigm, client and server are computational entities usually located on different hosts. Clients can access resources located on the server host by invoking remotely (e.g., through message passing or remote procedure call) services that comply with the interfaces provided by the server. The code describing how to perform the services (on the server) and how to request remote services (on the client) is bound statically to the host where it will be executed. Experience with the CS paradigm in large scale distributed systems has shown that enhancements are needed at least for the following concerns:

Server flexibility In CS applications, the set of services offered by the server is fixed, defined *a priori* by the application designer, and accessible through interfaces *defined statically*. The services provided or the particular interface may not be suitable for different unforeseen user needs. In addition, evolution of the application usually involves high-cost activities and may limit availability. For instance, in the network management approaches described so far, if the protocol, the information base structure, or the functionality of the agent are changed, the agent have to be extended and rebuilt. In other words, there is no way to dynamically extend the capabilities of the server side, in terms of code describing its actual behavior.

Bandwidth use Particular tasks involving continuous and intensive CS interaction through the network may result in bandwidth waste. For instance, monitoring stock information maintained by a server may require continuous polling by the client. As we described before, this is a major problem of micro management in SNMP where the management station polls continuously the agent, thus wasting bandwidth and, even worse, increasing network overloading.

Mobile code paradigms do not bind statically the code performing services to one or more hosts, rather they allow *migration* of code describing a service (and possibly the associated state of execution) to a different host, enabling the design of distributed *mobile code applications* (MCAs). At least three design paradigms are conceivable [1] to support this idea, namely:

Code on Demand (COD) The code that describes the behavior of a component of an MCA can change over time. A component running on a given host can download and link on-the-fly the code to perform a given task from a different (remote) component that acts as a "code server" (Fig. 2a). Hence, in a COD paradigm, the client owns the resources needed to perform a service, but lacks part of the code needed to perform it.

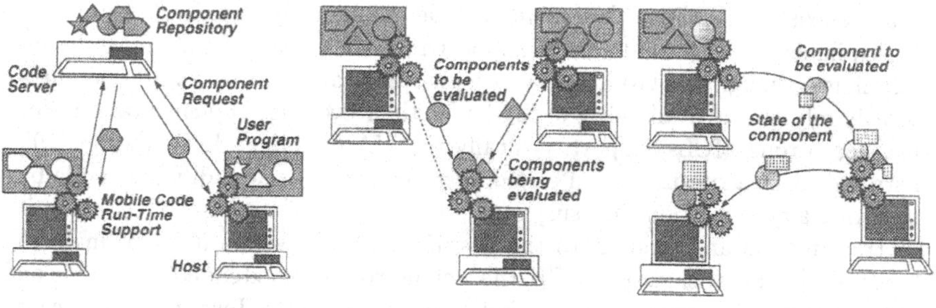

(a) Code on Demand. (b) Remote Evaluation. (c) Mobile Agent.

Fig. 2. Mobile code design paradigms.

Remote Evaluation (REV) In this paradigm, inspired by the pioneering work described in [8], any component of an MCA can invoke services provided by other components distributed among the hosts, like in a CS paradigm. The clients, in addition to the name of the service requested and the input parameters, send also the code describing the service to be executed. Upon execution on the server, this code will be allowed to access resources co-located with it (Fig. 2b). Hence, the clients own the code needed to perform a service, while the servers own the resources and offer a unique service constituted by the execution of client code.

Mobile Agent (MA) The term "agent" has presently many different meanings according to the research domains where it is used. In the scope of this work, a mobile agent is basically an *execution unit* (EU), like a UNIX process or a thread in a multi-threaded environment, that, while in execution at a given network node, is able to *migrate autonomously* to a different node and there resume execution seamlessly, as depicted in Fig. 2c. Hence, the agents in a MA paradigm own the code to perform a service, but do not own the resources needed to accomplish it. They are allowed to migrate their whole virtual machine on a different host (at least from a conceptual point of view), where the needed resources are located.

The paradigms above have been derived from the analysis of current MCLs, which provide for code mobility under two different forms, as discussed in [4]. If *strong mobility* is supported (by a *strong MCL*), the EUs coded in the MCL can move their code *and execution state* to a different host. The execution state contains the information related to the state of the EU, e.g., the instruction pointer. Migration is transparent, i.e., the EU resumes execution on the new host after the instruction that triggered migration. If *weak mobility* is provided (by a *weak MCL*), the EUs on a host can be bound dynamically to code coming from a different host. In currently available MCLs this encompasses two cases. Either the EU dynamically links code downloaded from the network, or the EU receives its code from another EU. In the latter case, two more options are possible. Either the EU in the destination site is created from scratch to run the incoming code, or a pre-existing EU links the incoming code dynamically and executes it.

Available MCLs provide direct support for at least one of the above design paradigms, though the latter are at a higher abstraction level and do not necessarily rely on the availability of MCLs for their eventual implementation. For instance, strong MCLs support naturally the MA paradigm. In Telescript [19], a strong MCL, a special thread called *agent* can migrate to a different node by executing a `go` operation that suspends the execution of the thread, serializes it for transmission and sends it to the destination node, where it is resumed. In Agent Tcl [7], another strong MCL, the Tcl interpreter is extended to provide an additional `jump` command, whose effect is analogous to the Telescript `go`, except that it freezes the whole UNIX process containing the interpreter rather than a single thread. In turn, Java [14] is an example of a weak MCL that supports directly the COD paradigm. The Java class loader, responsible for resolving class names at run-time, can be modified by the programmer to retrieve the corresponding code from a remote host. Finally, TACOMA [9], Facile [11], M0 [17], and Mole [5] are weak MCLs that support the REV paradigm. In these MCLs, a procedure or function can be sent to a remote host, at most with the portion of the global environment needed for their remote execution.

4 Network Management and Code Mobility Put Together

In this section we discuss how code mobility can be successfully exploited for the provision of decentralized and flexible solutions for network management.

Code on Demand: Flexibility In the IETF approach the MIB structure is implemented by the code of the management agent and cannot be changed at run-time. This lack of flexibility represents a limit, in particular for event notification, because the definition of significant events is hard-wired in the MIB structure and customized events cannot be defined. On the contrary, the ISO approach allows the MIT to be changed dynamically, thus providing higher flexibility at the expense of an increased complexity in the management agents.

Code on Demand can increase flexibility while keeping agents simple and small, thus combining the advantages of IETF and ISO approaches. In this setting, an agent becomes an extensible component of an MCA. Whenever the structure of the local information base needs to be changed, e.g., to modify the criteria to detect an event, the corresponding portion of the agent code can be invalidated and replaced automatically with a new one retrieved from a code server. Hence, the agent can be "patched" without any need to rebuild and reinstall it. Even more important, the update need not to be done manually by the network administrator for each agent on each network device, rather it can be made once on the code server and propagated *on demand* on every node. Consequently, this approach can be exploited to perform *i) perfective* maintenance as in this case, *ii) adaptive* maintenance, i.e., to upgrade the agent code as a consequence of a change in the underlying software platform, e.g., a change in the operating system version. As an aside, it can be noted that a COD paradigm

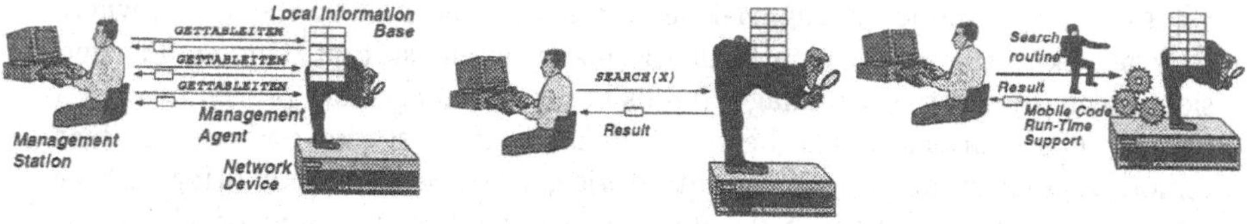

(a) Client-server. (b) Client-server. (c) Mobile code.

Fig. 3. Three different ways to perform table lookup.

is likely to be of great help also in network domains other than network management. For example, a new protocol module could be added to a router in a fairly automated way by downloading it on demand from a central repository.

Remote Evaluation: Bandwidth Saving and Processing Distribution In mainstream network management approaches, data are moved from agents to the management station and there processed. Afterwards, some data are possibly sent back to agents. Again, this aims at keeping agents small, without overloading them with the code implementing the operations the management station is in charge of. As an example, let us consider the case in which the management station has to search for a single value in a table, which is commonly used to store information inside devices. With mainstream approaches this can be done in one of the following ways:

1. The whole table is transferred into the management station, where its rows are searched for the value (Fig. 3a). Hence, the larger the table the more bandwidth is wasted and the more computational overload is generated on the management station.
2. The searching routine can be implemented into the agent code (Fig. 3b) and activated either by a remote action invocation (ISO approach) or as a side effect triggered by a change of some value in the MIB (IETF approach). Again, the agent tends to become big and complex as a larger number of routines are implemented. Even worse, the payoff of this increased size may be very little if many of these routines are executed only now and then.

Using a REV paradigm, the search routine could be sent to the device on which the table is stored and executed there, as shown in Fig. 3c. Hence, the table could be searched locally and only the result should be sent back to the management station. This solution saves bandwidth, since only the result is shipped back, and distributes the computational load among the agents, rather than concentrating it on the management station. Another benefit that can be achieved by REV is to raise the level of abstraction for the interaction between the management station and the agents. As mentioned in Sect. 2, the operations available to the management station are usually very low level, particularly in the IETF approach, where the management station can only get and set values on the agents' MIB. Using REV, sequences of primitive operations that do not require a direct processing by the management station (e.g., to retrieve a sequence of values) can be grouped in higher-level operations and sent to the agent, where they are executed independently of the management station. One could envision a scenario where the manager builds her own management procedures upon lower-level operations, stores them on the management station and invokes their remote evaluation on the appropriate device, when needed. This brings a nice side-effect of modularity into the management architecture, and provides better performance by reducing the number of messages exchanged between the agent and the management station, thus limiting the load in the area around it. Management by delegation [6] which is subsumed in our paradigms, highlighted as a shortcoming the explicit invocation of remote execution on each node. We agree with this observation as we do not propose to exploit REV for the decentralization of every management task. The REV paradigm, as well as the other design paradigms proposed here, is not a silver bullet and its use has to be assessed case by case according to a set of parameters, specific to the functionality that has to be implemented. For example, in the searching example above, a REV paradigm is justified—from the point of view of the traffic generated on the network—only if the table to be searched is big and the search routine code (as it is likely) is short. Under these assumptions the bandwidth needed for management is reduced, otherwise CS will probably perform just as well.

Mobile Agent: Autonomous and Mobile Management Functionality The capability to send the same code consecutively to many nodes maintaining its state from one hop to another can be of great help in enhancing the decentralization of the management functionality over the managed network nodes. The management station, instead of querying each node to gather the information needed to perform some operation, could inject a mobile agent into the network. The mobile agent should have the goal of visiting all the nodes which have the needed information and processing it locally (thus performing semantic compression of data), retaining the state of its computation whenever it moves to a different node. This could be beneficial in:

- Increasing flexibility, since access to resources on network nodes is obtained through the mobile agents, whose behavior can be determined by the management station on a customized basis, like in the REV paradigm.
- Reducing traffic around the management station, because each query to the network device is performed locally by the mobile agent without involving a message on the net. Moreover, once in place the agent can perform its processing independently of the connectivity between the management station and the device—a useful feature for dealing with unreliable or lossy links.
- Distributing processing load, because operations usually performed by the management station are executed on the devices by the mobile agent.

The management station can leave even more freedom to the agent, omitting the nodes on which the agent can access the needed information and allowing the agent to determine them according to its current state. Nevertheless, as in the case of REV, the various options provided by code mobility must be assessed

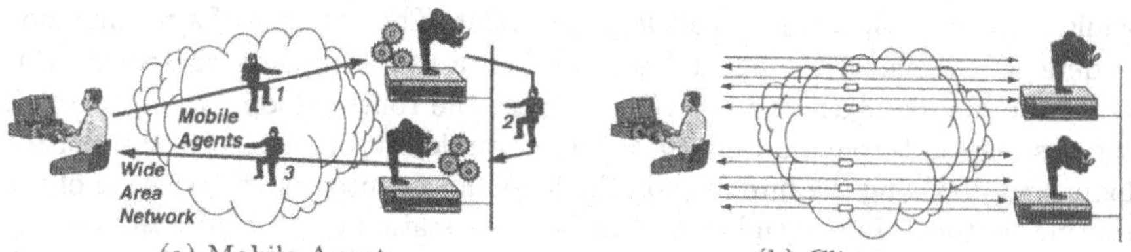

(a) Mobile Agent. (b) Client-server.

Fig. 4. Interaction between management station and devices.

carefully before implementation. For example, if the agent must collect information about a set of nodes, its state (containing such information) is likely to grow as the agent travels to various nodes. Furthermore, if the agent is free to determine its own destination, its code is likely to be quite complex and produce a high overhead, since it must be carried at each node. Hence, in these conditions and when a great number of nodes are involved, MA may not be the right approach—at least from a traffic overhead perspective. Of course, communication overhead is not the only criteria involved in the decision; the topology and physical characteristics of the network fragment under responsibility of a mobile agent, the particular management task to be performed, and the requirements for flexibility and reconfigurability are likely to be driving factors as well. For example, consider a scenario where some of the managed devices reside in a LAN, on which bandwidth is plentiful and cheap. The management station is far from the managed devices and reachable only through a (large) number of expensive (slow) links. In this case, mobile agents bring a considerable benefit because they provide the capability of collecting information about the set of network devices in an autonomous fashion, without being connected to the management station (Fig. 4a). Even though their movement from device to device requires a lot of bandwidth, it takes place in the local area (step 2 in Fig. 4a) where bandwidth is not a concern. In the traditional approaches this operation would require many data exchanges on slow links between the management station and the devices (Fig. 4b) with higher latency and risk of partial failure.

The mainstream approaches to network management presented in Sect. 2 exploit transport layer protocols to carry management messages. This allows the management station to communicate transparently with agents all over the network but, on the other hand, it makes management completely impossible when network level routing is disrupted. Mobile agents can help in overcoming this problem. If the management station does not have network level connectivity with a node to be managed through an agent, it can provide its agent with a route calculated from historical routing information and send it to the first hop on the route. Whenever the agent resumes execution on an intermediate hop, it tries to reach one of the next hops towards the target node using its internal route, until it reaches the target and performs its management task.

Finally, mobile agents can also be effective in detecting and bypassing routing loops. If the management station has clues to the presence of a loop, it can send a mobile agent to the first router towards the destination. This agent uses the information in its local routing table to move closer to the destination, while keeping track of the routers it is traversing. The presence of a routing loop is detected whenever the agent finds itself on a router already visited. At this point the mobile agent can try to: *i)* bypass the routing loop, trying to reach the destination through an interface chosen randomly, or *ii)* resolve the routing loop, e.g., disabling the interface on the loop and monitoring the reaction of the routing protocol. In principle, the management station could detect the routing loop on its own by reading the routing tables with the management protocol. Nevertheless, due to the presence of routing problems, it is likely that the management station does not have connectivity to some of the routers, and thus the partial or out-of-date information is not sufficient to identify the loop.

Feasibility Considerations and Interim Solutions The lack of network devices supporting direct execution of MCLs, which require a dedicated and often heavy run-time support, is today a major obstacle to the exploitation of code mobility in network management. Nevertheless, the opportunities offered by code mobility within the networking domain are becoming recognized by an increasing number of researchers and organizations, and the first efforts to embed code mobility at the network device level are beginning to appear [15]. In parallel, network device manufacturers are placing more and more computational power devoted to network management into their devices, thus enabling mobile code support to take advantage of existing hardware. For instance, the switches of some manufacturers are already equipped with a processor devoted to packet analysis and other functionalities required by RMON. Moreover, the problem of having a common format to ensure interoperability among the devices of different vendors, possibly using different languages, will exist. This problem is already evident in the mobile code arena, where the adoption of translation strategies based on an intermediate language has boosted portability but, on another hand, requires agreement on such a language in order to achieve full interoperability among different mobile code environments.

However, some interim solutions can be devised which, although less effective, are easier to implement and do not require support for code mobility on every node. These interim solutions could be a test-bed for code mobility in network management, in order to assess its effectiveness and possibly raise interest among the equipment manufacturers. Furthermore, they could be useful to manage legacy systems without built-in support for mobile code. In the remainder of this section we sketch briefly three architectures which can be used separately or in conjunction for this goals. A scenario where all the interim solutions are applied to the same network is shown in Fig. 5b.

1. Code mobility can be exploited to interact with SNMPv2 proxy agents running on workstations equipped with mobile code run-time support. In the interaction with proxy agents the management station gets the advantages previously described for the interaction with management agents. For example, management functions can be evaluated on the proxy agents' workstations (Fig. 5a) with a REV or MA paradigm, or the functionality of the proxy agent can be updated using a COD paradigm.

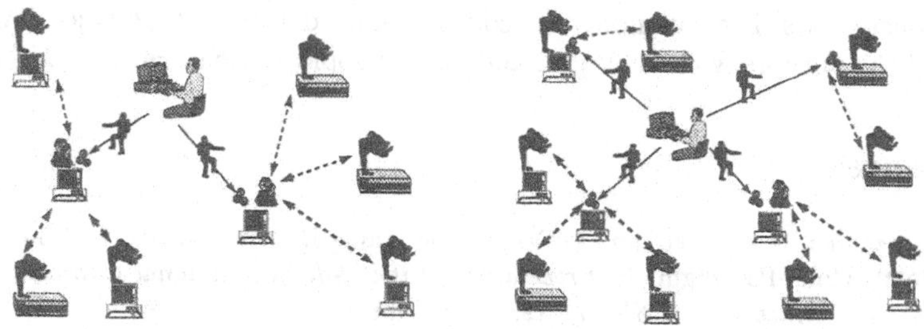

(a) Mobile code and proxy agents. (b) Mixed interim solutions.

Fig. 5. Interim solutions.

2. Mobile code could be sent to workstations with proper support which are installed in the managed area. As shown on the left in Fig. 5b, this code should interact with management agents on the nodes in the area around such workstations by using a conventional management protocol, e.g., SNMP or CMIP. This solution is not as beneficial as mobile code executing directly on network devices. Nevertheless, it enables local exchange of management protocol messages (e.g., useful on LANs with large capacity), having mobile code traveling from the management station to the managed areas. This solution is being implemented in a prototype study at our university.
3. When network devices will be equipped with mobile code run-time support (upper right part of Fig. 5b), this will be exploited in place of the workstations above. Mobile code will interact not only with the devices hosting the run-time support, but also with legacy ones installed in their neighborhoods, using conventional management protocols.

5 Conclusions and Future Work

In this work we investigated how new developments in design paradigms and technologies based on code mobility can be used to provide decentralized and flexible network management solutions, and discussed the benefits expected by their application. Nevertheless, we believe that network management would benefit from a combination of paradigms whose convenient use must be assessed case by case according to the functionality to be implemented, taking into account the CS paradigm as well. Finally, we discussed some of the obstacles to immediate applicability of these ideas on a large scale. Our work is at an initial stage, and we are currently investigating different research threads, including:

- *Development of a quantitative model* to identify which parameters of a network management application must be taken into account in order to select the most convenient approach, along the lines depicted in [1].
- *Prototyping with mobile code technology.* We are presently investigating the use of code mobility paradigms with one of the interim solutions sketched earlier using Agent Tcl [7] as our implementation language.
- *Probing of quantitative data* to demonstrate the effectiveness of the approach with respect to generated traffic.

Acknowledgments The taxonomy for code mobility discussed here is joint work of one of the authors with G. Vigna and other people at Politecnico di Milano.

References

1. A. Carzaniga, G.P. Picco, and G. Vigna. Designing Distributed Applications with a Mobile Code Paradigm. In *Proceedings of the 19th International Conference on Software Engineering (ICSE'97)*, 1997. To appear.
2. J. Case, K. McCloghrie, M. Rose, and S. Waldbusser. Structure of Management Information for version 2 of the Simple Network Management Protocol. RFC 1902, January 1996.
3. J. D. Case, M. Fedor, M. L. Schoffstall, and C. Davin. Simple Network Management Protocol. RFC 1157, May 1990.
4. G. Cugola, C. Ghezzi, G.P. Picco, and G. Vigna. Analyzing Mobile Code Languages. In [16].
5. M. Straßer, J. Baumann, and F. Hohl. MOLE—A Java Based Mobile Agent System. In [16].
6. G. Goldszmidt and Y. Yemini. Distributed Management by Delegation. In *15th International Conference on Distributed Computing*, June 1995.
7. R.S. Gray. Agent Tcl: A transportable agent system. In *Proceedings of the CIKM'95 Workshop on Intelligent Information Agents.*
8. J. W. Stamos and D. K. Gifford. Remote Evaluation. *ACM Transactions on Programming Languages and Systems*, 12(4):537–565, October 1990.
9. D. Johansen, R. van Renesse, and F.B. Schneider. An Introduction to the TACOMA Distributed System - Version 1.0. Technical Report 95-23, University of Tromsø and Cornell University, June 1995.
10. K. Jones. Internet's SNMP and ISO's CMIP Protocols for Network Management. *International Journal of Network Management*, pages 130–137, September 1994.
11. F.C. Knabe. Language Support for Mobile Agents. Technical Report ECRC-95-36, European Computer-Industry Research Centre, Germany, December 1995.
12. T. Magedanz, K. Rothermel, and S. Krause. Intelligent Agents: An Emerging Technology for Next Generation Telecommunications? In *INFOCOM'96*, San Francisco, CA, USA, March 1996.
13. OSI. ISO 9595 Information Technology, Open System Interconnection, Common Management Information Protocol Specification, 1991.
14. Sun Microsystems. *The Java Language Specification*, October 1995.
15. D.L. Tennenhouse and D.J. Wetherall. Towards an Active Network Architecture. *ACM SIGCOMM Computer Communication Review*, 26(2), April 1996.
16. C. Tschudin and J. Vitek, editors. *Mobile Object Systems*, Lecture Notes on Computer Science. Springer-Verlag, 1997. To appear.
17. C. F. Tschudin. *An Introduction to the* `MO` *Messenger Language*. University of Geneva, Switzerland, 1994.
18. S. Waldbusser. Remote Network Monitoring Management Information Base. RFC 1757, February 1995.
19. J.E. White. Mobile Agents. In *Software Agents*. MIT Press, 1996.
20. Y. Yemini. The OSI Network Management Model. *IEEE Communications Magazine*, pages 20–29, May 1993.

Java-Based Mobile Agents — How to Migrate, Persist, and Interact on Electronic Service Markets

B. Liberman, F. Griffel, M. Merz, W. Lamersdorf
Hamburg University - Department of Computer Science- Distributed Systems Group
[1liberma | griffel | merz | lamersd] @ informatik.uni-hamburg.de

Abstract

This paper presents a mobile agent approach that aims at satisfying the following requirements of open Internet-based electronic service markets: the mobile agent system should be usable by any Internet user without a need for specifically configurated non-standard software tools. It should reduce costs in mobile computing environments and therefore enhance overall efficiency. It should suit well to an electronic service market where local services are commercially offered and business transactions predominate the interaction between customers and suppliers.

As a part of the project OSM (Open Service Model), mobile agents are built on top of two well-established technologies: CORBA and Java. The first is used as a conceptual framework for interoperability, the latter as the programming environment. Since Java does not provide the necessary persistency of execution state, the concept of *OSM service profiles* is used to embed Java classes and to transfer a coarse-grained execution context in a secure and efficient manner.

1 Introduction

Electronic service markets allow customers and suppliers to exchange services against payment through business transactions [Mer96, Schm93]. It is assumed that both individual and standardized services are offered in an electronic service market. However, to satisfy evolution as one of the most fundamental requirement for the market mechanism, the ability to gain ad-hoc visibility and availability — despite of a possibly complex service offer — is an important precondition for service suppliers.

The OSM (Open Service Model) architecture aims at integrating the following mechanisms that allow to perform business transactions in a flexible way:

- Generic user access to remote services is provided by a browsing tool, called the *generic client* [MML94]. It supports customers to establish sessions with suppliers, to integrate them visually at the desktop-level, and to store, transfer, and resume sessions on different network sites.
- The ad-hoc *configuration of supporting services* such as payment, authentication, or notary services. Each time a business transaction is to be established this con-

figuration takes place using a unified description technique and a matching mechanism to specify the transaction partners' needs.

- *Value chains* emerge in the following two ways: first, through the establishment of mediators, i.e. services that provide service references to their clients. Mediators may either supply a query interface (such as in the case of the trading service [MML94]) or a browsing interface (on-line catalogues or directories). Secondly, value chains may emerge by enriching, combining, or coordinating existing services.
- The *service profile* is established as a common vehicle for service offer description and as a persistent data store. This allows all involved OSM components to dynamically provide or obtain specific information in a well-structured way: traders may process service type definitions, catalogues may extract icons and description texts, or the generic client may obtain information on the support service requirements of the transaction partner [MTL96].
- Finally, the OSM architecture aims at supporting *service negotiation* between client and server by structuring conversations into a limited set of speech-acts [CFF+92]. This helps to reduce the complexity that is principally given when two parties agree step-by-step on a set of service attributes and allows for a higher level of automation.

It has been discussed in [MML96] that *mobile agents* fit to this architecture if they are considered as value-added service providers: they are developed either by a service supplier or a third party in order to utilize the call interface of a single server or a set of servers that is necessary for a distinct task to be accomplished. To give an example, information retrieval at remote database servers may be performed by a single migrating agent visiting all appropriate database sites. Then, from a conceptual point of view, the mobile agent provides to the customer the independence from server-specific interfaces and semantics. It acts as a value-added service since the possibly complex data query interfaces may be reduced to a simple user entry form that allows only to enter some keywords. Also the possible heterogeneity of different database servers may be hidden by the agent in this way. However, in contrast to an immobile value-added server, the agent is able to actively interact with other agents to solve the given problem cooperatively.

Another important domain which promotes appliance of mobile software appears in connection with mobile computing. The nature of such an environment entails some questions mobile agents are tailored to cope with. Concerning communication costs particularly, the advantage of mobile agents lies in the minimizing of the on-line time and therefore cost reduction.

The rest of this paper is organized as follows: section 2 gives an overview of the design space for mobile agent systems and motivates the selection of Java as the implementation language. Possible problems of this decision are discussed and the service profile concept is introduced as a possible approach for their circumvention. Section 3 focuses on the chosen mobile agent architecture and some of its technical details. A concise example in Section 4 illustrates the integration of the agent system within the overall OSM architecture's mechanisms in a typical scenario. The outlook summarizes the resulting system and gives a perspective for future research directions.

2 Design choices for agent systems

Mobile agents are alleged to provide suitable techniques for the implementation of electronic market systems that allow both demanders and suppliers of services and goods to exchange them freely based on electronic contract settlement and execution [CGH+95, MRK96]. This application domain determines the requirements which are imposed on agents.

Definition:

In the following, we define a *mobile agent* as an encapsulation of *code, data,* and *execution context* that is able to *migrate autonomously* and *purposefully* within computer networks *during execution.*

An agent is able to react sophisticatedly on external events. It may be persistent in the sense that it can suspend execution and keep local data in stable storage. After resuming activity, an agent's execution is continued — but not necessarily at the same location.

Designing agents

In the following, the term *persistent execution state* — as a postulated basis for migration technology — means that the agent should comprise a control flow definition at a coarse level of granularity. This allows not only persistent programming language systems to be capable of representing mobile agents but also conventional ones, which may only be able to provide object-level persistency. These objects may control execution after a migrated agent has been revived at the target host. It must be noted that this relaxation does not really impose any constraints on the agent functionality since a reasonable activity usually comprises at least one method invoking — a high level operation.

The possible spectrum for mobile agent implementations therefore spans:

1. Persistent programming languages such as *Smalltalk* (with a persistent image), *pJava* [Jor96], or *Telescript* [Whi94]. Here, an abstract machine is used to execute portable bytecode that may be transferred forth and back within the network. A fine-grained migration capability is given since the agent may initiate migration at any point of execution (at the *micro-level*). However, persistent programming languages usually require support by databases or object stores, which, in turn, represent a language-specific environment that is not ubiquitously given on each computer in the network.

2. To factor out control flow definitions, workflow-management systems use petri nets or finite automatons, etc. (at the *macro level*). No local processing is done by the agent, which is, in fact, a data structure that is interpreted by each (local) engine in order to invoke a coarse-grained function at the respective network

site. This approach does not require any sophisticated language support, however, the main disadvantage lies in the necessity to factor-out any program logic to the stationary server — even simple arithmetic operations.

3. A well-balanced compromise of the previous two extremes seems to blend the advantages of mobile code with those of persistent data structures that determine control flow. In this case, local operations can still be performed efficiently by the agent code, but migrations will only be possible from distinct migration hooks that define the next entry point and indicate to the executing engine that a transfer of the agent is requested.

In contrast to *language-level persistence* (as given, e.g., in the case of pJava), persistence in Java is currently restricted to selected data objects that are manipulated through dedicated library functions. For this reason, this approach is called *library-level persistence*.

In the following, the third approach will be supported on the basis of Java. As a portable interpreted language, Java allows dynamical loading and binding of classes. The importance of this feature in the agent system environment is derived from the requirement of ad-hoc providing of individual services. Thus, the classes that provide the server's functionality can not be expected to be ubiquitous. Rather, they are tailored to the server's demands. Therefore a way must be found to load classes as they are needed. In Java, classes that are referenced in an applet are loaded through the network from the applet's home site. Applying this to the mobile agent approach means at least prolonged on-line sessions and successive connection attempts. This evidently violates some of the basic mobile agent requirements. Other problems emerging in this context will be explained in the next section. A better solution is to support the packaging of a set of classes into a common transport vehicle. Here, the OSM *service profile* appears as an appropriate persistency mechanism that provides sufficient flexibility to embed Java classes as well as control flow objects.

Additionally, the following characteristics lead to the choice of Java as the language environment for the mobile agent system implementation:

- ubiquity of the Java virtual machine and thus supporting environments,
- close integration into the World Wide Web infrastructure,
- sophisticated and standardized supporting libraries.

The following section discusses how mobile agents are represented in OSM, how migration is effected, and how agents interact with one another. Finally, the overall agent architecture is sketched.

3 The OSM mobile agent architecture

This section presents the fundamental ideas of a Java-based agent system that has been devised in the scope the OSM project. Since the profile mechanism as a persistent *and* movable storage plays the key role in the implementation a closer look is taken at this technique first.

3.1 Service profile

The original requirement to the service profile was the ability to describe any services that can be offered in the electronic market. This comprises the server interface, server representation to the user (GUI elements) and eventually method invocation sequences allowed. Since the profile is transferred to and processed at the user's local computer, it must be possible to serialize all profile elements. This means that the service profile in its current state can also be saved on the user's disk. The session with the server can therefore be resumed later, probably on another host.

Since it can not be foreseen what elements are needed to describe a specified service offer, the profile must be general enough to allow new types to be defined. This implies that some meta information must be included in profile as well: for each element it must be possible to dynamically determine its type and its name. For this, the profile is structured as follows (see Fig. 1):

- There are three levels that make up the profile:
    1. The meta information that describes standardized type constructors. Examples are OsmInteger, OsmRecord, OsmArray and s.o. These are also called type objects.
    2. The meta information about concrete types e.g. ClassRecord — a record with two fields: name of type String and ClassDefinition of type Opaque. The concrete types are created with the help of the type objects. Thus they are called object types.
    3. The actual information. This is constituted from the instances of the object types. For example, there can be an instance „Agent" of the type ClassRecord.
- Every instance has a reference to its object type and vice versa. This enables dynamic inspection of the profile contents. Also, it promotes the standardization of some elements other OSM components expect to find in the profile.
- A user is allowed to change the profile content in an individual manner. In the case of profile serialization, all changes are saved persistently or transferred to another location within the profile.

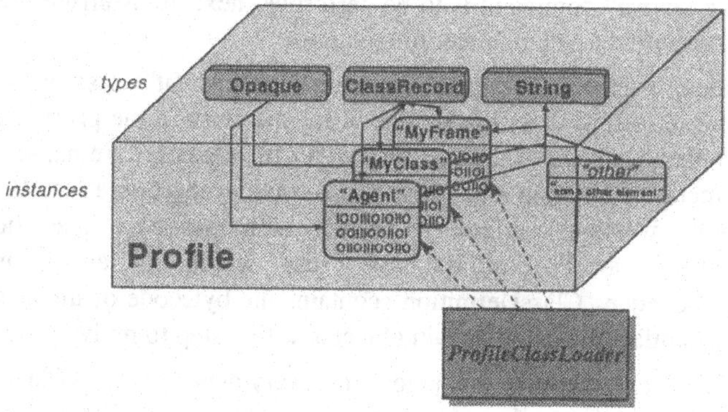

Fig. 1: Internal profile structure

It must be noted that a control description can also be embedded in the profile. The form of the description may be chosen from a wide range of concepts (from a petri net assuming an evaluator, up to coordinating Java classes) in a flexible way. Thus the profile can be used not only as a passive service offer specification but also as an active component in a workflow or mobile agent system as will be described in the rest of this section.

3.2 Standardization level

The introduction claimed that the usage of the agent system should not require any special configurations but only ubiquitously available technology (Java virtual machines are considered as such. Manipulation of the virtual machine to implement an agent system is not a choice in this paper). However, this cannot be fulfilled in its entirety since it requires at least some standardized conventions. For the sake of flexibility and autonomy it is desirable to minimize the level of such a standardization. Especially the classes constituting an agent should not be standardized, since this would restrict the personalization of an agent and may entail some operational constraints on its functionality. This implies that the agent must carry some meta information about classes it uses with it. Although it is not advisable to standardize classes themselves it is still possible to agree on a name of a main class that is used to create the first object of the agent without a loss of operational autonomy. Names of other classes whose objects may constitute the agent should not be standardized since it can not be predicted how many classes can be involved and what semantics is associated with them.

3.3 Embedding classes

What does this mean for the packaging of classes during agent migration? The suggested general execution sequence for (re-)building an agent is as follows. At the beginning, a class with a standardized name, say „Agent“, is loaded, and a new instance of this class is instantiated. This instance receives also a reference to the profile so it can build up itself up to the state it had before migration using other profile elements. Then the instance's execution is started as a Java thread and continues until a „move“ command is to be performed next, transferring the profile to the location specified as a parameter of the „move“.

As a first idea, it appears reasonable to store Java „Agent“ class bytecode in the profile and to let a Java class loader search for the class in the profile. For it, it is possible to take advantage of the fact that all profile elements are named. This concerns both meta information and instances. Assuming there is a standardized type „ClassRecord“ which describes a record with at least one field called „ClassDefinition“, a „ProfileClassLoader“ can search for an instance called „Agent“. The opaque „ClassDefinition“ contains the bytecode of the class that will be used to instantiate the agent's main object as a first step to revive it.

It is not difficult to generalize this algorithm: every class (say „MyClass“) which is used in „Agent“ has to be stored as an instance „MyClass“ of the type „ClassRecord“. This is continued recursively for other classes (e.g. classes used in

„MyClass"). The following code illustrates this algorithm as it is currently found in the implementation of the profile class loader:

```
public Class LoadClass( String sClassName ) {
...
OsmType      ot = profile.getType("ClassRecord");
Enumeration en = ot.enumOverInst();
boolean      proceed = true;
OsmInstance oi = null;

while( proceed )
  if( en.hasMoreElements() ) {
    oi = (OsmInstance)en.nextElement();
    // the instance must have the same name as the class

    // e.g. sClassName="Agent"
    if( ( oi.getName() ).equals( sClassName ) )
      proceed = false;
    else
      oi = null;
  } else
      proceed = false;
if( oi == null ) {
  throw new ClassNotFoundException("Could not find class" +
sClassName);
}
// get the array of bytes that is the class's byte code
OsmInstance oioClass = (OsmInstance) (
  (OsmRecordInstance)oi).getElement("ClassDefinition");
byte barClass[] = (byte [])oioClass.getValue();
// define the class
Class clDefinition = defineClass( barClass, 0, bar-
Class.length);
return clDefinition;
...
}
```

There are several advantages of using this technique:

1. Only the „Agent" class must be mentioned explicitly while searching for classes. All other classes are found using the common Java mechanism: the class loader of the object's class is asked if some type is unknown. This means, the programmer does not have to worry about class loading provided all classes are stored in profile under consistent names.
2. Class name conflicts are prevented: suppose, there are two agents that both have objects of classes with the same name although the classes are different (say „MyFrame"). Since the Java loading mechanism uses a different loader for each class applying the wrong class is avoided. Some approaches to implement Java-based agent systems suggest to find out whether all necessary classes are present at the remote host before the actual agent is transferred [Kov96]. The question here is how to cope with the situation where a wrong class with the correct name

is found at the destination. Additionally, this approach requires prolonged online communication, a fact which contradicts to the agent-oriented paradigms.

Using this profile class loader concept, the general scenario can be refined as follows. The profile class loader returns the „Agent“ class and the system creates an instance of the class. The result of the operation is casted to a predefined interface (say „BaseAgentInterface“) which is indeed a part of a fixed convention. Note however, that the agent code can still be any class that implements this Java interface. The interface provides a method to revive the agent. This means, all information that is necessary for the agent to restore its old state and to continue execution is passed to it. This mechanism is described in more detail in the next two subsections.

3.4 Agent migration

The problem of state recovering occurs only in the context of agent migration. Before an agent is transferred to another location it must be converted into a form that

- is platform independent
- preserves the current agent state
- preserves the agent's integrity

The profile mechanism fulfills all these requirements. Thus, the following agent migration procedure is supported. During its execution the agent writes all information that it will need at other locations in its profile. This information will be available after the transmission has taken place. Since the agent writes the data itself, it knows where it will find it within the profile afterwards. After the profile has successfully arrived at the specified new location the local (old) agent thread is terminated. The further execution will take place at the destination host.

All components involved in agent processing are listed below (see also Fig. 2). These actually constitute the current OSM agent system.

- The *Engine*: receives agents, manages them and allows for their communication. The class Engine must provide a functionality defined by a „BaseEngineInterface“ which is subject to standardization.
- The *Assembler*: created by the engine on the agent arrival, sets up the agent for execution.
- The *ProfileClassLoader*: created by the assembler, locates and loads agent's classes.
- The *Dispatcher*: created by the engine, is responsible for agent splitting.
- The *Forwarder*: created by the engine or dispatcher in the case the agent wants to move.
- The *Synchronizer*: created by the engine, responsible for agent synchronization.

Compared to the „all-in-one-engine“ approach, this structuring avoids bottlenecks and allows for higher autonomy and security as shown below. The following, more detailed discussion, aims at making the cooperation of these components clearer.

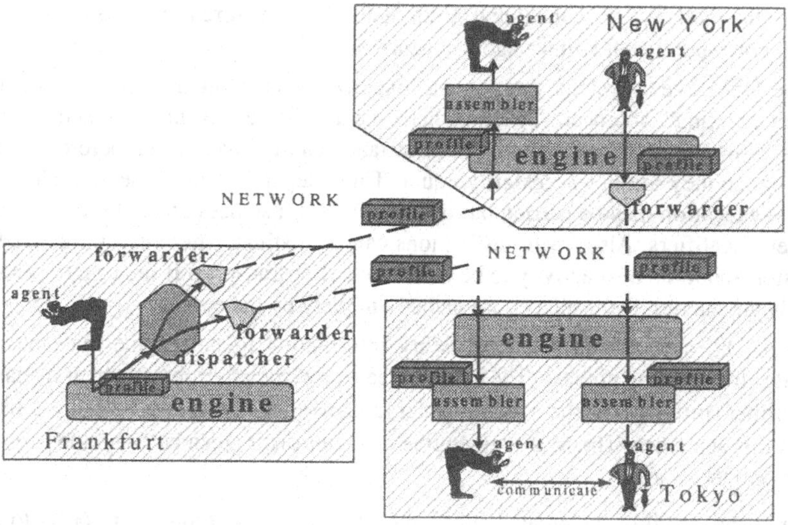

Fig. 2: Agent System Components

Bootstrapping

On indication of an incoming agent, the engine creates an assembler object that actually receives the agent and sets it up. The information passed to the agent by the assembler includes the reference to the engine and to the profile. The corresponding agent method is called „`reviveAgent`" and is part of the „`BaseAgentInterface`". This method is overloaded in a manner that the agent fetches the information which is relevant to its state from the profile. If the agent needs some information from the environment (at the new location) it contacts the engine. The agent presumes that the engine provide certain functionality to access the environment. Due to this indirection, a better level of security is achieved since the locally installed engine can be specified, tested and controlled by the local service provider — who should trust it then without being afraid of direct manipulation of his environment by incoming agents. At the end of the „`reviveAgent`" method, the agent starts its execution as a Java thread. A „`run`" method determines the next activity to be performed by the agent. The local activity continues until a „`move`" method is invoked. Another way to terminate execution is to call the „`destroy`" method being part of the „`BaseAgentInterface`". All resources associated with the agent and managed by the engine are freed then and the agent's thread is destroyed.

The next paragraphs describe other methods provided by „`BaseAgentInterface`". These constitute the fundamentals for inter-agent concurrency and communication approaches.

Concurrent agent inter-working

It was claimed above that electronic markets present the domains where agents can be employed as „value-adders" by simplifying service access or combining more than one service automatically within a single task given to them. Additionally, electronic markets are constituted from naturally concurrent business processes which correspond well to inter-agent concurrency.

In the OSM agent system, inter-agent concurrency is implemented based on the „agent splitting“ approach. Splitting here means that an agent is cloned several times. However, local variables of each instance can be overwritten before or after cloning, so they are not necessarily equal. Thus, depending on these variables, the further execution may be carried out differently. All instances created differ at least in their identifiers. Also, their destinations can be distinct. These can influence the decision about the next activity to be performed after transport. If the agent does not supply any names, the instances are named uniquely by the engine.

A „`split`“ method passes all necessary information to the engine that actually initiates the splitting process: The engine creates a *dispatcher* object which manages the further splitting. For the actual transfer, a *forwarder* is employed. Figure 2 illustrates this sequence. The receiving engine does not distinguish between the original agent and the clones.

Often, some or all of the created subagents need to be synchronized in order to exchange information collected. For it, it is necessary to make an agent wait for another one. This can be another subagent created by an earlier split or it can be a completely different agent. In any case, the agent must be able to identify the other agent it is waiting for. In the OSM agent system, the agent's unique identifier is currently used for this. Since it may not be desirable that the agent is able to access the information about what agents are present at the local host, the synchronization is carried out indirectly by a *synchronizer* object. For this, the agent invokes a „`synchronizeAgents`“ method being part of the „`BaseEngine-Interface`“ again. Then it suspends itself.

The engine creates a synchronizer object and passes to it information about which agent is waiting, which agent is being expected to arrive and information about all agents at this location. If agents being expected have not arrived yet, the synchronizer periodically fetches information about present agents from the engine. As soon as the agent awaited arrives or after a specified timeout the synchronizer wakes up the waiting agent. It is anticipated that the agents synchronize themselves in order to exchange some data. This means, after the synchronization, agents will probably set up communication with each other.

Inter-Agent Communication

Since it can not be predicted what information should be exchanged by the agents, it is desirable to develop a very generic communication technique. A first idea is to require a reference to the communication partner from the engine and then to cast the reference from the „BaseAgentInterface“ to the actual agent type. This approach supposes that the communication entities are informed about the implementation details of each other. This is not too unrealistic, especially in the case of formerly splitted agents. However, the current serialization package implementation does not allow such references to be casted to the agent's actual type although the types are equal. Thus, in the current agent system implementation, a less elegant but generic approach is utilized. A method „`communicate`" (with a parameter of type „`Object`") is provided by the „BaseAgentInterface". It should be noted, that the agent communication does not involve third instances like the engine. Therefore it can be kept confidential and be considered as a secure channel. As a part of the given object parameter, credentials could be passed that authorize and authenticate one agent to the other.

This subsection closes the discussion about the OSM agent system functionality. As it is stated above, agents present a technique that seamlessly fit into electronic market technologies. This is illustrated by the example in the next section showing where the other concepts of the OSM environment may support the use of agent.

4 An information retrieval scenario

For now, the usual way to find some information, e.g., about stone-age wooden-made tools is by asking a user's favorite search engine. The OSM infrastructure could instead offer a *catalogue* of specialized agents. The choice of the agent that seems to be most appropriate is done with the *generic client* which may also be used to parameterize the agent by the contents of the user's request. The agent's own program analyses the request and determines that at least two different areas of interest are involved. Therefore it splits itself and one of the clones migrates to a site containing a historical database in New York and the other visits a technical library in Tokyo (see also Figure 2). After arrival, these agents contact the sites' local resources and retrieve information they are interested in. This process also involves the OSM payment supporting services since the information resources might be offered commercially. This in turn includes the OSM security features to keep the information delivered confidential. Since the historical database is a rather large one, the first agent may like to send some intermediate results to Tokyo where the information is merged with those retrieved by the second agent. This transfer could be done by a different agent (say an *information messenger*). Finally the Tokyo agent goes back to the user's home at Frankfurt and reports its result to the user.

5 Conclusion and outlook

This paper gave a view of the motivation for Java-based mobile agent systems and some important implementation aspects. It was shown how agent persistence, migration, synchronization, and communication have been integrated into an electronic market architecture.

The most important features of the OSM mobile agent system can be summarized as follows. A minimal standardization level is given that does not hinder the customer in highly individualized application development. Also class naming autonomy is guaranteed for agents. By encapsulating its own classes, the agent is able to warrant a certain level of security.

This contribution emphasized the question of agent persistency and interaction. Further aspects, such as the authentication infrastructure, payment aspects, or agent-based negotiation support are addressed by the OSM architecture, but not discussed in detail. On the other hand, the question of agent programming tools still remains open: In the current version, an agent is programmed manually — including design and manipulation of the control flow. One of the next tasks is thus to ease the work of the programmer on control flow specification by applying special software tools. These tools will then be a part of the overall OSM agent development environment.

6 References

[CFF+92] H. Chalupsky, T. Finin, R. Fritzson, D. McKay, S. Shapiro, G. Wiederhold: "An overview of KQML: A knowledge query and manipulation language". Technical Report, April 1992

[CGH+95] D. Chess, B. Grosof, C. Harrison, D. Levine, C. Paris, G. Tsudik: "Itinerant Agents for Mobile Computing". IBM Research Report RC 20010

[Jor96] Jordan, M.: „Early Experiences with Persistent Java". In Proc. of the first International Workshop on Persistence and Java, University of Glasgow, 1996

[Kov96] E. Kovács: Advanced Trading Service Through Mobile Agents. In: *Proc. Trends in Distributed Systems '96*, Aachen 1996, pp. 112-124

[MRK96] T. Magedanz, K. Rothermel, S. Kruse: "Intelligent Agents: an Emerging Technology for Next Generation Telecommunications?". In: Proc. IEEE INFOCOM, San Francisco, USA, März 1996

[Mer96] M. Merz: "Elektronische Dienstemärkte - Modelle und Mechanismen zur Unterstützung von Handelstransaktionen in offen verteilten Systemen". Diss., Universität Hamburg, November 1996

[MML94] M. Merz, K. Müller-Jones, W. Lamersdorf: „Service Trading and Mediation in Distributed Computing Systems". In: L. Svobodova, Ed., Proc. 14th 'International Conference on Distributed Computing Systems', Poznan, Poland, IEEE Computer Society Press, 1994, S. 450-457

[MML96] M. Merz, K. Müller-Jones, W. Lamersdorf: „Agents, services, and electronic markets — how do they integrate?". In: A. Schill, O. Spaniol, Ed., *Proc. International Conference on Distributed Platforms ICDP '96*, Feb. 1996 (XXX bei Lamersd)

[MTL96] M. Merz, T. Tu, W. Lamersdorf: „Dynamic Support Service Selection for Business Transactions in Electronic Service Markets". In: *Proc. Intl. Workhop on Trends in Distributed Systems*, Aachen 1996, Springer, Berlin, Heidelberg New York 1996, pp. 183-195

[Schm93] B. Schmid: "Electronic Markets". In: *Wirtschaftsinformatik*, 35 (1993) 5, S. 465-480.

[Whi94] J.E. White: „Telescript Technology: The Foundation for the Electronic Marketplace". White Paper, General Magic, Inc., 1994

Mobile Code Paradigms and Technologies: A Case Study

Carlo Ghezzi and Giovanni Vigna

Dip. Elettronica e Informazione, Politecnico di Milano
P.za L. Da Vinci 23, 20100 Milano, Italy
[ghezzi | vigna]@elet.polimi.it.

Abstract. The opportunities offered by the Internet are encouraging research aimed at the creation of a computational infrastructure that exploits the wide spread communication infrastructure. The mobile computation paradigm is a proposal to build a computational infrastructure that goes beyond the well-known client-server paradigm and increases dynamicity and flexibility. Despite the promising first steps, there is still confusion on the role of paradigms and technology in the development on applications based on the mobile computation paradigm. We present a case study in which we develop several versions of an application using different paradigms and different technologies in order to show when these concepts come into play and which are their relationships.
Keywords: mobile code, design paradigms, case study

1 Introduction

The Internet has now become the largest distributed system ever built. While the deployed *communication infrastructure* is evolving at a fast pace providing larger bandwidth by means of new network technologies and protocols, the *computational infrastructure* is still rather primitive and only recently has become the focus of systematic research activities. By computational infrastructure we mean both the *technologies* available to implement and support execution of network-centric applications and the design *paradigms* according to which such applications can be structured. Although application developments are literally exploding on the Internet, such applications are mostly developed using unstable and evolving technologies, and very little is known regarding design paradigms, besides the conventional client-server model.

To consolidate the explosion of network-centric applications, we believe that research is needed both at the level of enabling technologies and at the level of design paradigms. In fact, in order to fill this gap, the concept of *mobile computations* has become the focus of much recent research [1]. In this framework, the computational infrastructure is composed of a (possibly world-wide) distributed environment with several *computational environments* (CEs) that support the computations of *executing units* (EUs). Such EUs may change their computational environment and even the code they execute dynamically. Several technologies, like Telescript [16], Messengers [15], and Java [10] have been proposed. Still, the development of applications based on the mobile computation paradigm (shortly, ***Mobile Code Applications*** or MCAs) lacks a methodological background.

We envision an idealized process by which software designers are equipped with methods that allow them to select the most appropriate design paradigm for any specific application. The software architecture designed according to the selected design paradigm should then be mapped onto an implementation using the technology (languages and their support tools) that best fit the chosen paradigm.

Unfortunately, the distinction between paradigms [4] and technologies [5] is often blurred and not well understood. The focus of our work is exactly on understanding the conceptual foundations of mobile computations, trying to identify the specific issues that characterize mobile code applications at all stages of their development process. In particular, in this paper we address the issue of design paradigms and technologies. We identify a repertoire of paradigms that are suitable for several kinds of mobile code applications and we discuss their relationships with technologies. We will show how the different paradigms can be implemented using different technologies. We will also show that certain paradigms are supported more easily and efficiently by certain technologies. As a result, one might develop guidelines that help to choose the most appropriate technologies for each paradigm. This may be viewed as an initial step in the direction of the above mentioned idealized process.

The paper is organized as follows. In Section 2 we introduce a case study that will be used throughout the paper to discuss both possible design paradigms and implementation issues. The case study is the search of information in a distributed database. In Section 3 we identify an initial repertoire of different design paradigms for mobile applications. Based on such paradigms, Section 4 presents different design alternatives for our case study. In Section 5 we present some classes of technologies, while in Sections 6, 7, 8, we shortly present the different implementations of our application. In Section 9 we discuss implementation issues. Section 10 draws some conclusions and illustrates future work.

2 A Case Study

Our study application is a distributed information retrieval system. The application is composed of several *Database Management Systems* (DBMSs) and of a *Search Engine*. DBMSs are distributed over a set of computational environments. They are identified by a location, i.e., the computational environment they are running on, and a symbolic name that uniquely identifies a particular DBMS in the corresponding CE. Each DBMS manages a single table composed of two fields: *keyword* and *data*. The keyword is an identifier of an entity. The data field may either be some kind of information related to the entity denoted by the keyword or the identifier of another database that may contain additional information about the corresponding keyword.

The Search Engine's task is to gather the largest amount of information associated with a particular keyword, given an initial set of DMBSs. If during the query of these initial DBMSs some references to other DBMSs are found, the Search Engine continues the search on those DBMSs.

3 Mobile Code Paradigms

The design of MCAs is a challenging task. Such applications are highly dynamic from the point of view of both code and location and therefore it is necessary to take into account these concepts at the design level. We identified three main paradigms for mobile computations: *Remote Evaluation* (REV), *Code on Demand* (COD), and *Mobile Agent* (MA) [4]. Although we don't claim that such paradigms cover all possible design structuring styles for network-centric applications, they can be viewed as the most typical representatives.

Given two interacting components A and B of a distributed architecture, these paradigms differ in how the *know-how* of the application, i.e., the code that is necessary to accomplish the computation, the *resources*, i.e., the inputs/outputs of the computation, and the *processor*, i.e., the abstract machine that executes the code and holds the state of the computation, are distributed between the components. In order to let this computation to take place, all the three capabilities above have to be present at one location *at the same time*. We assume A to be the entity that causes the interaction and the one that is interested in its effects. Table 1 shows how the paradigms behave with respect to the capabilities described above. The table also lists the *Client-Server* (CS) paradigm. Although conceptually CS cannot be viewed as a paradigm for mobile computations (no mobility takes place), we included it because it is a highly used paradigm on network-centric applications.

Paradigm	*A side*	*B side*
client-server	–	know-how resources * processor
remote evaluation	know-how	resources processor *
code on demand	* resources processor	know-how
mobile agent	know-how processor	resources *

Table 1. Mobile code paradigms. This table shows the location of the capabilities just before the interaction takes place. The star (*) indicates where the capabilities meet, i.e., where computation associated with the interaction takes place.

In the CS paradigm, a server component (B in Table 1) exports a set of services. The code that implements such services is owned by the server component, thus, we say that the server holds the ***know-how***. It is the server itself that executes the service, thus it has the ***processor*** capability. The client (A in Table 1) is interested in accessing some entity managed by the server, and therefore it is the server that has the ***resources***.

In the REV paradigm, the executor component (B) offers its computational power (the ***processor***) and its ***resources***, but does not provide any "specific" service. It is A that sends the service code (the ***know-how***) that will be executed by B in its location.

In the COD paradigm, component A initially is unable to execute its task. It is B that provides the code (i.e., the ***know-how***). Once the code is received by A, the computation is carried out on A's location, thus, A holds the ***processor*** capability. The computation involves only local files and local devices; thus, A holds the ***resources***.

In the MA paradigm, A has the ***know-how*** and ***processor*** capabilities. The computation associated with the interaction takes place on B's location where the ***resources*** involved reside.

4 Designing an Application

Usually, an application (or parts thereof) may be designed following different paradigms. In our case study, we have designed our application using the well-known Client-Server paradigm and two mobile code paradigms, namely, Remote Evaluation and Mobile Agent.

4.1 Client-Server Design

According to the CS paradigm, DBMSs play the role of servers while the Search Engine is a single component that acts as a client. Each DBMS offers a *query* operation that, given a particular keyword and an index n, returns the information contained in the nth tuple containing the specified keyword or an error if such tuple does not exist. The Search Engine queries the DBMSs contained in its initial set and then updates such set with possible new databases whose identifiers have been found by previous queries. This process goes on until there are no more unqueried DBMSs.

4.2 Remote Evaluation Design

According to the REV paradigm, the Search Engine component sends a code fragment to the location of each DBMSs it has to query. Such fragments are evaluated on the remote locations where DBMSs are located, i.e., new components are created to execute the code on the destination sites. Such components query their local DBMSs using the same primitives that DBMSs export in the CS case. When a remote component terminates its task, it sends back to the

Search Engine the results of queries. If the results contain some references to other DBMSs new REV interactions with these locations are started.

4.3 Mobile Agent Design

Following the MA paradigm, the Search Engine is modeled as a series of components that roam through the locations of the DBMSs in order to collect information about the given keyword. Initially, as in the case of REV, a component is sent to the location of each DBMS of the given DBMSs set. Each component has an initially empty "to-be-visited" list containing the DBMSs that have to be searched and an empty "visited" list containing the DBMSs that have already been visited. On each location that hosts a DBMS there is a "history" list that each visiting component updates with the list of its visited DBMSs.

A component A migrates to the location of the first DBMS in its "to-be-visited" list. There, it performs the following actions:

1. it checks the local "history" and prunes its "to-be-visited" list accordingly;
2. it updates the local "history" with its "visited" list;
3. it checks if another component B is presently searching the local DBMS. If it is so, A interacts with B following these steps:
   (a) A provides B with its own "visited" list, so that B can update its "to-be-visited" list accordingly;
   (b) A balances its "to-be-visited" list with the B's one;
   (c) A removes the current DBMS from its "to-be-visited" list;
4. if its "to-be-visited" list does not contain the current DBMS anymore, A skips to step 7;
5. if the list still contains the current DBMS, it searches the DBMS, possibly enriching its "to-be-visited" list;
6. adds the visited DBMS to the local "history";
7. migrates to the location of the first DBMS of the "to-be-visited" list if any; otherwise it goes back to the starting location and reports its results.

5 Implementation Technologies

Having designed a MCA according to some paradigm, one has to choose a technology to implement it. Given a particular paradigm, which technology should be used?

We identify three classes of technologies [7]:

Message-based These technologies enable the communication between remote EUs in the form of message exchange. A typical example is RPC [2].

Weakly mobile These technologies provide mechanisms that enable an EU to send code to be executed in a remote CE together with some initialization data or to bind dynamically code downloaded from a remote EU. Examples of such technologies are the *rsh* facility in UNIX, languages like M0 [14] and Obliq [3], or systems like TACOMA [9] and Mole [13].

Strongly mobile These technologies enable EUs to move with their code and execution state to a different CE. An example is represented by the Telescript technology.

We implemented the different architectures of our application using different types of technologies. We chose Tcl-DP [12], Obliq [3], and Agent Tcl [8].

Tcl-DP is an extension of the Tcl language [11] for distributed programming. Tcl-DP provides support for TCP/IP and RPC programming. It is a message-based technology.

Obliq is an untyped, object-based, lexically scoped, interpreted language. It supports remote method invocation and remote evaluation of code. Therefore it is both a message-based and a weakly mobile technology.

Agent Tcl provides a Tcl interpreter extended with support for EU migration. An executing Tcl script can move from one host to another with a single `jump` instruction. A `jump` freezes the program execution context and transmits it to a different host which resumes the script execution from the instruction that follows the `jump`. Therefore Agent Tcl can be viewed as a strongly mobile technology.

Sections 6 through 8 provide an informal and succinct description of how the designs based on the CS, REV, and MA paradigms can be implemented using Tcl-DP, Obliq, and Agent Tcl.

6 Implementing the Client-Server Architecture

6.1 Message-based Technology

In this version of the application, we used Tcl-DP to implement the CS architecture. The DBMS component is implemented as a process running a Tcl-DP interpreter acting as an RPC server that exports a single *query* service with the characteristics described in Section 2. The Search Engine component is implemented as another process running a Tcl-DP interpreter that acts as an RPC client. The client queries the server using RPC primitives. The CEs are represented by UNIX hosts.

6.2 Weakly Mobile Technology

We used the Obliq language to implement this version of the application architecture. Even if Obliq enables the remote invocation of methods, we decided to use the mechanisms for remote evaluation of code offered by the language, since our goal here was to evaluate how a technology based on the remote evaluation of code supports the CS paradigm. We have implemented locations as Obliq interpreters that export *engines* (i.e., execution services), and DBMSs as objects that enclose the database data and provide a query method. The Search Engine is a thread in an interpreter that uses the *engines* exported by other interpreters in order to evaluate segments of code remotely. At run-time the Search Engine chooses a DBMS and sends a piece of code containing a single query method invocation to the remote engine of the interpreter containing the DBMS. The single invocation is performed in the remote interpreter by a newly created thread and then the results are delivered back.

6.3 Strongly Mobile Technology

We used Agent Tcl to implement the Client-Server architecture. In this setting the DBMSs are stationary agents that accept queries from agents located on the same site (represented by a UNIX host extended with the Agent Tcl run-time support). The Search Engine is a moving agent that, in order to query a DBMS, jumps to the corresponding site, performs a single query, and then jumps back to its starting site.

7 Implementing the Remote Evaluation Architecture

7.1 Message-Based Technology

We used the Tcl-DP language to implement the REV architecture. In this case, the remote site is extended with a process running the Tcl-DP interpreter that acts as a code executor. It is an RPC server that exports the service *execute*. Such service takes as a parameter a Tcl-DP script . DBMSs are Tcl-DP interpreters that export the *query* service as in the CS case, but only to local processes. When the Search Engine wants to evaluate remotely the code that performs a set of queries, it sends to the remote executor a service request containing the query script. In turn, the executor interprets the script that queries the DBMS and then returns the results back.

7.2 Weakly Mobile Technology

We used Obliq to implement the REV architecture. In this implementation, the Search Engine thread requests the execution of the query code to the remote engine corresponding to a particular DBMS. A new thread is created to execute the code. The newly created thread performs all the needed queries to the local DBMS, which, as in the case of CS, is an object owned by the remote interpreter. Then, the results are delivered back to the source site.

7.3 Strongly Mobile Technology

We used Agent Tcl to implement the REV architecture. In this implementation the Search Engine creates a set of agents that jump to the sites of each DBMS in the initial set, perform the set of query on the local DBMSs, and then return to the original site with the results. Such results are analyzed and then a new "squad" of agents is sent to the sites of the DBMSs whose identifiers have been found during the execution of previous query process.

8 Implementing the Mobile Agent Architecture

8.1 Message-Based Technology

We used Tcl-DP to implement the MA architecture. In this case, the DBMSs are RPC servers that accept queries from local processes while Search Engine mobile components are Tcl-DP scripts. In order to move from site to site, such mobile components pack their code and state (i.e., their "to-be-visited" and "visited" lists and the values of some state variables that keep trace of their computation) into a message and then send the message to an executor that unpacks the message and creates a new component. The new component uses the information stored in the state part of the message in order to restore its execution flow. After dispatching the message to the remote executor, the sender terminates.

8.2 Weakly Mobile Technology

We used Obliq to implement the MA architecture. Since Obliq threads cannot migrate from one interpreter to another, when a Search Engine component must migrate to another interpreter it creates a copy of itself on the remote site and then terminates. In order to keep track of the execution, an object is used to maintain the state of the component. After each "jump", the newly created thread must create a local copy of the object representing the state and perform some operations based on its contents in order to re-establish the state of the computation.

8.3 Strongly Mobile Technology

We used Agent Tcl to implement the MA architecture. The Search Engine is composed of a set of agents. At startup, such agents migrate to the locations of the given set of DBMSs. There, they perform the steps described in Section 4.3, i.e., they query the local DBMS and, if references to other DBMSs are found, they migrate to such locations, until their "to-be-visited" list becomes empty. Eventually, they jump back to their starting site and report their findings.

9 Discussion

The case study described in the previous sections shows that paradigms and technologies are not completely orthogonal. In principle, it is possible to implement applications developed with any paradigm by using any kind of technology, given that such technologies allow for the communication between EUs. However, we have found that some technologies are more suitable to implement applications designed using particular paradigms. Unsuitable technologies force the developer to program, at the application level, some mobility mechanisms or force an inefficient, counter-intuitive use of the existing ones.

As shown in Table 2, message-based technologies are well suited for implementing architectures based on the CS paradigm. If they are used to implement REV-based architectures, they force the implementor to use (unnaturally) code as data and to program the evaluation of such code explicitly. Even worse, if message-based technologies are used to implement MA-based architectures, the programmer has also to code state management, i.e., auxiliary variables must be used to keep the state of the computation and unnatural code structures must be used to restore the state of a component after migrating to a different site.

Weakly mobile technologies that allow to execute segments of code remotely are naturally oriented towards the implementation of MCAs designed according to the REV paradigm. These technologies are inefficient to implement CS architectures since they force the remote execution of segments of code composed of a single instruction. Therefore a new EU is created in order to execute this "degenerate" code. On the contrary, in order to implement MCAs based on the MA paradigm, the programmer has to manage, at the program level, the packing/unpacking of the variables representing the state and the restoring of the EU execution flow.

Strongly mobile technologies are oriented towards MA-based applications while they are not suited for implementing applications based on the CS and REV paradigms. In the former case, the programmer has to "overcode" an agent in order to have it moved to the server site, execute a single operation and jump back with the results. Such implementations could be rather inefficient since the whole EU state is transmitted back and forth across the network. In the latter case, in addition to the code to be executed remotely, the implementor has to add the migration procedures. Furthermore, the state of the EU is to be transmitted over the network.

Summing up, technologies may reveal to be too powerful or too limited to implement a particular architecture. In the first case resources are wasted, resulting in inefficiency. In the second case the programmer has to code all mechanisms and policies that the technology does not provide.

10 Conclusions

The ever-increasing growth of MCAs has stimulated research on methodologies and technologies that constitute the computational infrastructure of this new class of applications. Several technologies, with different characteristics have been proposed. Yet, a clear methodological framework is still missing; many concepts are not clearly defined and there is often confusion about paradigms and technologies

Mobile code paradigms are the styles according to which the software architecture of an application can be designed in terms of interacting components. Technologies provide mechanisms that can be used to implement network-centric distributed applications.

We have developed a case study in order to understand in which phase of the development these concepts come in play and which are the relationships between paradigms and technologies.

Technologies	Paradigms CS	REV	MA
Message-based	Well suited	Code as data Program interpretation	Code and state as data Program state restoring Program interpretation
Weakly mobile	Code is a single instruction Creates unnecessary execution units	Well suited	State as data Program state restoring
Strongly mobile	Code is a single instruction Creates unnecessary execution units Move state back and forth	Manage migration Move state back and forth	Well suited

Table 2. Relationships among paradigms and technologies.

We have identified which class of technologies are well suited to implement applications designed using a particular paradigm and which are the difficulties or the inefficiencies that stem out from the use the inappropriate technology.

Our case study is a "toy" application of limited complexity. Future work could consider the study of a real-life mobile code application. In addition, more technologies and paradigms might be considered, other than those discussed here. At present, we are extending our work by developing a case study that includes the COD paradigm, which was not covered here, and uses other technologies like Java and TACOMA.

We did not cover phases of the development process other than design and implementation. As an example, testing and debugging phases are strongly influenced by the introduction of mobility. Testing of MCAs is much more difficult than testing of "traditional" applications since the configuration of components and the binding among components and code is dynamic. In addition, debugging code that is executed remotely is a challenging task. Further work is needed to fully understand the effect of the new computational infrastructure provided by the network on the entire lifecycle of MCAs.

Acknowledgments

A preliminary treatment of the issues discussed in this paper can be found in [6]. We wish to thank Tullio Dovera and Roberto Nespoli for implementing most of the experiments illustrated here. The previous work about classification of mobile code languages and paradigms was carried out with G. Cugola, A. Carzaniga, G. P. Picco, and A. Fuggetta.

References

1. J. Baumann, C. Tschudin, and J. Vitek, editors. *Proceedings of the 2nd ECOOP Workshop on Mobile Objects ("Agents on the Move")*, 1996.
2. A. D. Birrell and B. J. Nelson. Implementing remote procedure calls. Technical Report CSL-83-7, XEROX, October 1983.
3. L. Cardelli. Obliq: A language with distributed scope. Technical report, Digital Equipment Corporation, Systems Research Center, May 1995.
4. A. Carzaniga, G. P. Picco, and G. Vigna. Designing Distributed Applications using Mobile Code Paradigms. In *Proceedings of the 1997 International Conference on Software Engineering*, May 1997.
5. G. Cugola, C. Ghezzi, G.P. Picco, and G. Vigna. Analyzing Mobile Code Languages. In *Special Issue on Mobile Object Systems*, LNCS. Springer-Verlag, 1997. To appear.
6. T. Dovera and R. Nespoli. Paradigmi e tecnologie per lo sviluppo di applicazioni basate su codice mobile. Master's thesis, Politecnico di Milano, 1996.
7. C. Ghezzi, G. Cugola, G. P. Picco, and G. Vigna. A Characterization of Mobility and State Distribution in Mobile Code Languages. In *Proceedings of the 2nd ECOOP Workshop on Mobile Object Systems*, July 1996.
8. R.S. Gray. Agent Tcl: A Transportable Agent System. In *Proceedings of the CIKM'95 Workshop on Intelligent Information Agents*, 1995.
9. D. Johansen, R. van Renesse, and F.B. Schneider. An Introduction to the TACOMA Distributed System - Version 1.0. Technical Report 95-23, "University of Tromsø and Cornell University", June 1995.
10. Sun Microsystems. The Java Language: A White Paper. Technical report, Sun Microsystems, 1994.
11. J.K. Ousterhout. *Tcl and the Tk Toolkit*. Addison-Wesley, 1994.
12. B. Smith and L. Rowe. Tcl-DP. Documentation, 1996.
13. M. Straßer, J. Baumann, and F. Hohl. MOLE: A Java Based Mobile Agent System. In *Proceedings of the $2^{n}d$ ECOOP Workshop on Mobile Objects ("Agents on the Move")*, 1996.
14. C. F. Tschudin. *An Introduction to the* MO *Messenger Language*. University of Geneva, Switzerland, 1994.
15. Christian F. Tschudin. OO-Agents and Messengers. In *ECOOP'95 Workshop on Objects and Agents*, August 1995.
16. James E. White. Telescript Technology: The Foundation for the Electronic Marketplace. Technical report, General Magic, Inc., 1994. White Paper.

The Architecture of the Ara Platform for Mobile Agents

Holger Peine and Torsten Stolpmann
Dept. of Computer Science
University of Kaiserslautern, Germany
{peine, stolp}@informatik.uni-kl.de

Abstract: We describe a platform for the portable and secure execution of mobile agents written in various interpreted languages on top of a common run-time core. Agents may migrate at any point in their execution, fully preserving their state, and may exchange messages with other agents. One system may contain many virtual places, each establishing a domain of logically related services under a common security policy governing all agents at this place. Agents are equipped with allowances limiting their resource accesses, both globally per agent lifetime and locally per place. We discuss aspects of this architecture and report about ongoing work.

Keywords: migration, multi-language, interpreter, Tcl, C, byte code, Java, persistence, authentication, security domain.

1. Introduction

Mobile agents have raised considerable interest as a new concept for networked computing, and numerous software platforms for various forms of mobile code have recently appeared and are still appearing [CGH95, CMR+96, GRA96, HMD+96, LAN96, LDD95, JRS95, RAS+97, SBH96]. While there seems to have emerged a wide agreement about the general requirements for such systems, most notably portability and security of agent execution, many issues are still debated, as witnessed by the numerous approaches exploring diverging solutions. Prominent issues here include the right balance between necessary functionality and incurred complexity, and the degree of compatibility with existing models, languages, and software.

The Ara[1] system is a mobile agent platform under development at the University of Kaiserslautern. Its design rationale is to *add* mobility to the well-developed world of programming, rather than attempt to build a new realm of "mobile programming". Mobility should be integrated as comfortably and unintrusively as possible with existing programming concepts — algorithms, languages, and programs. A mobile agent in Ara is a program able to move at its own choice and without interfering with its execution, utilizing various established programming languages. Complementing this, the platform provides facilities for access to system resources and agent communication under the characteristic security and portability requirements for mobile agents in heterogeneous networks.

The rest of this paper is structured as follows: The subsequent main section will describe the system architecture of Ara, featuring agent execution, mobility, communication, security, and fault tolerance. This is followed by a section discussing selected

1. "Agents for Remote Action"

aspects of mobile agent architecture. A subsequent section gives an account of the ongoing work with Ara, and the paper closes with a conclusion section. An extensive description of the Ara system will appear in [PEI97].

2. The Ara Architecture

The programming model of Ara consists of agents moving between and staying at places, where they use certain services, provided by the host or other agents, to do their job. A place is physically located on some host machine, and may impose specific security restrictions on the agents staying at that place. Keeping this in mind, agents are programmed much like conventional programs in all other respects, i.e. they work with a file system, user interface and network interface. Corresponding to the rationale stated above, the Ara architecture deliberately abstains both from high-level agent-specific concepts, such as support for intelligent interaction patterns, and from complex distributed services, such as found in distributed operating systems.

2.1 System Core and Interpreters

Portability and security of agent execution are the most fundamental requirements for mobile agent platforms, portability being an issue because mobile agents should be able to move in heterogeneous networks to be really useful, and security being at stake because the agent's host effectively hands over control to a foreign program of basically unknown effect[1]. Most existing platforms, while differing considerably in the realization, use the same basic solution for portability and security: They do not run the agents on the real machine of processor, memory and operating system, but on some virtual one, usually an interpreter and a run-time system, which both hides the details of the host system architecture as well as confines the actions of the agents to that restricted environment.

This is also the approach adopted in Ara: Mobile agents are programmed in some interpreted language and executed within an interpreter for this language, using a special run-time system for agents, called the *core* in Ara terms. The relation between core and interpreters is characteristic here: Isolate the language-specific issues (e.g. how to capture the Tcl-specific state of an agent programmed in the Tcl programming language) in the interpreter, while concentrating all language-independent functionality (e.g. how to capture the general state of an Ara agent and use that for moving the agent) in the core. To support compatibility with existing programming models and software, Ara does not prescribe an agent programming language, but instead provides an interface to attach existing languages. In contrast to most other systems, such as Telescript [GEM95] or Java [ARG96], this separation of concerns makes it possible to employ several interpreters for different programming languages at the same time on

1. There is also the reverse problem of the agent's security against undue actions of the host. There is, however, no general solution for this problem; see section 2.4, "Security" for a discussion of this.

top of the common, generic core, which makes its services, e.g. agent mobility or communication, uniformly available to agents in all languages.

Since part of an agent's execution state is inevitably contained in its interpreter, a given interpreter necessarily has to be extended by state capturing functions if the full transfer of the executing agent is desired. Currently, interpreters for the *Tcl* scripting language as well as for *C/C++*, the latter by means of precompilation to an efficiently interpretable byte code [STO95], have been adapted to the Ara core, opening up a wide spectrum of applications. An adaption of the *Java* language is on the way, and other languages such as Pascal and Lisp are being considered.

The functionality of the system core is kept to the necessary minimum, with higher-level services provided by dedicated server agents. The complete ensemble of agents, interpreters and core runs as a single application process on top of an unmodified host operating system. Fig. 1 shows this relation of agents, core, and interpreters for languages called $\mathcal{A}$ and $\mathcal{B}$.

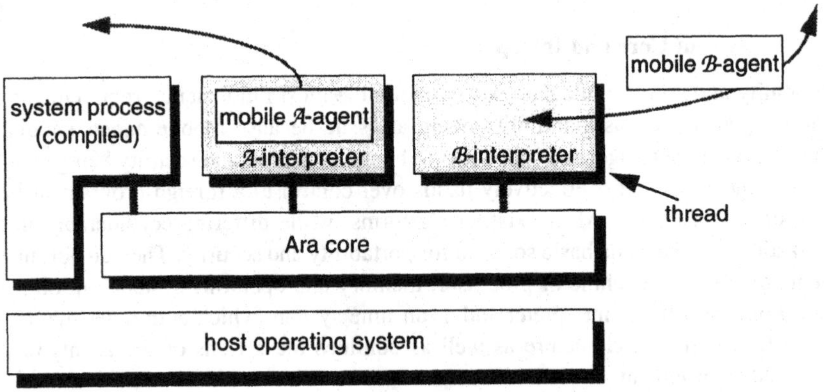

Fig. 1. High-level view of the Ara system architecture

Ara agents are executed as parallel processes, using a fast *thread* package, and are transparently transformed into a portable representation whenever they choose to move. The system also employs processes for certain internal tasks ("*system processes*") in order to modularize the architecture[1]. Employing threads as opposed to host operating system processes keeps the agent management completely under control of the core and achieves superior performance. The use of multiple threads in a common address space does not induce a memory protection problem here, as protection is already ensured on a higher level by the interpreters (see below), independent of hardware facilities such as privileged processor modes or page protection.

1. If such processes are trusted and not mobile, they may also be compiled to native machine code for undiminished performance.

Adapting a given interpreter for some programming language to the Ara core is a clearly defined procedure. First, it requires the definition of calling interfaces (*stubs*) in this language for the functions of the core API, and conversely the provision of functions for interpreter management (*upcalls*) to the core. The job of the stubs is mostly a matter of data format conversions and similar interface translations. Regarding the interpreter upcalls, the most prominent functions are those for the extraction of an executing interpreter's state as it is necessary to transfer the agent being interpreted, and conversely for the restoration of such a state on arrival of a migrated agent. Further, during execution the interpreter must ensure that the agent program will not call illegal code or access illegal memory locations; interpreters for languages without physical memory access such as Tcl or Java will ensure this anyway. Finally, the interpreter has to assist the core in the preemptive execution of the agent programs by performing regular calls to a core function for time slice surveillance.

2.2 Mobility

Many applications require agents to be moved not only once from their source to a destination site, but to move further, based upon their intermediate results and perceived environment, and continue their task across several sites. For such purposes a moving agent needs to carry its execution state along, effectively making it a migrating process. In contrast to systems moving code exclusively prior to execution, e.g. Java, Ara agents can migrate at any point in their execution through a special core call, named `ara_go` in Ara's Tcl interface[1]:

```
ara_agent {puts "Going to ida"; ara_go ida; puts "Hello at ida!"}
```

This creates a new agent, giving it a Tcl program (enclosed in braces) to execute. The agent will migrate to a place named `ida` (simply a host name, in this case) and then print the greeting message there. The *migration* instruction moves the agent in whole to the indicated place and resumes in the exact state from where it left off, i.e. directly after this instruction, while hiding the complexity of extracting the agent from the local system, marshaling it to another, possibly heterogeneous, machine and reinstalling it there. Furthermore, the act of migration does not affect the agent's flow of execution nor its set of data (including local variables), allowing the programmer to make the agent migrate whenever it seems appropriate, without having to deal with preparation or reinstallation measures.

Note that while the internal state of a moving agent is transferred transparently, this does not hold for its "external state", i.e. its relations to other, stationary system objects and resources like files or communication end points. It might be tempting to add a software layer over such stationary resources making them appear as mobile, effectively creating a distributed operating system. However, Ara opted against this, since the complex protocols and tight coupling involved with this approach do not seem well adapted to the low-bandwidth and heterogeneous networks targeted by mobile agents.

1. The same could be achieved in a C agent a by calling a C function `Ara_Go()` etc.

Ara agents move between *places*, which are both an obvious association to physical location and a concept of the architecture. Places are virtual locations within an Ara system, which in turn is running on a certain machine. In fact an agent is always staying at some place, except when in the process of moving between two of them. In practice, a place might be run by an individual or an organization, presenting its services. Service points (see subsequent section), for instance, are always located at a specific place. More importantly besides structuring, however, places also exercise control over the agents they admit and host (see section 2.4, "Security").

Places have names which make them uniquely identifiable and serve as the destination of a migration. A place name in Ara is, in the most general case, a list of *URLs*, corresponding to the different transport protocols[1] by which the site hosting the designated place might be reached, e.g. MIME mail, HTTP or raw TCP. On migration, the system will try the indicated protocols until one of them succeeds. Apart from designating a protocol and site, place name URLs will contain a local name of meaning to the targeted Ara system only. This local name will identify the specific place, using a simple hierarchical name space.

Agents bear names as well, consisting of a globally unique id, an identification of their principal, and an optional symbolic name from a hierarchical name space (disjoint from the place name space).

2.3 Communication

It can be argued whether agent communication should be remote or restricted to agents on the same machine. Considering that one of the main motivations for mobile agents was to avoid remote communication in the first place, Ara emphasizes local agent interaction. This is not to say that agents should be barred from network access (which depends on the policy of the hosting place, see section 2.4). Rather, the system encourages local communication. There are various options for this, including disk files, more or less structured shared memory areas ("tuple space", "blackboard"), direct message exchange, or special procedure calls, each entailing different ways of access and addressing. For reasons of efficiency and simplicity, Ara chose a variant of message exchange between agents, providing client/server style interaction. The core provides the concept of a *service point* for this. This is a meeting point with a well-known name where agents located at a specific place can interact as clients and servers through an *n:1* exchange of synchronous request and reply messages. Each request is stamped with the name of the client agent, and the server may use that in deciding on the reply.

Service points provide a simple and efficient mechanism for interaction between heterogeneous agents. However, for a widely deployed real-world mobile agent system an integration with existing, more structured service interfaces such as CORBA [OMG96] would certainly be a preferable alternative.

In spite of the emphasis on local interaction, a simple asynchronous remote *messaging*

1. Currently, only raw TCP is supported.

facility between agents will be added for pragmatic reasons, appropriate e.g. for simple status reports, error messages or acknowledgments which do not reward the overhead of sending an agent. However, to avoid remote coupling, the messaging facility will not involve itself in any guarantees against message losses. Messages will be addressed to an agent at a place, named as explained above. A message will be delivered to all agents at the indicated place whose names are subordinates of the indicated recipient name in the sense of the hierarchical agent name space. This addressing scheme may be used to send place-wide multicast messages or implement application-level transparent message forwarding by installing a subordinate proxy agent.

Quite apart from programming the agents' actions, the term "agent language" is sometimes also applied to the language interacting agents, in particular "intelligent" ones, use for mutual communication. However, there is no set of agreed basic functionality for such languages, and it is a current issue of research to find powerful, yet general patterns of agent communication (see [MLF95] for an example). Ara, in particular, leaves the choice of communication language open, offering only a general data exchange mechanism; applications may implement their own customized interaction scheme on top of this.

2.4 Security

The most basic layer of security in the Ara architecture is the memory protection through the interpreters as described in section 2.1. Besides this fundamental and undiscriminating protection, the different places existing on an Ara system play the central role in the Ara security concept. An Ara place establishes a *domain* of logically related services under a common security policy governing all agents at that place.

Allowances to Limit Resource Access

The central function of a place is to decide on the conditions of admission, if at all, of an agent applying to enter. These conditions are expressed in the form of an *allowance* conceded to the agent for the time of its stay at this place. An allowance is a vector of access rights to various system resources, such as files, CPU time, memory, or disk space. The elements of such a vector constitute resource access limits, which may be quantitative (e.g. for CPU time) or qualitative (e.g. for the network domains to where connection is allowed). An agent migrating to a place specifies the allowance it desires for its task there, and the place in turn decides what allowance to actually concede to the applicant and imposes this on the entering agent. The system core will ensure that an agent never oversteps its allowance.

Besides the local allowance conceded by an agent's current place, every agent may also be equipped with a global allowance at the time of creation. The global allowance puts overall limits to an agent's actions throughout its lifetime, effectively limiting its principal's liability. The system core ensures that a place will never concede a local allowance to an agent which exceeds the agent's global one. Agents may inquire about their current global and local allowance at any time, and may transfer amounts of it among each other under certain conditions. Agents may also form groups sharing a common allowance.

Entering a Place

Places may be created dynamically, by specifying a name and an *admission function*. The admission function has a predefined interface, receiving the agent's name and *authentication* status (i.e. the strength, if any, of its authentication), along with its desired local allowance as input parameters, possibly accompanied by further security attributes such as the agent's past itinerary record. The admission function returns either the local allowance to be imposed on this agent, or a denial of admission. Each place may thus implement its own specific security policy, discriminating between individual agents, principals, or source domains, and controlling resource access with the appropriate granularity.

When an agent resumes after a successful migration and admission procedure, it may check its local allowance, discovering to what extent the place has honored its desires. This enables the agent to decide on its own what to do if it finds the conceded local allowance insufficient. An agent which has been denied access to the destination place of a desired migration is sent back to its source place, there to discover the failure in the form of an error return from its migration call.

General resource access restrictions as imposed by allowances are an adequate mechanism for securing common accesses like allocating memory, writing a file or sending to a certain network location. However, certain higher-level security requirements such as enforcing that only data of a specific format are sent, or that consistency conditions across several files are preserved, require correspondingly higher-level access restrictions. This may be achieved by using service points as controlled outlets of the security domain, served by a trusted agent maintaining those high-level requirements. In particular with respect to such outlets, the security domain concept of Ara places is somewhat similar to the *padded cell* security model of Safe-Tcl [OLW96], but realized independent of a specific language and also somewhat more comprehensive, regarding allowances for CPU time and memory consumption.

Open Problems

The implementation of authentication will be based on digital signatures using public key cryptography. However, since a mobile agent usually changes during its itinerary, it cannot be signed in whole by its principal, which makes it difficult to authenticate the changing parts of the agent. It seems most desirable that the agent's code should be signed by the principal; this, however, would preclude dynamically generated code as it is common e.g. in the Tcl programming language. Other security-relevant components of a mobile agent might be authenticated by dedicated schemes, e.g. its itinerary record can be incrementally signed by the nodes the agent has passed through. In addition to authentication, public key cryptography will also be used to optionally *encrypt* Ara agents during migration to protect against eavesdropping.

As with any cryptographic scheme, the question of key distribution must be resolved. As this is a general problem not specific to mobile agents in any way, Ara does not define specific support for this, but assumes the existence of a well-known trusted public key server.

Quite apart from the security of the host system against malfunctioning or malicious agents, which is indispensable for any mobile agent platform to be practically accepted, there is also the reverse problem of the agent's security against undue actions of the host, e.g. spying on the agent's content or modifying it to an harmful effect. It is fortunate that the agent's security requirements are not as severe in practice as those of the host, since there is no general solution for the problem of agent security. The Ara system will provide certain measures, such as protecting immutable parts of the agent (e.g. its code) against tampering by a digital signature of its principal; other threats, however, such as spying on the agent's content, cannot usually be solved by technical means.

2.5 Fault Tolerance

When moving through a large and unreliable network such as the Internet, mobile agents may fall a prey to manifold accidents, e.g. host crashes or line breakdowns. Rather than trying to anticipate all potential pitfalls, Ara offers a basic means of recovery from such accidents: An agent can create a *checkpoint*, i.e. a complete record of its current internal state, at any time in its execution. Checkpoints are stored on some persistent media (usually a disk), and can be used to later restore the agent to its state at the time of checkpointing. The obvious application for this scheme is for an agent to leave a checkpoint behind as a "back-up copy" before undertaking a risky operation. Applications may build their own fault tolerance schemes upon this. The system will, however, provide a facility to implicitly checkpoint all locally existing agents in the event of an emergency shutdown.

3. Discussion

Most of the technical problems involved with mobile agents appear solvable in principle. However, considerable work is still needed to arrive at solutions which strike a satisfactory balance between conflicting requirements, such as necessary functionality vs. incurred complexity, security vs. flexibility and performance, or conceptual purity vs. compatibility with existing models, languages, and software. This section discusses three selected issues of debate and makes a case for Ara's decisions.

Language Integration

Mobile agent systems are often discussed from point of view of programming languages, suggested by prominent examples [GEM95, ARG96]. However, integrating concept and language blurs the differences between both and raises the hurdle for widespread use by requiring new skills and tools and hindering the interoperation with existing software. Analogous experience from distributed programming rather suggests to employ libraries and run-time systems instead of enhanced programming languages, interfaced from whatever languages seem appropriate for the application. Experience has shown here that distribution handling is not intertwined so intimately with the local processing as to require language support very strongly[1], relative to the disadvantages of changing the language. It is remarkable in this respect that even the seminal Telescript system, a typical example of the integration of language and system, has recently been suggested by its creator to play the role of one of several language environments on top of a common platform [WHI96].

Location Transparence

Distributed object systems and distributed operating systems often strive towards the goal of location transparence, i.e. the property of a logical object that its physical location is neither discernible nor important. It might be argued that a mobile agent platform seek such transparency, too, for maximum convenience. However, the wide area networks targeted by mobile agents tend to make distributed objects unwieldy to use. Moreover, there is a conceptual mismatch between location transparency and the principle of mobile agents to explicitly move between locations. Both problems are rooted in the different underlying network assumptions, since hiding distances is only practicable assuming reasonable network bandwidth and reliability; otherwise it seems sensible to admit the distance and deal with it. Accordingly, the distributed functions in a mobile agent system should be kept to a minimum.

Performance

Performance has not been as much in the focus of mobile agent systems as, say, operating systems. This may stem from the idea of an agent performing relatively few and high-level operations, such that its performance is mostly determined by that of the underlying host system. While this may be true for an individual agent, the performance overhead of an agent platform on a server executing hundreds of agents may be crucial. Analogous experience from WWW servers strongly suggests the use of threads instead of operating system processes. Using threads in a common address space allows highly efficient context creation and switching without sacrificing protection, since the latter may conveniently be ensured by the agent interpreters. Moreover, the threads may be scheduled non-preemptively while preserving sufficiently fine-grained preemption semantics from point of view of the agents, achievable by performing time slice checking synchronously in the run-time system (as opposed to an asynchronous interrupt handler). Non-preemptive thread scheduling enables parallelism without synchronization within the run-time system, further benefiting performance.

4. Ongoing Work

Both the core mobile agent platform functionality as well as tools and applications building on top of this are active areas of work. Most components of the Ara platform have been implemented, including the larger part of the core providing agent execution, service points, checkpointing, and migration; the same holds for the Tcl and C interpreters.

1. Parallelism, as opposed to distribution, constitutes an instructive counter example: Parallelizing languages and compilers are well-established in high-performance computing. This can be attributed to the fact that parallelism appears and can be realistically exploited in a more fine-grained form than distribution.

The focus of current work at the platform is on the security implementation. Agents will be able to create places with programmable admission policies implemented by application code; at the moment, however, there is only one implicit default place supported per system. Accordingly, place names currently reduce more or less to machine names[1]. The default place has a fixed behavior; it admits all arriving agents and fully honors their desires for local allowance. Consequently, there is no authentication of agents yet. However, allowance enforcement is implemented, and the set of resources currently controlled by allowances (CPU time and memory consumption) will be enlarged by files, network connections, disk space, bandwidth, and visited places.

Apart from the core system functionality, two other areas of work are tools and applications. We are developing a visual on-line monitoring and control tool for a set of Ara systems distributed across a network, which will include control and debugging of remote agents. As a first application based on mobile agents, we are implementing a service for searching and retrieving Usenet news articles [HOA87], a class of application we consider typical for mobile agents. Usenet is a network of servers exchanging news articles, where each server possesses only a constantly changing subset of all articles. Mobile agents visit servers in search for interesting articles, adapting their search objective and itinerary based on the contents of articles they already found, by means of exploiting meta information in the article headers such as article propagation path or cross references.

5. Conclusion

Ara is a system platform trying to provide mobile processes in heterogeneous networks in an efficient and secure way while retaining as much as possible of established programming models and languages. This paper has laid out the architecture of the system, based on a run-time core, on top of which mobile agents are executed inside interpreters to support portability and security. The system offers a clear interface to adapt interpreters for established programming languages to the core, demonstrated by the adaption of interpreters for such diverse languages as C/C++ and Tcl. Ara offers full migration of agents, i.e. orthogonal to the conventional program execution, which relieves the programmer of all details involved with remote communication and state transfer.

The security model of Ara is flexible in that domains of protected resources can be dynamically created in the form of places, and that the admission of agents to such a domain, as well as their actual rights at that place, can be controlled in a fine grained manner down to individual agents and resources.

However, the described architecture is still lacking in the area of structured agent interoperation. Further, supportive services for distributed resource discovery will be needed for real world applications.

---

1. To be precise, a place name currently designates one (of possibly several) specific Ara systems on a specific machine.

A usable development snapshot of the Ara platform is expected to be available in full source code from the Ara WWW pages[1] by the time of this publication. The system has been ported to the Solaris, SunOS and Linux operating systems so far.

References

[ARG96] ARNOLD, K. and GOSLING, J. (1996) *The Java Programming Language*, Addison-Wesley, Reading (MA), USA.

[CGH95] CHESS, D., GROSOF, B. and HARRISON, C (1995) *Itinerant Agents for Mobile Computing*, Research Report RC-20010, IBM Th. J. Watson Research Center. http://www.research.ibm.com:8080/main-cgi-bin/gunzip_paper.pl?/PS/172.ps.gz

[CMR+96] CONDICT, M., MILOJICIC, D., REYNOLDS, F. and BOLINGER, D. (1996) *Towards a World-Wide Civilization of Objects*, Proc. of the 7th ACM SIGOPS European Workshop, September 9-11th, Connemara, Ireland. http://www.osf.org/RI/DMO/WebOs.ps.

[GEM95] GENERAL MAGIC, Inc. (1995) *The Telescript Language Reference*, Sunnyvale (CA), USA. http://cnn.genmagic.com/Telescript/TDE/TDEDOCS_HTML/telescript.html

[GRA96] GRAY, R. (1996) *Agent-Tcl: A Flexible and Secure Mobile Agent system*, Proc. of the 4th annual Tcl/Tk workshop (ed. by M. Diekhans and M. Roseman), July, Monterey, CA, USA. http://www.cs.dartmouth.edu/~agent/papers/tcl96.ps.Z

[HMD+96] HYLTON, J., MANHEIMER, K., DRAKE, F., WARSAW, B., MASSE, R., and VAN ROSSUM, G. (1996) *Knowbot Programming: System support for mobile agents*, Proceedings of the Fifth IEEE International Workshop on Object Orientation in Operating Systems, Oct. 27-28, Seattle, WA, USA. http://the-tech.mit.edu/~jeremy/iwooos.ps.gz

[HOA87] HORTON, M.R. and ADAMS, R. (1987) *Standard for interchange of USENET messages*, Internet RFC 1036, AT&T Bell Laboratories and Center for Seismic Studies, December. http://ds.internic.net/rfc/rfc1036.txt.

[JRS95] JOHANSEN, D., van RENESSE, R. and SCHNEIDER, F. B. (1995) *An Introduction to the TACOMA Distributed System*, Technical Report 95-23, Dept. of Computer Science, University of Tromsø, Norway. http://www.cs.uit.no/Lokalt/Rapporter/Reports/9523.html.

[LAN96] LANGE, D. (1996) *Programming Mobile Agents in Java - A White Paper*, IBM Corp. http://www.ibm.co.jp/trl/aglets/whitepaper.htm

---

1. http://www.uni-kl.de/AG-Nehmer/Ara/

[LDD95] LINGNAU, A. DROBNIK, O. and DÖMEL, P. (1995) *An HTTP-based Infrastructure for Mobile Agents,* Proc. of the 4th International WWW Conference, December, Boston (MA), USA. http://www.w3.org/pub/Conferences/WWW4/Papers/150/.

[MLF95] MAYFIELD, J., LABROU, Y. and FININ, T. (1995) *Desiderata for Agent Communication Languages,* Proc. of the AAAI Symposium on Information Gathering from Heterogeneous, Distributed Environments, AAAI-95 Spring Symposium, Stanford University, Stanford (CA). March 27-29, 1995. http://www.cs.umbc.edu/kqml/papers/desiderata-acl/root.html.

[OMG96] OBJECT MANAGEMENT GROUP (1996) *CORBA 2.0 specification*, OMG document ptc/96-03-04, http://www.omg.org/docs/ptc/96-03-04.ps.

[OLW96] OUSTERHOUT, J. K., LEVY, J., and WELCH, B. (1996) *The Safe-Tcl Security Model*, draft, Sun Microsystems Labs, Mountain View, CA, USA. http://www.sunlabs.com/research/tcl/safeTcl.ps

[PEI97] PEINE, H. (1997) *Ara – Agents for Remote Action*, in *Itinerant Agents: Explanations and Examples with CD-ROM*, ed. by W. Cockayne and M. Zyda, Manning/Prentice Hall. To appear[1].

[RAS+97] RANGANATHAN, M., ACHARYA, A., SHARMA, S., and SALTZ, J. (1997) *Network-Aware Mobile Programs*, Dept. of Computer Science, University of Maryland, MD, USA. To appear in USENIX'97. http://www.cs.umd.edu/~acha/papers/usenix97-submitted.html

[SBH96] STRASSER, M., BAUMANN, J. and HOHL, F. (1996) *Mole – A Java Based Mobile Agent System*, Proc. of the 2nd ECOOP Workshop on Mobile Object Systems, University of Linz, Austria, July 8-9. http://www.informatik.uni-stuttgart.de/ipvr/vs/Publications/1996-strasser-01.ps.gz

[STO95] STOLPMANN, T. (1995) MACE - *Eine abstrakte Maschine als Basis mobiler Anwendungen*, diploma thesis, Department of Computer Science, University of Kaiserslautern, Germany. German text and English abstract at http://www.uni-kl.de/AG-Nehmer/Ara/mace.html.

[WHI96] WHITE, J. (1996) *A Common Agent Platform*, position paper for the Joint WWW Consortium / OMG Workshop on Distributed Objects and Mobile Code, June 24-25, Boston, MA, USA. http://www.genmagic.com/internet/cap/w3c-paper.htm.

1. A preprint can be obtained from the author (see cover page of this paper for address).

A Multi-Agent Architecture Supporting Services Access

Anthony Sang-Bum PARK, Stefan LEUKER

ap@i4.informatik.rwth-aachen.de

Department of Computer Science 4 (Communication Systems)
Aachen University of Technology • 52056 Aachen • Germany

Key words: mobile agent, agent server, multi-agent system, agent services

Abstract: *This paper proposes a multi-agent system comprising of mobile agents communicating with a fixed infrastructure of agent servers. This script-based multi-agent system enables easy access to Internet services and combines remote execution to support mobile users and migration of agents within the agent server network. Such an environment offers a higher degree of flexibility and efficiency to the user by performing much of the work on the server located in the fixed network. The focus of this paper lies on the description of the agent server architecture and the agent definition methods.*

1 Introduction

The recent explosive development of wireless networks and the still growing popularity of the Internet leads to closer examination of efficient Internet services access technologies through wireless access networks. To fulfill the support of mobile users with a higher degree of flexibility and efficiency, we need an environment that performs much of the work on the server of the fixed network. In this context the most interesting property is referred to as Remote Programming. This approach differs fundamentally from the classical form of client/server computing, helps to reduce required network resources and thus supports systems that do not have permanent network connections, such as mobile computers [1]. A multi-agent system using the remote programming paradigm offers an environment that perfectly fits to the above mentioned requirements. This paper focuses on the architecture of a multi-agent system that supports mobile users taking the variety of possible mobile terminals into account which are designed for different requirements and could be a simple mobile phone, a Personal Digital Assistant (PDA) or a high end multimedia notebook. An agent moving through this multi-agent system is understood as a program that takes over some/most of the users', applications' or even other agents' tasks. If necessary, agents communicate with each other, and/or the environment. They are able to move from server to server and even launch new agents during their migration to accomplish their task.

First implementations of systems supporting mobile agents already exist and some of them are commercially available, e.g. General Magic's Magic Cap [2] and Tabriz [3]. France Telecom is going to test a network based on Magic Cap agents for the general public. Magic Cap is intended for the use as a platform for PDA/Desktop communication systems, whereas Tabriz is for creating electronic market place applications based on the World Wide Web (WWW). However, use of these commercial products restricts the open access to the agent network and, particularly, interferes with the highly desirable use of services available on the Internet. The Aglets Workbench [4] is another research project at IBM labs Japan and also realizes agents that move from one browser to another by means of a special Agent Transfer Protocol (ATP). Using Java as its implementation language and SUN's Remote Method Invocation (RMI) library [5], it gains a much wider acceptance.

The multi-agent environment, that we are going to introduce is currently designed and will be implemented at Aachen University of Technology [6]. The prototype aims to integrate agent technology, used in a wireless environment, and open access to the Internet. This open multi-agent system architecture will be based on the widespread language Java. The advantages of a Java based multi-agent system include its platform independence and the easy access to the Internet. One of the major goals is to make services provided through the Internet accessible to mobile users via the multi-agent system. Additional research is made on how to utilize already existing and standardized services, like Trader concepts for distributed service access [7].

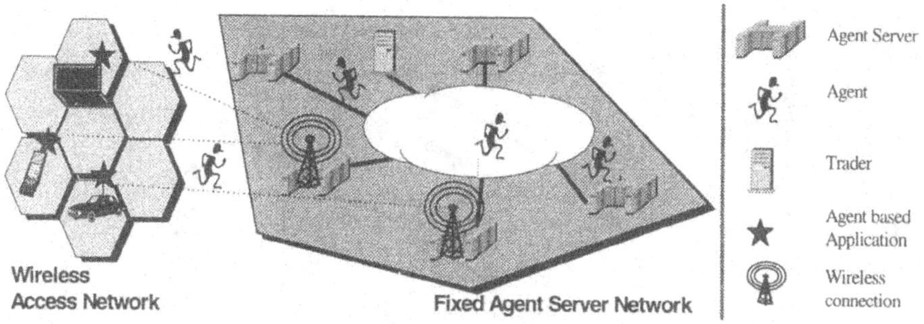

Figure 1: Multi-Agent Environment

Long-standing research at our department on Trader concepts will help us considering distributed systems according to the Reference Model of Open Distributed Processing (ODP) [8] or the Common Object Request Broker Architecture (CORBA) [9]. A trader acts as a kind of mediator that matches user requirements against the available range of services. The matching is based upon so-called service properties that describe all significant features of a service. In an electronic service market, properties are of overwhelming importance, because service providers competing among each other advertise qualitative features of their services using service properties.

Figure 1 depicts an environment of a multi-agent system with the wireless access network and the fixed agent server network. Within this environment the mobile agents act on behalf of their mobile users through simple transactions via a wireless access network. Agent servers on the fixed network side actually deal with the tasks to be performed, including for example looking for the required services, duplicating mobile agents to send them to various agent servers, invoking remote services, evaluating returning agents and taking into account that those returning agents cannot be delivered immediately to the mobile user. Thus, mechanisms have to be made available to inform mobile users that new messages or returning agents have arrived at the agent server in the fixed network. In addition, a small agent server for the client side has to be developed, since it is safe to assume that Java Bytecode processors will be available in PDAs and mobile phones shortly.

2 JAE - The Java Agent Environment

2.1 System Overview

The Java Agent Environment (JAE) is a foundation for developing and deploying mobile agent based applications. It contains the core technology for security, services, and mobility, and allows the easy implementation of user created agents. This will be shown in an example in chapter 3. Before we will discuss the implementation and reusable parts of JAE however, here are some words on the concept of JAE.

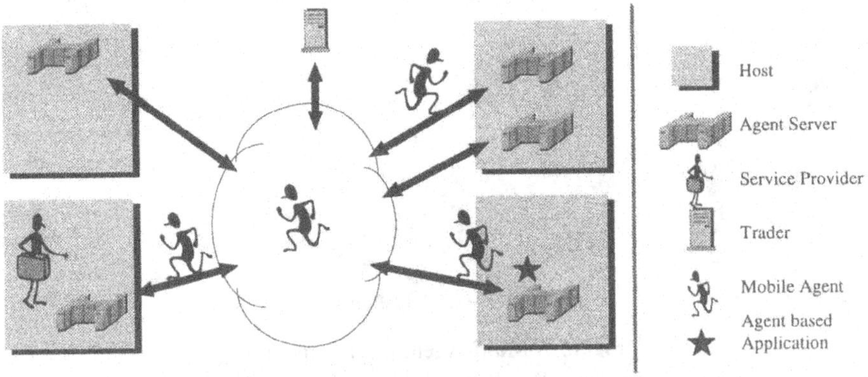

Figure 2: Components of the Multi-Agent Environment

Figure 2 shows the components that multi-agent environments are built of, the network, and the physical machines hosting the environment. Agents are created and sent out by applications to perform tasks, moving to agent servers on different machines and finding service providers that assist them. The actual deployment of the agent to an agent server by the application is an act of remote execution, whereas the migration of agents is code mobility.

Agent Server Architecture

The most central concept of an agent environment is the agent server, which is started as a resistent process and represents the agent environment on a host. As Figure 2 above depicts, there can be more than one agent server running on the same host at a time, but usually there is only one necessary.

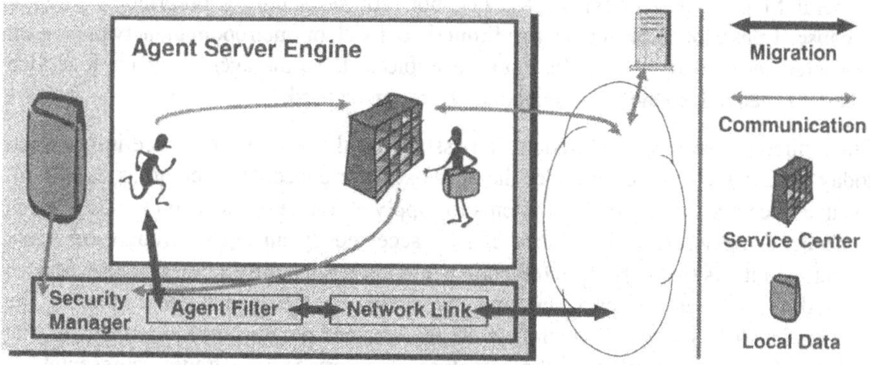

Figure 3: Agent Server Architecture

Figure 3 shows a single agent server in the context of its local host and the network. Agent servers take care of the network communication, maintain a connection to the services on the host, and handle the incoming and outgoing mobile agents. JAE's agent server hosts two different kinds of agents: the mobile agents which can enter the engine at any time and leave it after performing some operation they came for, and service agents that stay resident on the engine to provide the mobile agents with services.

As the place where agents come to live and execute commands, the engine is the most critical part of the system. On the one hand, agents should not be deployed in a foreign system without a mechanism to protect the supposedly sensitive data (or program logic) it is carrying with it. On the other hand, a malicious agent may try to harm the agent server, other agents, or it's hosting system [12]. To prevent at least the latter, the JAE engine includes a security manager which controls all injurious operations as manipulating files or unrestricted network access. For a mobile agent, only actions that effect its own data are permitted, plus calls to special functions of the agent server and the service center. Special, non mobile agents on the agent server, called service agents, may also access local properties of the host system, but no network access is allowed.

As for the security of the agent and its data, the agent server must be trusted, because there is no prevention for the server's access to the agent in the current conception. However, agents cannot read or write each others' properties. In most cases, an agent does not even know who else is on the agent server.

Communication

Since agents are not able to communicate with the network, nor can they access local properties of the host system, they totally rely on services that the agent server offers. A common way in agent environments is to provide service information — what is available and where to find it — in the agent program code. This approach is used by General Magic with Telescript [10, 11], but represents only a proprietary solution because Telescript applications are limited to local or metropolitan networks with restricted services only. It is far more desirable to have the agent look for a service when it is needed, so the latest available offers can be used.

Since directory services and traders can assist with the search for service information today, JAE's agent server provides the *ServiceCenter* concept that communicates with local service agents and trading systems to supply a mobile agent with the information it needs. A *ServiceCenter* instance can be accessed by an agent through the agent server, and it has methods to search and update the service directory. For every service offered by a service provider and available in the agent environment, the *ServiceCenter* has a record which lists the features and parameter requirements of that service. This list is similar to the signature of a service in a trader representation, including the engine controlling the service, the service type, the type of returned values, and the parameter specification, but goes beyond that, in also being of help in creating the right kind of input for the service. An agent then can invoke the service with the help of this record and the server that hosts the service.

2.2 Agent Programming Concepts

JAE is implemented as a Java library package, which consists of classes that represent the agent environment components. The table below lists the most important classes in the library and some of their methods.

Engine	Implementation of the agent server, including the security aspects. • **useService** invokes a *ServiceAgent* on the agent server.
Launcher	The basic class for every application that creates and remotely executes agents. It uses remote execution to deploy created agents on a designated agent server.
ServiceCenter	Facility for storing and retrieving *Service* objects. See chapter 2.2 for further information about *ServiceCenter*'s methods.
PropertiesStreamable	Java interface for the streaming mechanism provided by JAE.
Agent	Abstract class which contains most of the methods for mobility and persistence, but does not perform any task. • **go** lets an agent migrate to a remote agent server • **send** clones an agent and sends the clones to several agent servers

StreamableProperties	Key-value pairs that are streamable.
Ticket	Information about a destination for **go** or **send** invocations.
Service	A StreamableProperties subclass that stores the feature and parameter descriptions of a service. • **ticketForService** returns a Ticket with the destination of the agent server offering the required service
Provider	Generalized Java interface for service providers. The only method is • **use** which takes a *StreamableProperties* list of parameters to the service

Agents are actually programmed by subclassing the *Agent* class. Programmers only have to declare needed instance variables and implement two methods that are abstract in *Agent*, on the one hand the **initialize** method for initialization purposes and on the other hand the agent's program logic named **live**. These methods are written in regular Java code, making the creation of user agents easy for all programmers with some experience in C++ or other object oriented languages. However, some restrictions exist:

- Programmers must use the JAE storage classes like for persistent data in agents, since JAE implements its own, system independent persistence concept. In general, every class describing objects that belongs to a migrating agent has to implement the *PropertiesStreamable* interface.
- In the first prototype version, local variables are not permitted in the **live** method, because they are located on the Java Virtual Machine stack and could not be properly restored after the migration process. It is possible however to move the functionality that would need local variables to a calculation method and to call it from the **live** method.
- **go** may only be called from the user agent's **live** method. This is to ensure a save state when the agent migrates, allowing an exact code reentry.
- **send** uses an unusual syntax for the code to be executed by the cloned agents. The method call is not terminated by a semicolon, but is followed by an execution block in curled braces; this is the code that is executed by the clones. A return statement is required in this execution block. **send** returns a list of all returned results.

Since JAE uses Java as its agent language, some security aspects come for free. In Java it is impossible to access memory directly, call methods in objects you allow or load program code that would crash the runtime system. In addition, Java already contains the concept of a security manager to overlook critical operations, which is used in the JAE agent server to prevent agents from direct network access and local file manipulation.

Services

The JAE library contains a generic service exporter class called *ServiceAgent*, which implements the same underlying behavior of agents, but does not directly relate to the *Agent* class since it is not mobile but stays resident. All *ServiceAgents* implement the service invocation interface *Provider* that is the common link between all service providing facilities and the engine.

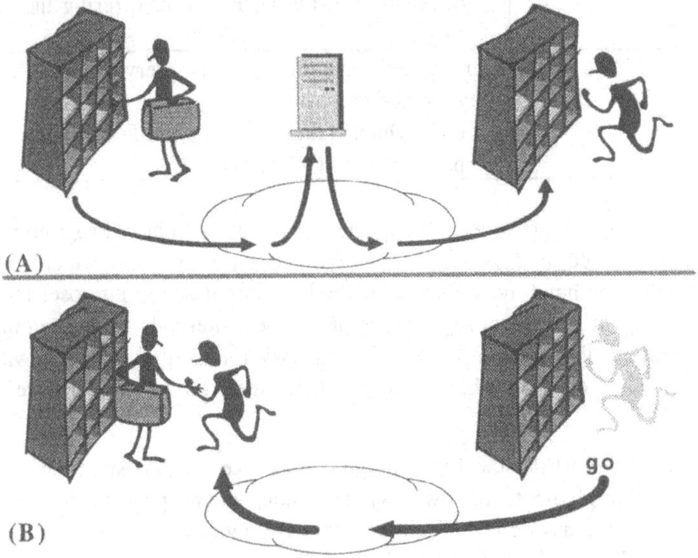

Figure 4: **Service registration and invocation**

When the agent server is started, service agents which are loaded by the server, register their services through the service center by calling the **registerService** method. A *Service* object given to the service center with this method must be able to create a complete parameter list with default values that allow a successful service invocation. Service agents can either perform the offered task themselves or call an external, but local application, because network communication is not allowed for services inside the agent server. Mobile agents are also able to register their own services through the same mechanism. Their registration, however, is only valid as long as the agent resists on the same agent server. To provide a registered service, the service agent or mobile agent has to implement the generalized *Provider* interface that has only one method called **use**. Since agents cannot see each other on an agent server however, the actual invocation of a service is done by calling the **useService** method of *Engine*, which itself knows the right service agent and forwards the parameters to **use**.

Figure 4 (A) shows a service agent registering its service with the local service center, which exports the information to the environment's trading system and on this way to all other service centers. A mobile agent then can access the service information on its current agent server through the local service center. Service providers can cancel the support for a service by calling the **withdrawService** method, signaling that this service will be no longer available.

Mobile agents use the *ServiceCenter* to search for a specified service with the **servicesFor** method, giving a property list of requirements as an argument. These requirements can be the return type or the type of service required. With the **firstServiceFor** method it is also possible to access only one service that matches the requirements. It returns the first service found by the service center. The service center however does not store all the service records itself, but relies on a trader community that stores the services for the whole agent environment.

A mobile agent on another agent server can get the *Service* record from its local service center using the lookup methods described above. With the *Service* records returned by **servicesFor** or **firstServiceFor**, the mobile agent can **go** to the service's engine, as depicted in Figure 4 (B), create a default invocation record, modify it for its needs and call the service with the generalized **useService** method of the engine.

3 An Example Agent

Imagine an agent that is able to fetch the email address of someone you might want to write but do not remember her address. This agent is equipped with the search string, i.e. the name of the recipient, and additional information like the company she is working with. Then the agent migrates to the nearest agent server, gets information of the email address search services from the service center and migrates to the listed engines to collect data. This data must be compiled and an agent containing all email addresses matching that name returns to your system. How is such an agent implemented with JAE?

First of all, the agent's instance variables must be defined. Remember that it is important to use the container types defined in the JAE library. Here is the declaration of the variables needed by the email fetching agent:

```
StreamableProperties  searchProperties;
StreamableProperties  emailAddresses;
StreamableList        serviceTickets;
StreamableProperties  serviceParameters;
StreamableList        returnedResults;
StreamableString      searchString;
```

These variables need to be initialized in the **initialize** method. This is done as usual in Java, by calling the new operator following a constructor method for the appropriate class.

```
void initialize()
{
    searchProperties = new StreamableProperties();
    (etc.)
}
```

EmailSearcher also needs a method that defines the search string.

```
void setSearchString(String aSearchString)
{
    searchString = StreamableString.fromString(aSearchString);
}
```

The more interesting part is the implementation of the **live** method including the invocation of services. Certainly the programmer does not know all services on the whole Internet that can look up email addresses, but that is not required for a JAE agent anyway. The service center can find this information from its own service information storage or by contacting a trader network when it is needed. The only thing that is indispensable for a successful search is to know how to build a good search record.

The information about the desired service is:

- The search string of the person's name.
- The email address is returned.

This means the **servicesFor** method requires a property list containing the following specification:

ServiceType	email-search
Price	0
ReturnType	String/email-address

The **servicesFor** method of the ServiceCenter returns a list containing all service records available in the environment, so the next step is to create a valid service invocation property list for each of them, fill in the additional information, and get service information from the service center:

```
public StreamableProperties
live()
{
    // Build the search properties list
    searchProperties = new StreamableProperties();
    searchProperties.put("ServiceType", "email-search");
    searchProperties.put("Price", "0");
    searchProperties.put("ReturnType", "String/email-address");

    // and do the search; this returns a StreamableList of Services.
    searchResult =
engine.serviceCenter().servicesFor(searchProperties);
```

Now **searchResult** contains *Service* records describing the services available in the agent environment that can return an email address from a search string. The only thing remaining to invoke the services are tickets to each service location. Due to the fact, that there might be many locations to migrate to, the **send** method is used to create and deliver the clones. **Send** requires a list of tickets as its parameter, thus this has to be created first.

```
private void
processServiceList(StreamableList services)
{
   Service aService;
   Enumeration cursor = services.allObjects;
   while (cursor.hasMoreElements())
   {
      aService = (Service)cursor.nextElement();
      serviceTickets.addObject(aService.ticketForService());
   }
}
```

processServiceList creates tickets out of a list of service objects and stores them in the **serviceTickets** instance variable of the email agent. **Live** calls the method `ProcessServiceList(searchResult)`.

Now it's time to invoke **send**. Remember that JAE requires a syntax slightly different from the usual Java code after **send**, defining which code will be executed by the clones on remote systems. **Send** returns a list of *StreamableProperties* that are the results of each clone created. The second parameter to **send** is also a list; it contains objects that are passed to **sendParameter** and can be accessed by the clones. In the example the *Service* objects are passed as the **sendParameter**, since each clone will invoke one of the services.

```
returnedResults = send(serviceTickets, searchResult)
{
   // This happens on the remote host where the service is located
   // The agent being cloned never executes this code.
   serviceParameters = ((Service)sendParameter).parameters();
   serviceParameters.put("SearchString", searchString);
   returnedResults =
      engine.useService((Service)sendParameter,serviceParameters);
   return returnedResults;
   // All the results are returned to the original agent instance
}
```

The task of the agent clones is very easy: get the invocation parameters for the service, fill in the search string and return the service results. After all clones have either returned successfully or failed, their results or error codes are listed in **returnedResults** and the original agent continues execution after the **send** statement. Since **live** must return an instance of *StreamableProperties*, a method for transforming several results is implemented as following.

```
emailAddresses = processResults(returnedResults);
return emailAddresses;
```

The method **processResults** will not be discussed any further in this example, but here is the skeleton anyway.

```
private StreamableProperties
processResults(StreamableList serviceResults)
{
   StreamableProperties someResults = new StreamableProperties();
```

```
    /* fill in someResults with the serviceResults from our clones */
    /* ... */
    return someResults;
}
```

Of course it is possible that the agent returns with many addresses when looking for a common name. The agent programmer has then to decide how and which address to choose or display to the user.

4 Future Work

JAE is currently under development at Aachen University of Technology with demonstrations already running regarding the agent mobility, remote execution of agents and registering services in multi-agent systems. Recent work includes defining the interfaces for service invocation and agent server communication and the complete implementation of the JAE library. Future work will be done in implementing an agent development environment based on JAE including an agent compiler as well as an interface to trading systems that comply with the CORBA standard for distributed systems.

5 References

[1] T. Magedanz: Intelligent Agents - State of the Art and Potential Application Areas in Future Telecommunications. High Speed Networks and Open Distributed Platforms, St. Petersburg 1995

[2] General Magic: *Magic Cap Developer Resources, Technical Documentation.* General Magic Inc., 1996, http://www.genmagic.com/Develop/MagicCap/Docs/

[3] General Magic: *Tabriz White Paper.* General Magic Inc., 1996

[4] Danny B. Lange and Daniel T. Chang: *IBM Aglets Workbench, Programming Mobile Agents in Java.* IBM White Paper, 1996

[5] Java Soft: *Java™ Remote Method Invocation Specification.* Sun Microsystems Inc., Revision 1.0, Draft Oct. 2, 1996

[6] A. S. Park, J. Meggers: *Mobile Middleware: Additional functionalities to cover wireless terminals.* 3rd International Workshop on Mobile Multimedia Communications, Princeton, NJ, Sept. 1996

[7] Küpper, A.; Herzog, H.: *Deploying Trading Services in WWW-based Electronic Service Markets.* (in German). Accepted for KiVS '97, Braunschweig, 1997

[8] Draft Rec. X.950 | ISO/IEC DIS 13235 - *ODP Trading Function,* 1996

[9] OMG Document orbos: *OMG RFP5 Submission, Trading Object Service,* 1996

[10] James E. White: *Telescript Technology: An Introduction to the Language*. General Magic White Paper, 1995

[11] James E. White: *Telescript Technology: Mobile Agents*. General Magic White Paper, 1996

[12] C.G.Harrison, D.M. Chess, A. Kershenbaum: *Mobile Agents: Are they a good idea?* IBM T.J. Watson Research Center, NY, 1995

Contracting and Moving Agents in Distributed Applications Based on a Service-Oriented Architecture

B.Schulze[1,2], E.R.M.Madeira[1]

1.Institute of Computing / UNICAMP PO Box 6176 13083-970 Campinas, SP - Brazil
2.Brazilian Center for Physics Research / CNPq, 22290-180 Rio de Janeiro, RJ - Brazil
Email: [schulze | edmundo]@dcc.unicamp.br

Abstract. This paper presents a service-oriented platform for development and execution of distributed applications based on contracting stationary and migrating services. Services are seen as active objects build on top of a middleware using OMG/CORBA and added features. Customized services add to the middleware the ability to handle transparently application start-up and distribution according to load-balancing and inverse caching application demand. Services can be considered of any kind ranging from scientific specialized processing to data archiving juke-boxes. An application on system management in scientific experimental environment drives the work on some aspects of the architecture.
Keywords. mobile agents, service-oriented architecture, agents distribution, distributed processing, ORB, load-balancing.

1 Introduction

Service-oriented applications make use of available services as much as possible and start new services when they are not available. Just like in any other environment one can make use of services from the shelf and self customize what is not available.

Some of the aspects regarding the development and execution of such a service-oriented application include: initial contracting of services, distribution and setup of additional services not encountered anywhere on the authorized servers. At runtime, the application handles: querying, replying and substituting services. Specific services are redistributed at runtime, regarding load-balancing and inverse-caching [5], i.e., code is moved close to data. Finally, the application has to be shutdown at some point.

Section 2 presents insights from AI and OO suggesting simplifications to distributed programming. Section 3 describes the service-oriented architecture and some services. Section 4 describes implementation details and Section 5 presents concluding remarks.

2 Insights from AI and OO

An interesting notion is the one of *components* [17] as stand-alone objects that can plug-and-play across networks, applications, languages, tools and operating systems. Distributed objects are, by definition, components because of the way they are packed.

An analogy [20] regarding knowledge engineering and programming gives an interesting insight to the paradigm of programming at a higher level of abstraction. The approach is that it requires less work deciding only what objects and relations are worth representing and which relations hold among which objects. There is no need to compute the relations between objects. There is the need only to specify what is true while an inference procedure figures out turning facts into a solution of the problem. If we consider that a fact is true regardless of what task is trying to be solved, then knowledge bases can be reused for a variety of different tasks without modification. The debugging task is expected to be easier because any given sentence is true or false by itself, while the correctness of a program statement depends strongly on its context.

The notions above introduce the field of agent-based software programming [4], as an attempt to make all sorts of systems and resources interoperable by providing a declarative interface based on 1st-order logic.

2.1 Distributed Problem Solving (DPS) and Multi-Agent Systems (MAS)

In DPS, distributed computing environments are used to solve problems which are naturally distributed while complex. Here agents are pre-programmed for cooperation with methods to guarantee this under: coherence, robustness and efficiency. The quality of a DPS system is the global performance in solving the specific problem.

It is not simple to establish these new properties in a collection of individuals, as demonstrated in experiences in Social Sciences, and so, Multi-Agent Systems concentrate studies on basic assumptions about agents for a possible cooperation in society.

In MAS[13], agents range from simple automata to knowledge-based systems, while interactions between agents go from physics-based models to speech acts. Agents organizations are incorporated into complex systems and environments are guided by the type of application.

2.2 Agent Classification

An agent need not to be a program at all [3], but software agents are, by definition, programs that must measure up to several marks to be an agent, presented in Table 2.

"The notion of an agent is meant to be a tool for analyzing systems, not an absolute characterization that divides the world into agents and non-agents." [20].

Table 1. Agent classification [3].

Property	Other Names	Meaning
reactive	(sensing & acting)	timely fashioned response to changes in the environment
autonomous	--	exercises control over its own actions
goal-oriented	pro-active purposeful	does not simply act in response to the environment
temporally-continuous	--	is a continuously running process
communicative	socially able	communicates with other agents, maybe people
learning	adaptive	changes its behavior based on its previous experience
mobile	--	able to transport itself from one machine to another
flexible	--	actions are not scripted
character	--	believable "personality" and emotional state.

2.3 Problem Solving Architecture

An ideal architecture would solve any problem by knowing everything and interacting with any other system. To be practical, an architecture has to come up in time to a good solution of a problem in a particular environment and be able to communicate accordingly in order to sense and react.

Inter communication is a good example of extremes that an architecture has to fit in between. Regarding security on one side, there should exist a fully secure encryption while regarding interoperability on the other side, there should exist a general adaptative protocol, i.e., de-encryption. In fact the moderator between these extremes is *time*, i.e., the time to come to a solution which is still useful in time.

An interesting proposal presented in [2] suggests the understanding and building of interactive knowledge media or collaborative problem solving environments rather then the traditional goal of understanding and building autonomous, intelligent thinking machines. In such a collaborative problem solving systems, users and the system share the problem solving and decision making while different role distributions may be chosen depending on the user's goal, the user's knowledge and the task domain.

A collaborative system should address the point of what part of the responsibility has to be exercised by human beings, and how to organize things for an effective human communication with the computational system.

- a partial understanding and knowledge of complex task domains is acceptable;
- two agents can achieve more than one, by exploring the asymmetry between them;
- breakdowns are not as detrimental, especially if the system provides resources for dealing with the unexpected;
- semi-formal system architectures are appropriate, and
- humans enjoy "doing" and "deciding" by being involved in the process.

In the following sections the notion of agents presented up to here is associated to a notion of services and the building of service-oriented applications, exploring agents' mobile property. In MAS approach agents are contracted from a set of already existing agents willing to collaborate on a common negotiated objective. Mobility therefore is treated as an ability of an agent needed in the fulfillment of a common objective.

3 A Service-Oriented Architecture

The proposed service-oriented architecture is based on the OMG/CORBA(Common Object Request Broker Architecture) and the building components are agents which can be in a stationary phase or in a pre-stationary (mobile) phase. These are associated to services already available and services in the process of being put available.

If an application can not find all needed services it can either wait, abort or customize a replacing service which will certainly demand code migration. Therefore, processing performance can improve with code migration for the purpose of load-balancing of processing and communication.

In the CORBA model, components are addressed transparently and an application can run without having to care where components are. This transparency is extended to agent mobility in such a way that the application doesn't care about specific addresses to move the code, but instead it searches for specific resources needed to load a service and which are offered in an *availability service.*

Using the load-balancing metrics together with the availability service and a mobility service, agents' migration can occur in a transparent way. An additional feature is that initial code distribution at application start-up also happens transparently.

The simple diagram of Fig. 1 illustrates some services in service-oriented applications with the following basic blocks and associations:

• *agents* are all kind of services used by an application

...*available* services are offered by an agency;

...*non-available* services are customized by the application at some site and afterwards treated as an available services;

• *agency* is a basic component able to offer services to an application;

• *negotiation* of services are handled by a *trader* [14];

• *trader* is yet a service for locating other services in a pool of contracted agencies.

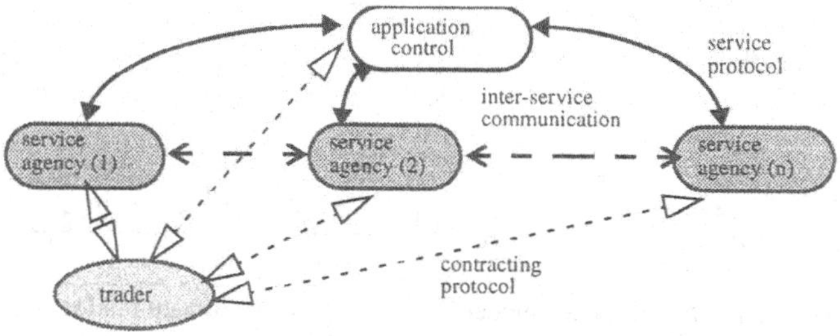

Fig. 1. Service-Oriented Application.

3.1 Services

Computing with services is a higher level of abstraction in implementing any application allowing a reduction of the development effort to the specific objects not available anywhere and to the interconnection of all the active objects regarding the application. The interconnection of these objects will deal with: *contracting*, *locating*, *requesting* and *replying*. The term *active objects* [1, 17, 21] is also equivalent to agents in a multi-agent environment.

Available services. Can be of any kind, like remote: co-processors, databases, data crunching, archiving, specialized processing, etc.

Non-available services. Can be of any kind, like the above, but for some reasons it is just not available in the context. Non-availability can have different meanings like:

• the application has non-authorized access to a service;

• a specific service is not available where needed;

• a service is temporarily disconnected;

• a service is a too specific computation of the application and has to be customized.

The application has to handle this unavailability accordingly and customize the missing service. The customization of a service will handle with: code transportation, resource allocation for execution, naming and registering of the service. After customization the application can deal with the customized service just as it deals with any other already available service. Any service can make use of other remote services and for that there is an inter-service communication.

3.2 Service-Oriented Agency

The agency architecture is composed of an object broker and a collection of agent services, which may include or not an *agent mobility service* and an *availability service*.

An agency with agent mobility and availability services is able to run new services loaded by the application itself, i.e., the agency is open to new services or agents to be loaded by an application demanding this kind of service. In straight relation to the CORBA model and its object services, a service offered by an agency can be called agent and the collection of services called agent services, as sketched in Fig. 2.

Middleware. The Multiware platform [11] sketched in Fig. 3 is the platform on top of which this work is being done. CORBA allows for a good degree of flexibility in the implementation of the core ORB. It can be implemented as a set of runtime libraries, a set of daemon processes, a server machine, or part of an operating system [7].

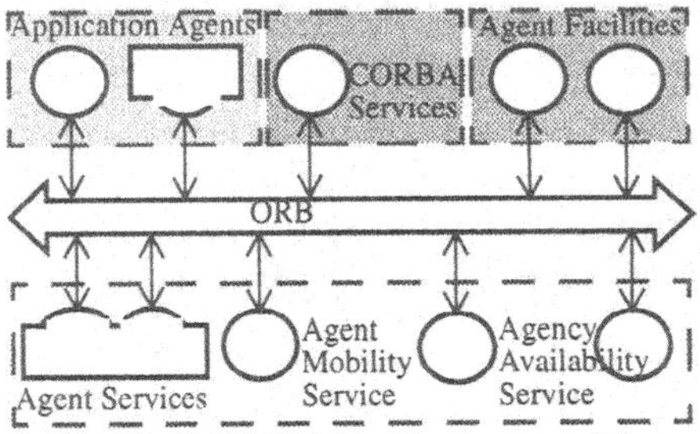

Fig. 2. A CORBA based agency model.

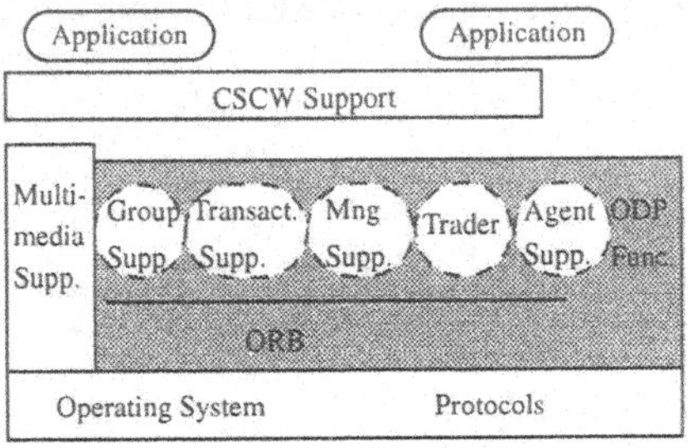

Fig. 3. Multiware Platform.

3.3 Life-Cycle and Persistence

Up to here services can be identified in different phases during its life-cycle:

Start-up. It involves contracting and distribution like considered for any application.

Stationary. This phase of a service can be temporary or indefinite according to the characteristics of the service. Making services available for general usage involves management and distribution of these services in order to guarantee availability as much as possible. One can think of these services as stationary most of the time as long there is no major problem with the network or host on which these services are running. But thinking of services as *always available* demands a natural need to make smooth moves in case of some failure in the environment.

Migration. It is demanded by the environment or the service itself and in attendance to load-balancing, inverse caching or redistribution due to some failure.

Migration involves persistence of code and status, i.e., before moving the agent has to save the variables defining its status and persistently store them. Both, status and code, are moved as sequences and persistently stored at the receiving site, followed by a removal at the sending site after a successfull completed move. At the very moment when the agent is instantiated, it reads back its status into the original variables.

In all situations, after the agent´s arrival, it is instantiated by the *agent support*. This is done in order to recover from the status file the memory on what the agent has to do. If it has just to do nothing and go idle that is coded in the status.

Removal. It follows shutdown or migration of a service. In this phase, there is the possibility of using a migratory agent passed as a token in order to handle any application termination and proper shutdown. A token agent is composed of code and data.

3.4 Mobility Service

Mobility service supports the reception of an agent, its persistent storage and the registration of its interface on the ORB. Basic setup and execution steps are as follows:

- at the sending / receiving end:
  ...ORB running;
  ...registering the mobility service;
  ...calling the mobility service;
  ...marshalling / un-marshalling & sending / receiving of agent;
  ...remove/store agent from persistent storage.

There are some additional steps for moving an agent:

- at the sender
  ...disabling any new request by removing the interface registration;
  ...putting the agent on a dispatch queue;
  ...the service (agent) persisting until conclusion of requests previously attended;
  ...being killed when it goes idle.
- at the receiver
  ...publishing of agent interface;
  ...instantiating when receiving a request.

The persistence service is needed for code and status storage of moving agents.

3.5 Availability Service

When a new service is going to be setup at some site, there is the need to locate and allocate resources on an agency. In order to identify agencies which are open to new services, another service is included in the agency itself: an *availability service* which informs the level of availability of the agency.

The availability service evaluates the loading of an agency using the performance metrics included in the instrumentation facility [19]: *response time*, *throughput*, and *utilization*. Utilization allows different parameters to evaluate loading in terms of: CPU, memory, disk, networking activity, number of users / processes. These numbers are computed including the *specmark* of the particular host in order to allow a comparative value to other hosts. The availability level of the agency is published in order that this parameter can be obtained from a querying to the agency or via a *trader.*

Availability Evaluation. One can think of an evaluation process or daemon just being started when there is an availability request, however, availability has to consider a certain backtracking in time, reflecting the time the application will execute. Considering this approach, availability evaluation demands a continuous running daemon on every host which puts its resources available with a logging of the host loading history.

Continuous running process doing logging are not always welcome because they demand CPU time and storage resources. However, one can think of a dedicated firmware based co-processor(s) on general purpose hosts doing this kind of task while logging can be constrained to a maximum number of history samples, by removing intermediate samples from the history archive as time passes by.

Cheap firmware co-processors remotely programmable, like Sun´s Java chips [24], can help in distributed monitoring tasks and management applications.

3.6 Trading Service

In case of querying via a trader [10, 14], the query includes a range of availability of a specific kind of resource. The trader replies returning a list or simply the most available agency. The selection phase can include a direct interrogation before contracting for the loading of the new service by the application. An additional step at this point allows fine tuning, by using a customized agent to evaluate the agency more closely in case of a very sensible application. This can be added as a trading extended service at the trader side or at the application level itself.

4 Some Implementation Details

Above, the concepts of agents as known in AI were linked with the concepts of distributed OO in OMG's Common Object Request Broker Architecture (CORBA) and here this linking is extended to a middleware implementation and to the ORB it is based on.

4.1 The Object Request Broker (ORB)

The commercial ORB used is an Orbix and next is how it translates the CORBA model:

It consists of library functions linked with clients and servers together with the runtime system, for improved throughput and application distribution. The *server library* can *issue* and *receive* remote object operation requests, while the *client library* can only initiate them. A *daemon* is responsible for launching server processes dynamically as required, according to the various activation policies described in the CORBA specification. Non-distributed client/server applications in the same address space, can use server library alone. Fig. 4 shows how Orbix handles client/server connections.

API. An important step in generating a distributed application is the definition of the interfaces by which clients and servers will communicateis. IDL interfaces are formal standardized interfaces defining the services and how clients shall invoke them. Fig. 5 sketches inter-service communication on the ORB.

IDL. This compiler uses the IDL file to generate the client stubs and the server skeletons. If client and server are going to be on different platforms then the same IDL will be compiled for both platforms with appropriate client and server code.

Stubs & Skeletons. Stubs can be used within the client application as local object method invocations, while on the Server side these methods, i.e., skeletons must be implemented to produce the desired result. Server developers work completely independent of client developers.

Dynamic Invocation. An invocation by a client establishes client/server communication transparently initiated by the daemon. The daemon establishes a connection with the server, passes it back to the host and drops out. In all cases, the client/server interoperability is established while the location and nature of the server's host is kept transparent. The daemon is only concerned with the appropriate servers to be running and with the client/server connections to be established; it is not an ORB itself.

BOA. The basic object adaptor functions are: *putit*-publishes the interface of an object in the implementation repository, *rmit*-removes it, *lsit*-lists all registered interfaces, *catit*-lists details of interfaces, *psit*-shows active objects' status, *killit*-kills an active object.

The *locator* service is used for transparent inter-agency service location. On Orbix, it is possible to include a set of interfaces in a group and also create a group of hosts.

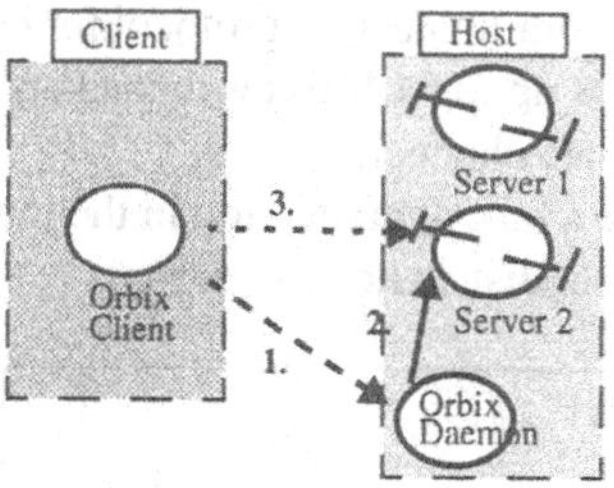

1.Client contacts daemon, explicitly defined or identified via Locator or Name Server.

2.Daemon opens connection to server.

3.Connection to server passed to client. The daemo has no further role to play.

#Daemon waits for new request.

Fig. 4. Client/Server connection with orbix daemon.

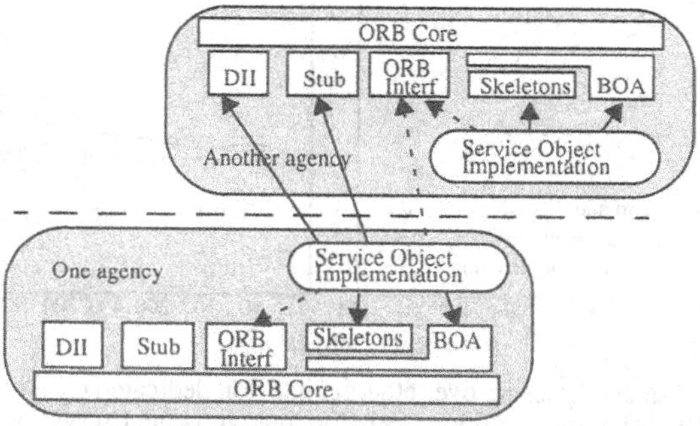

Fig. 5. CORBA Server / Server communication.

4.2 Passing code messages

There is currently an OMG's request for proposal on *passing object by value.* The subject of passing objects [9] is handled here on an Orbix platform passing code as a message in sequence type parameter format. Current results are based on Orbix 1.3.

The object to be sent is read from the persistent *Implementation Repository* at the sending site as a binary sequence into an IDL sequence type parameter. The sequence is sent as a normal parameter to the receiving site and persistently stored locally.

The *Implementation Repository* (IR) is based on a file system, which imposes a separate file for every agent, specially for agents to be moved. A better approach is an OO database to persistently store status and code, specially for increasing number of agents. This is directly related with *persistence service* but not the subject of this work.

Messages of ascii type and binary type up to the size of 1MByte are considered for most applications and are being passed without major problem. In order to estimate an upper bound on the message size and a lower bound on the transfer rate, the performance was measured on the less performing machines in the considered network. The plots in Fig. 6 are based on *sparc*1+ and sparc2 machines non-dedicated to the test, connected over ethernet and using sequence sizes from 10KB to 10MB.

In Fig. 6 (a), the transfer rate drops quickly as the message size goes above 2 MB due to memory allocation and because client and server share the same machine reaching higher rates then in Fig. 6 (b) where client and server run on different machines.

Actually memory allocation for the sequence imposes a message size limit and an alternative is spliting the full message into packets reflecting a buffer size. This technique is well known and should mirror the underlying communication protocol for better performance. In [23], the transmission of image files up to 64 MBytes in packets of 124 KBytes is improved with an external high speed data channel.

Local and remote client/server results in Fig. 6 give a hint of contention in the load-balancing of processing versus communication in global distributed execution.

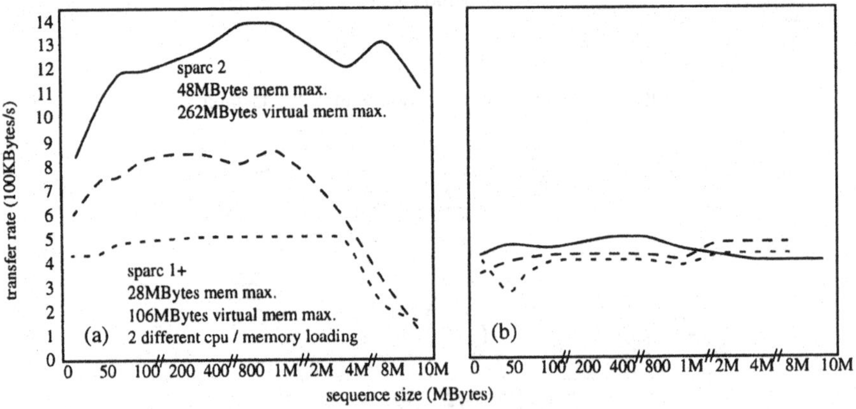

Fig. 6. **(a)** IDL-sequence passing over ethernet in a non dedicated environment and client/server running locally. **(b)** Same conditions as before but with client/server on different hosts..

4.3 Application start-up

The steps regarding start-up of an application under the described environment is resolved by the same mechanism described for the contracting of available services and the loading of new services, i.e., existing services are contracted and unavailable services are distributed to selected agencies departing from an implementation repository site. No relation with OMG's Object Start-up Service describing ORB's start-up.

4.4 Implementation Repository (IR)

There are different possibilities for the distribution of unavailable services regarding their location at start-up. In a simple case, the IR of the application is hold locally at the user's machine and the new services are redistributed as the application demands.

In a more complex application demanding stronger reliability, an IR server can be added, holding a copy of all services to be distributed in this context. At start-up, (re)distribution of services can be done from this server while it is the last server of every list of possible IR used by applications in this context. This server guaranties an available IR copy even in case of failing hosts. It may failure but another server can increase redundancy and so on up to level of the acceptable cost/reliability ratio.

4.5 Unavailable services distribution

Independently of the kind of implementation repository, the new services are redistributed according to the application's demand on load balancing and / or inverse caching. This means that if distribution is not demanded by the application in the current environment circumstances, then it runs just locally. Another possibility is that the application has to wait in the start-up queue for sufficient resources.

4.6 Results on application distribution

An application start-up result is presented next, for two already mentioned situations demanding migration of objects: load balancing and inverse caching.

Inverse caching. These conditions are considered as follows:

- an object needs to move to a specific site to run attached to a contracted service;
- the moving object has to contract the local agent support and demand migration to where the specific service is;
- the agent support locates the specific service and sends the agent calling the remote agent support as a inherited class / method.

Load-balancing. These conditions are similar to the previous ones plus some considerations:

- an appropriate agency is contracted under the availability service query criteria;
- availability services are identified in a unique way by concatenation with the host name and invocation using multicast;
- the selected availability service name is passed to the local agent support which locates the specific service and sends the agent whose migration was requested.

Evaluation. It is based on a stationary client sharing the execution of a problem with a moving server. The client searches for memory and CPU availability for the moving server execution, contacting every host in the group, including itself. Execution status is kept by the client while the server restarts on a new host in its initial state.

The actual code of the server is made available on every host so that only the execution is passed to the server on the next selected host. This decouples this test from the previous one of code passing performance in Section 4.2. The transparent distribution of the application allows exactly the same application to be started several times running concurrently with every other new one started.

Testing was done in a homogeneous environment with migrating agents implemented in a common C++, but Java [18] features and similarities to C++ make it attractive while running interpreted code is not necessarily a major constraint.

4.7 Updating, Debugging and Management Aspects

A translation of concepts of Section 2 related to debugging, updating and management is possible. To update a long-living application once it is released and running, can be very cumbersome, specially to bring it down and the subsequent start-up. Debugging and updating of a full application build with agents are simplified to the replacement of separate components/agents since each one can be shutdown and restarted separately without a global shutdown/start-up.

Management of applications stands for task management but management of a collection of services (agencies) is outside the application's authority and if looking from the service provider, stands to distributed system management. However, services interacting with other remote services is an application itself using task management.

Some fixed services for management were implemented [19] and new services will take advantage of mobility. Agents with different problem solving strategies in management can be allowed, remaining the most effective.

Management levels are proposed for a step wise allowance in sensing and reacting. The history of the system participates on every new hint issued and a learning phase followed by an execution phase in a successive repetition keeps the system up-to-date.

5 Conclusion

The proposed architecture introduces an *availability service* as a way to combine the usage of fixed services and moving services in an environment where available services are contracted and unavailable services are customized and then contracted. This is clearly illustrated by an application start-up where transparent code distribution and later redistribution is possible. Every machine open for new applications in a certain context has to have the availability service built as a fixed service. The trader and the mobility service are related and particularly important in heterogeneous environments.

Distributed Client / Server paradigm can be extended with the usage of code migration. Migration or mobility makes it possible to reduce network traffic, to optimize load balancing, and to provide better response time to the user. Mobility can be considered as an essential component of future open systems improving software distribution at large, specially if the technology runs across multiple platforms. Additional requirements are introduced, particularly on security and interoperability that make it hard to run with the same performance of native code. But, after all, native code is not mobile.

Some scientific applications [25] in experimental facilities need to run continuously for long periods, stand dynamic reconfigurations for upgrading hard/software and changes in the search for special events. Management of such applications demand the ability to upgrade platforms and software over the life-cycle of a process in a more flexible manner, replacing components over time and/or a complete software update.

Acknowledgments. This work is partially funded by: FAPESP, CAPES and CNPq.

References:

1. E. Cardozo, J.S. Sichman and Y. Demazeau. *Using the Active Object Model to Implement Multi-Agents Systems*, Proceeding of the 5th IEEE Conference on Tools with Artificial Intelligence, Boston, USA, pp 70-77, November 93.

2. G. Fischer. *Rethinking and Reinventing Artificial Intelligence from the Perspective of Human-Centered Computational Artifacts,* LNAI #991 Springer-Verlag, pp 1-11, 95.
3. S. Franklin and A. Graesser. I*s it an Agent, or just a Program?: A Taxonomy for Autonomous Agents,* 3rd Int. Workshop on Agent Theories, Architectures, and Languages, 96, www.msci.memphis.edu/~franklin/AgentProg.html.
4. M.R. Genesereth and S.P. Ketchpel. *Software agents.* Communication of the ACM, 37(7), July 94, pp 49-53, http://logic.stanford.edu/sharing/papers/agents.ps.
5. G.S. Goldszmidt. *Distributed Management by Delegation,* Ph.D. Thesis, Graduate School of Arts and Sciences, Columbia University, US, 96.
6. C.Iglesias, J.C.Gonzalez and J.R.Velasco, *MIX: A General Purpose Multiagent Architecture,* LNAI #1037 Springer-Verlag, pp 251-266, 96.
7. IONA Technologies, Ltd. *OrbixTalk: Management Overview,* April, 96, www.iona.com/ Orbix/Talk/MO/CorbaIntro.html.
8. S.Krause and T. Magedanz. *Mobile Service Agents enabling "Intelligence on Demand" in Telecommunications,* IEEE GLOBECOM'96, London, UK, pp 78-84, November 96.
9. D.B. Lange and D.T. Chang. *Aglets Workbench,* IBM Corporation, August, 96, www.ibm.co.jp/trl/aglets.
10. L.A.P. Lima Jr. and E.R.M. Madeira. *A Model for a Federative Trader,* Open Distributed Processing: Experiences with Distributed Environment, pp.173-184, Chapman&Hall, 95.
11. W.P.C. Loyolla, E.R.M. Madeira, M.J Mendes, E. Cardozo and M.F. Magalhães. *Multiware Platform: An Open Distributed Environment for Multimedia Cooperative Applications,* IEEE COMPSAC'94, Taipei, Taiwan, November, 94.
12. M.J Mendes et al. *Agents Skills and their roles in mobile computing and personal communications,* IFIP 14th World Computer Congress, World Conference on Mobile Communications, Canberra, Australia, September, 96.
13. MAGMA. cosmos.imag.fr/MAGMA/magma_research.html, 1st Feb., 95.
14. ODP. *Trading Functions,* ISO/IEC JTC1/SC 21, June, 95, ftp.dstc.edu.au/pub/arch/RM-ODP.
15. OMG. *Common Facilities Architecture, Rev. 4.0,* OMG Document # 95-1-2, January, 95.
16. OMG. *The Common Object Request Broker: Architecture and Specification,* rev 2.0, July, 95.
17. R.Orfali, Dan Harkey and J.Edwards. *The Essential Distributed Objects Survival Guide,* John Wiley & Sons, 96.
18. OSF. *Java Mobile Code Paper,* 15/01/96. www.gr.osf.org/projects/web/java/whit_pap.htm.
19. A. Queiroz and E.R.M. Madeira. *Management of CORBA objects monitoring for the Multiware platform,* ICODP'97, Toronto, Canada, May97, accepted for publication.
20. S. Russel, P. Norvig. *Artificial Intelligence, A Modern Approach,* Prentice Hall Series in Artificial Intelligence, New Jersey, pp 33, USA, 95.
21. J.S. Sichman and Y. Demazeau. *Exploiting Social Reasoning to Enhance Adaptation in Open Multi-Agent Systems,* LNAI #991 Springer, pp 253-263, October, 95.
22. D.C. Schmidt, S. Vinoski. *Object Interconnections: Modeling Distributed Object Applications (Column2),* SIGS C++ Report Magazine, February, 95.
23. D.C. Schmidt, T. Harrison, E. Al-Shaer. *Object Oriented Components for High-speed Network Programming,* Proc.Usenix Conf. on OO Technologies, Monterey, CA, USA, June, 95.
24. Sun Microsystems Inc. February 2, 96, www.sun.com/sparc/newsreleases/nr95-042.html.
25. DELPHI Trigger Group. *Architecture and performance of the DELPHI trigger system,* Nuclear Instruments and Methods in Physics Research A 362, pp 361-385, 95.

Concordia: An Infrastructure for Collaborating Mobile Agents

David Wong, Noemi Paciorek, Tom Walsh,
Joe DiCelie, Mike Young, Bill Peet
Mitsubishi Electric ITA
Horizon Systems Laboratory
1432 Main Street
Waltham, MA 02154, USA
email: {wong,noemi,walsh,dicelie,young,billp}@meitca.com

Abstract

Use of the Internet and the World-Wide-Web has become widespread in recent years and mobile agent technology has proliferated at an equally rapid rate. In this paper, we introduce the *Concordia* infrastructure for the development and management of network-efficient mobile agent applications for accessing information anytime, anywhere, and on any device.

Concordia has been implemented in the Java language to ensure platform independence among agent applications. The design goals of *Concordia* have focused on providing complete coverage of flexible agent mobility, support for agent collaboration, agent persistence, reliable agent transmission, and agent security.

Concordia offers a flexible scheme for dynamic invocation of arbitrary method entry points within a common agent application and extends the notion of simple agent interaction with support for agent collaboration, which allows agents to interact, modify external states (e.g., a database), as well as internal agent states. *Concordia* provides support for agent persistence and recovery and guarantees the transmission of agents across a network. *Concordia* has also been designed to provide for fairly complete security coverage from the outset. An alpha release of *Concordia* is available.

1. Introduction

Use of the Internet and the World-Wide-Web has become widespread in recent years and agent technology has proliferated at an equally rapid rate. There are two commonly accepted classes of agents in the literature: intelligent agents and mobile agents [25]. Intelligent agents are typically static entities with much built-in intelligence to perform a specific task. Mobile agents, on the other hand, are dynamic and have the ability to traverse an entire network, performing a number of tasks along the way, but with minimal intelligence. A number of recent efforts have been initiated to address the latter class of agents [1,14,15,21,23].

Concordia is a new framework for developing and executing highly mobile agents. *Concordia* offers a full-featured middleware infrastructure for the development and management of network-efficient mobile agent applications for accessing information anytime, anywhere, and on both wire-based and wireless devices. *Concordia* has been implemented in the Java language to ensure unimpeded interoperability and platform independence among agent applications. The design goals of *Concordia* have focused on providing complete coverage of flexible agent mobility, support for agent collaboration, persistence of agent state, reliable agent transmission, and agent security.

The remainder of the paper will proceed as follows. In Section 2, we discuss the overall system architecture of *Concordia*. In Section 3, we discuss *Concordia* agent mobility and transport. In Section 4, we present *Concordia* support for agent interaction. Finally, in Section 5, we discuss the current status of this work and the future directions that this work may take.

2. System Architecture

The *Concordia* infrastructure toolkit consists of a set of Java class libraries for server execution, agent application development, and agent activation. Each node in a *Concordia* system consists of a number of interacting component servers that could be executing on one or more Java virtual machines as shown in Fig. 1.

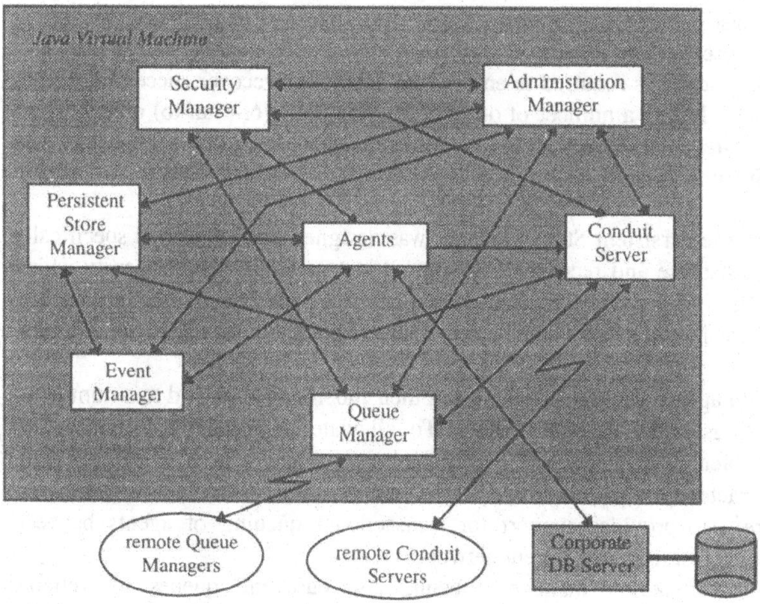

Concordia is similar to a number of existing agent infrastructures and toolkits with respect to its support for the basic communication plumbing that is required for agent mobility. For instance, both FTP Software's *CyberAgents* [5] and UC Berkeley's *Java-To-Go* [14] require the notion of a agent *propagation* server to propagate an agent. In *CyberAgents*, this server is called a *community*, while in *Java-To-Go*, this server is called the *Hall Server*. In the University of Stuttgart's *Project Mole*, this propagation service is embedded in the *location* server[13]. In *Concordia*, this propagation server is called the *Conduit Server*.

The Conduit Server serves as the communication server for agent transfer. An agent program initiates its transfer by invoking the Conduit Server's methods. The Conduit Server then proceeds to propagate the agent to the Conduit Server at another *Concordia* system. *Concordia's* agent mobility mechanism extends beyond the functionality provided in other Java-based agent systems by also offering a flexible scheme for dynamic invocation of arbitrary method entry points within a common agent application. This flexible scheme for agent mobility is discussed in more detail in Section 3.

While a number of efforts have provided support for agent interaction [1,5], *Concordia* extends this notion of simple agent interaction with support for two forms of inter-agent communication: asynchronous distributed events and agent *collaboration*. Asynchronous distributed events are scheduled and managed by the *Event Manager*, while agent collaboration requires the agent application programmer to specify a collaborating *AgentGroup* object through the utilization of the *Concordia* class libraries. Agent collaboration allows agents to interact, modify external states (e.g., a database), as well as internal agent states. Inter-agent communication is discussed in more detail in Section 4.

Agent persistence is required to ensure that agents can recover successfully from system crashes. Just as a number of other efforts currently (or plan to) offer support for agent persistence [1,7], *Concordia* also offers support for agent persistence. The *Persistent Store Manager* allows the internal state of agent objects to become persistable.

Although the Persistent Store Manager was designed and developed specifically to support persistence and recovery of agents, it is a general-purpose facility which may also be used to store internal state to facilitate recovery after server failure. The Persistent Store Manager implementation is based on the Java object serialization facilities.

Concordia agents are highly mobile and their mobility can extend to a number of local as well as wide area networks. To alleviate potential performance and reliability problems associated with the transmission of agents across networks with different characteristics in the underlying communication medium, the *Concordia* infrastructure also provides support for transactional queuing of agents between Conduit Servers residing on different networks.

The *Queue Manager* manages inbound and outbound queues for reliable transport of agents across a network. The Queue Manager communicates with its local Conduit Server and performs handshaking with other remote Queue Managers for reliable agent transmission. The Queue Manager design goals centered on achieving optimal disk space utilization, fast write operations, and fast recovery from server failure. Its implementation borrowed some ideas from the log-structured file systems research area [19,20] to employ a unique data architecture which ensures better overall performance over traditional message queuing systems [6,8,16]. The preservation of an object's class specification on disk is handled by the Java object serialization facilities while Queue Manager communication relies on the Java RMI package.

Concordia's security model provides support for two types of protection: (1) protection of agents from being tampered with, and (2) protection of server resources from unauthorized access.

Agents are protected from tampering while stored on client systems during transmission and while stored on the persistent store. Storage protection is handled by encryption. The only other system to address agent protection on both the client and server is the Itinerant Agents [4]. *Concordia* uses the SSLv3 protocol to transmit agent information from one system to another. Transmission protection is a de facto requirement for an agent application. In contrast, CyberAgents and Telescript appear to only provide secure internet transmission using encryption and digital signatures [5,23].

Concordia has implemented a highly flexible user-based security mechanism for server resource protection. The *Concordia Security Manager,* a Java object owned by the Java VM rather than a full-fledge process or thread, manages resource protection. Each agent is assigned an identity which allows the agent to access server resources. Resource permissions for agents can also be dynamically adjusted to increase or decrease an agent's security clearance. *Concordia's* resource protection differs from Aglets and CyberAgents in that it is based on the user of the agent rather than the developer of the agent. [1,5].

Concordia system administration is handled by the *Administration Manager.* The Administration Manager starts up and shuts down the other servers in the *Concordia* agent system. It also manages changes in the security profile of both agents and servers in the system and makes requests on behalf of the agent or server to the Security Manager. The Administration Manager also monitors the progress of agents through out the network and maintains agent and system statistics.

Users interact with a *Concordia* system by developing agent application programs. In the *Concordia* infrastructure, agent application programs are implemented as Java objects. Users would first need to write a Java class that specifies some action, such as accessing a database on a remote node. Once this Java class is written and compiled, the user can *launch* the agent program in three ways: (1) via a GUI Agent Launch Wizard, (2) via a command line tool, or (3) using the external API. The first two mechanisms are provided with *Concordia,* while the last one requires the user to write a customized launch class which makes use of the *Concordia* class libraries.

3. Agent Mobility

Since the agent objects are composed of a combination of code and data, object mobility means the network transportation of both code and data. As stated earlier, agent mobility is accomplished by the Conduit Server. Beyond providing for just the mobility of code and data, *Concordia* provides for the transmission of state information detailing where the agent has been and what it has accomplished as well as where it is going and what it still has to do. *Concordia* also provides interfaces allowing agents to create other agents and to clone themselves.

Some of the design goals for the Conduit Server were:

1. Provide for mobility that is transparent to users of the system.
2. Provide a programming model as close as possible to that of "regular" programming.
3. Build on existing infrastructure where available.

Within *Concordia*, an agent's travels are described by its *Itinerary*. The Itinerary is a data structure which is stored and maintained outside of the agent object itself. The Itinerary is composed of multiple *Destinations*. Each Destination describes a location to which an agent is to travel and the work the agent is to accomplish at that location. In the current implementation, location is defined by a hostname of a machine on the network and the work to accomplish is by a particular method of the agent class. Thus, if you had an agent class containing two methods, named *method1* and *method2*, a potential Itinerary for this agent could look like the following;

LOCATION	METHOD
server1.mycompany.com	method1
server2.mycompany.com	method2

When an agent is launched with this Itinerary, the agent would first travel to the machine identified by the TCP/IP hostname *server1.mycompany.com*. At that location the method *method1* would be invoked automatically by the agent system. After *method1* completes execution, the agent is transferred by the system to the node *server2.mycompany.com*. As the agent is transferred to the new location all of its internal state, meaning all of the information stored in its member variables, is transferred with it. This allows the agent to remember any computations it made at prior stops in its travels. Once the agent arrives at *server2* the system invokes its *method2* method which is allowed to run to completion.

There are some important characteristics of this Itinerary model that is worth noting. The Itinerary is a completely separate data structure from the agent itself. Thus where the agent travels is maintained in a separate logical location than what the agent does. This is very different than the Telescript [23] model where an agent's travel is initiated in its code by a call to its *go* method. A design decision was made to separate the agent's Itinerary from its code since this leads to a much more manageable system. Without extensive analysis of the Telescript code composing an agent and some knowledge of what runtime conditions will be like, it can be difficult to predict where a Telescript agent may travel. Further, it can be very difficult to locate where a Telescript agent has traveled after it has been launched. *Concordia*'s Itinerary model provides a simple mechanism for defining and tracking how an agent travels. For flexibility reasons, the system allows agent's to modify their Itineraries at runtime.

This Itinerary model also allows for multiple entry points into the agent to be executed at multiple locations. It appears that some existing agent systems, such as IBM's Aglets [2] or FTP Software's CyberAgents only support a single entry point into the agent. In these systems, at each stop in the agent's Itinerary, this entry point method is invoked when the agent arrives. Within the code of this one method, the agent must determine what work has previously been executed and then proceed to dispatch to the proper code to handle the work left to be completed.

This single entry point model unnecessarily presents the agent programmer with a different programming model than that of the non-mobile programming paradigm. For complex agent applications, this constraint can require the programmer to maintain a large amount of state information which can be better encapsulated within the agent's Itinerary.

Mobility of an agent's data was accomplished using the Java Object Serialization facility [17]. Transfer an agent state is a matter of serializing an agent's data down into a format suitable for network transmission, transmitting the data in this format, and then deserializing the data back into the original agent. This is very similar to the mechanism used by Java Remote Method Invocation (RMI) [18] for passing an object *by value* between distributed objects. RMI itself does not provide for true object mobility as it provides for no mobility of an object's code and in fact requires that the code for any objects passed by value be pre-installed on both sides of the network connection.

Java's Object Serialization features provide an almost transparent mechanism by which Java objects can be serialized into data streams and provided suitable technology for implementing agent mobility.

The problem of transmitting an Agent's code is solved in a manner similar to the way in which a web browser loads a Java applet. A browser will typically implement a special Java class called a called a *ClassLoader* [11]. The Java virtual machine makes a callback into the ClassLoader object whenever the system attempts to load the bytecodes for a Java class. In response to this callback, the ClassLoader implemented within the browser makes an HTTP request to a web browser in order to retrieve the file on the server containing the bytecodes for the class. The Java language provides a mechanism for converting the contents of this file into an actual Java class from which objects can be instantiated.

The *Concordia* infrastructure uses a very similar mechanism to support mobility of code. As an agent travels around a network its bytecodes and the bytecodes of any objects it creates and stores in its member variables are loaded via a special ClassLoader. This ClassLoader packages theses bytecodes into a special data structure which travels with the agent. During the deserialization of the agent, the bytecodes for the agent and its related classes can be retrieved from this data structure and are used to instantiate a new copy of the agent.

4. Agent Communication

Concordia includes two paradigms for inter-agent communication: asynchronous distributed events and collaboration. Its distributed events are, in many ways, similar to those offered by other systems. However, *Concordia*'s implementation of collaboration extends the events mechanisms in unique ways. Hence, this section examines both modes of communication, but explores collaboration in greater detail.

4.1. Events

Concordia provides two forms of asynchronous distributed events: selected events and group-oriented events. The event selection paradigm enables agents to define the types of events they wish to receive. In contrast, group-oriented events are distributed to a collection of agents (known as an event group) without any selection.

Selected Events

Concordia's *EventManager* object is the focal point for selected events. It accepts event registrations, listens for and receives events, and notifies interested parties of each event it receives. The EventManager filters each event it receives by notifying only those objects (e.g., agents) that have registered to receive events of that type.

Before an agent (or any other object) can receive selected events, it must register with the EventManager by sending it a list of event types it is interested in receiving and a reference to a location where it wishes events to be sent. This location is actually a distributed object. Hence, the EventManager can forward events to an agent even after it migrates to another system. Agents may choose to handle events synchronously in their main thread or asynchronously in an event handler thread.

The EventManager saves all registrations it receives in persistent storage via requests to the Persistent Store Manager. No registrations are lost during EventManager failures because it retrieves outstanding registrations from persistent storage whenever it restarts. Furthermore, EventManager failures and restarts are transparent to agents because they communicate via an *EventManagerProxy* object rather than directly with the EventManager. This proxy is responsible for re-establishing failed connections with the EventManager. (The EventManager itself is automatically restarted by an administration server that starts and monitors critical *Concordia* servers.)

The selected events programming paradigm is simple and easy to utilize in agent applications. As an example, an application may launch an agent that will notify it when the airfare between two cities drops below a certain price. The agent may migrate to a remote location and monitor a database containing travel information. When the agent detects the conditions have been met, it can notify the application via an event. Events are also commonly used to inform an application of exceptional conditions encountered by agents it launches. (In the future, this may also be accomplished via e-mail.)

Group-Oriented Events

As mentioned earlier, *Concordia* distributes group-oriented events to groups of objects without filtering them. Agents within an application that need to communicate or coordinate with each other often do so via group-oriented events. As an example, agents may wish to be notified when an agent within the same application encounters exceptional conditions. In particular, collaborating agents communicate via group-oriented events.

Joining an event group is a prerequisite for communicating via group-oriented events. Joining a group is similar to registering with the EventManager: each object (e.g., agent) joining the group sends it a reference to a distributed object where it wishes events to be forwarded. When the event group receives an event from one of its members, it forwards it to other objects in the group. Hence, all group-oriented events are distributed to the event group's entire membership.

Concordia offers two flavors of event groups: basic and persistent. The *EventGroup* object implements the basic functionality described above. The *PersistentEventGroup* object adds persistent group membership and reliable, transparent recovery from failures via proxy objects.

4.2. Collaboration

Distributed events have many applications, but they are not flexible enough to manage complex agent coordination. *Concordia*'s collaboration framework facilitates this type of interaction by enabling multiple agents to work together to solve complex problems.

Consider the following scenario: A user wishes to determine the best package price for a ski trip given the following criteria: a resort in the Alps, for a week in February, with slopeside lodging, and the lowest price for all expenses. To solve this problem, an agent obtains a list of appropriate ski resorts from a database before spawning other agents to query travel databases, possibly in different formats, for package prices at those resorts in February. Agents can perform this task more efficiently when they can correlate their results and adjust their computations based on the outcome of that collaboration.

Suppose the agents visit local travel agencies and then share their intermediate results and collaborate before migrating to travel agency sites in other cities. If an agent determines that a particular resort does not have any available lodging meeting the user's criteria, the agents may determine to drop queries about trips to that destination. As more information is gathered, agents may also make other decisions. As this example demonstrates, agents can perform complex distributed computations more effectively if they correlate their results and alter their behavior based on the combined results. *Concordia*'s collaboration framework facilitates this process.

The class of application described above divides a complex task into smaller pieces and delegates them to agents that migrate throughout the network to accomplish them. These agents perform computations, synchronously share results, and collaboratively determine any changes to future actions.

Concordia employs a simple programming paradigm for this type of collaboration. The goals of the collaboration framework include:

1. A simple programming interface for synchronous collaboration.
2. Asynchronous notification of exceptional conditions via events.
3. Reliable and robust implementation utilizing proxy objects to shield agents from the effects of software failures within the collaboration framework.
4. An infrastructure that enables location transparent inter-agent communication.

Agents within an application may form one or more collaboration units, known as agent groups. *Concordia* provides base classes for collaborating agents and agent groups (i.e., *CollaboratorAgent* and *AgentGroup*, respectively). AgentGroups are implemented as distributed objects which export a simple interface to CollaboratorAgents. These agents hold remote references to AgentGroup distributed objects and access them via Java's Remote Method Invocation (RMI) facility.

AgentGroup collaboration is implemented via a distributed synchronization point, known as a collaboration point, and a software method, *analyzeResults*. The AgentGroup abstraction provides the distributed synchronization. Each application need only supply its own implementation of analyzeResults to analyze the collective results of the agents in the group and to allow each agent to adapt its behavior based on those results. Both the synchronization point and invocation of analyzeResults are encapsulated within the AgentGroup's *collaborate* method.

This distributed synchronization scheme requires that each agent "arrive" at the collaboration point (by invoking the collaborate method on the AgentGroup distributed object) before collaboration may commence. Hence, it is ideally suited to applications that subdivide a complex problem into sub-tasks that correlate their results. When each agent arrives at the collaboration point, it posts the results of its computation to the AgentGroup and blocks until all the agents in the group arrive.

The AgentGroup collects the results of the agents' computations, and when all agents in the group arrive at a collaboration point, its collaborate method invokes analyzeResults on behalf of each agent, passing it the collective result set. The AgentGroup abstraction supports both parallel and serialized execution of the analysis stage of collaboration.

Concordia also provides both strong and weak collaboration models. Applications may specify (via an argument to the AgentGroup's constructor) whether collaboration should be allowed to continue if agents in the group fail to arrive at the collaboration point. The weak collaboration paradigm is useful for information-gathering agents that may wish to coordinate with each other even if some agents have terminated prematurely or encountered network failures. Agents that modify external states (e.g., updating a database) generally employ the strong collaboration paradigm, which aborts collaborations if all agents in the group do not arrive at the collaboration point.

The AgentGroup also utilizes time-outs to detect potential deadlocks. Note that since AgentGroup collaboration is designed for closely coordinated agents, deadlocks are generally caused by programming errors. Hence, the AgentGroup does not need to use a more sophisticated scheme for deadlock detection or avoidance.

An added benefit of AgentGroup collaboration is that it enables location-transparent inter-agent communication. As each agent migrates, it carries a remote reference to an AgentGroup distributed object and utilizes the AgentGroup as a gateway for communicating with the other members of the group.

As mentioned earlier, AgentGroups facilitate both synchronous collaboration and asynchronous notifications. This is possible because the AgentGroup object derives from the PeristentEventGroup object. AgentGroups forward any events they receive from their members (e.g., that an agent caught an exception) to the remainder of the group. Occasionally, they may also initiate events that they deliver to the group.

A benefit of this event management scheme is that AgentGroups temporarily queue events for in-transit agents and flush them after the agents arrive at their new destinations. Hence, no events are lost during agent migration.

The AgentGroup's persistent membership and agent status information also increase reliability. Whenever the group membership or the status of one of its agents changes, the AgentGroup saves the current state to persistent storage. If an AgentGroup terminates prematurely, it is restarted and restores the current state from persistent storage. Events queued for in-transit agents may optionally be saved to persistent storage.

AgentGroup restarts are transparently handled by *AgentGroupProxy* objects. Instead of communicating directly with an AgentGroup object, agents communicate via proxies which shield them from the effects of AgentGroup failures. Each agent creates its own AgentGroupProxy and the proxies coordinate to atomically re-create the AgentGroup, if it terminates or fails to communicate.

As detailed above, *Concordia*'s collaboration paradigm offers several benefits: a simple programming interface for synchronous collaboration; asynchronous distributed event management; support for agent mobility; location-transparent inter-agent communication; reliability, persistence, and transparent recovery from failure; deadlock detection; and a portable implementation. No other agent collaboration implementation offers all these features.

In contrast to *Concordia*'s simple programming interface in a language increasingly used for application development, Telescript is a language designed for writing mobile agents. It supports agent cloning and provides meeting places -- locations where mobile agents may communicate with stationary specialized agents (e.g., a mobile agent may request the lowest airfare between two points). Telescript does not, however, possess any support for agent collaboration. IBM's Itinerant Agents [4] also utilize an agent meeting point abstraction that is very similar to Telescript's meeting places.

The artificial intelligence community provides a broad range of agent collaboration features with an agent communication language (ACL) [10] (which actually consists of two different languages (KQML and KIF) [9]), combined with the development of an application-specific ontology [12]. Hence, it is much more difficult to program agent collaboration with ACL given its added complexity. In addition, ACL does not support mobile agents.

Other agent implementations [3,22,24] provide some of the features of *Concordia*'s collaboration framework, but fall short in several other areas.

5. Conclusion

In this paper, we have described the *Concordia* middleware infrastructure for collaborating mobile agents. *Concordia* offers a complete framework for the development and management of network-efficient mobile agent applications. The design goals of *Concordia* have centered on providing support for flexible agent mobility, agent collaboration, agent persistence, reliable agent transmission, and agent security.

Concordia's agent mobility mechanism extends beyond the functionality found in current Java-based agent systems by offering a flexible scheme for dynamic invocation of arbitrary method entry points within a common agent application. The *Concordia* framework offers support for agent interaction via the notion of agent *collaboration*, which allows agents to interact, modify external states, as well as internal agent states. *Concordia* also provides support for agent persistence and guarantees reliable transmission of agents across a network. *Concordia* has been designed to provide complete security coverage from the outset.

Concordia has been implemented in Java to ensure platform independence among agent applications. A alpha release of Concordia is available at the Mitsubishi Electric ITA Web site (URL=*http://www.meitca.com)*. Future extensions to the existing functionality may include support for transactional multi-agent applications and knowledge discovery for collaborating agents.

6. References

[1] *Aglets: Mobile Java Agents*, IBM Tokyo Research Lab, URL=http://www.ibm.co.jp/trl/projects/aglets

[2] D. T. Chang, D. B. Lange, "Programming Mobile Agents in Java" URL=*http://www.trl.ibm.co.jp/aglets/*

[3] D. T. Chang, D. B. Lange, "Mobile Agents: A New Paradigm for Distributed Object Computing on the WWW", In *Proceedings of the OOPSLA96 Workshop: Toward the Integration of WWW and Distributed Object Technology*, October 1996.

[4] D. Chess, B. Grosof, C. Harrison, D. Levine, C. Parris, "Itinerant Agents for Mobile Computing", *IEEE Personal Communications Magazine*, 2(5), October 1995.

[5] *CyberAgents* Documentation, FTP Software Inc., URL=http://www.ftp.com

[6] *DECmessageQ Programmer's Guide,* Digital Equipment Corporation, Maynard, Massachusetts, 1994.

[7] "Distributed and Mobile Object Projects", OSF Research Institute, URL=http://www.osf.org/RI/DMO/DMO.html

[8] *Encina RQS Programmer's Guide*, Transarc Corporation, Pittsburgh, Pennsylvania, 1994.

[9] T. Finin, R. Fritzson, D. McKay, "A Language and Protocol to Support Intelligent Agent Interoperability", In *Proceedings of the CE & CALS Washington '92 Conference*, June 1992.

[10] M. R. Genesereth, S. P. Ketchpel, "Software Agents", *Communications of the ACM*, 37(7):48-53, July 1994.

[11] J. Gosling, F. Yellin, The Java Team, "Java API Documentation Version 1.0.2 - Class ClassLoader", URL=*http://java.sun.com/products/JDK/1.0.2/api/*

[12] T. R. Gruber, "A Translation Approach to Portable Ontologies", *Knowledge Acquisition*, 5(2):199-220, 1993.

[13] F. Hohl, *Mole Alpha 1.0 Documentation*, URL= http://www.informatik.unistuttgart.de/ipvr/vs/projekte/mole.html

[14] W. Li, *Java-To-Go*, Univ. of California, Berkeley, URL= http://ptolemy.eecs.berkeley.edu/~wli/group/java2go/java-to-go.html

[15] D.S. Milojicic, M. Condict, F. Reynolds, D. Bolinger, and P. Date, "Mobile Objects and Agents", In *Proceedings of the Second USENIX Conference on Object Oriented Technologies and Systems (COOTS),* Toronto, Canada, June 1996.

[16] *MQSeries: Message Queuing Interface Technical Reference*, IBM Corporation, Armonk, New York, 1994.

[17] "Object Serialization for Java", Javasoft Corporation, URL=*http://chatsubo.javasoft.com/current/serial/index.html*

[18] "Remote Method Invocation for Java", Javasoft Corporation, URL=*http://chatsubo.javasoft.com/current/rmi/index.html*

[19] M. Seltzer, "Transaction Support in a Log-Struct ured File System", In *Proceedings of the Ninth International Conference on Data Engineering*, February, 1993.

[20] M. Seltzer, K. Bostic, M. McKusick, C. Staelin, "A Log-Structured File System for UNIX", In *Proceedings of the 1993 Winter Usenix Conference*.

[21] M. Straβer, J. Baumann, F. Hohl, "MOLE: A Java Based Mobile Agent System", In *Proceedings of the European Conference on Object Oriented Programming*, 1996.

[22] K. Sycara, K. Decker, A. Pannu, M. Williamson, D. Zeng, "Distributed Intelligent Agents", The Robotics Institute, Carnegie Mellon University Technical Report, 1996.

[23] J. E. White, "Telescript Technology: Mobile Agents", General Magic White Paper, 1996.

[24] D. Woelk, M. Huhns, C. Tomlinson, "InfoSleuth Agents: The Next Generation of Active Objects", Microelectronics and Computer Technology Corporation White Paper, 1996.

[25] M. Wooldridge, N.R. Jennings, *Intelligent Agents: Theories, Architectures, and Languages*, Lecture Notes in AI, Vol. 890, Springer-Verlag Publisher, Berlin, Germany,1995.

The OMG Mobile Agent Facility: A Submission

Daniel T. Chang and Stefan Covaci

IBM and GMD FOKUS
dtchang@vnet.ibm.com and covaci@fokus.gmd.de

Abstract

GMD FOKUS, IBM and The Open Group have jointly submitted to the OMG a specification on the Mobile Agent Facility for evaluation and adoption. This paper gives an overview of the technical requirements of the OMG Request for Proposal, the design goals of the joint submission, the architecture of the proposed Mobile Agent Facility, and the salient features of its interfaces.

1. Introduction

The Object Management Group (OMG) has been adopting and promoting technologies for distributed object computing since 1989. The central architecture and programming paradigm which tie all the adopted technologies together are defined in CORBA (The Common Object Request Broker: Architecture and Specification), currently in Revision 2.0 [1] [2]. CORBA defines a synchronous message passing paradigm whereby distributed objects, which are stationary, interact with each other through synchronous or deferred-synchronous message passing.

Recently the OMG has begun to address the need for new programming paradigms or extensions to the synchronous message passing paradigm, within the confine of CORBA. It has issued Request for Proposal (RFP) on: Mobile Agent Facility [3], Messing Service [4], and Object-by-Value [5]. In this paper, we focus on the RFP on the Mobile Agent Facility and particularly on the specification on the Mobile Agent Facility jointly submitted by GMD FOKUS, IBM and The Open Group to the OMG for evaluation and adoption [6].

Mobile agents are CORBA objects that have the ability to move and the ability to start executing autonomously and asynchronously. The ability to move can bring the agent closest to where it can best perform its tasks instead of performing them at some pre-determined sites.

The Mobile Agent Facility supports the mobility of agents and the invocation of specific agent systems by providing frameworks for manipulating agents and for handling agent transfer and agent execution. Agent communication and agent management are also areas of great interest on mobile agents but are outside the scope of the joint submission.

2. The Request for Proposal

The Request for Proposal states that the Mobile Agent Facility (or simply the Agent Facility) is used to support the mobility of agents and invocation of agent systems. Specifically, the Agent Facility should support for:

a. Marshalling and un-marshalling of agents

b. Encoding of agent containers for transport

c. Moving agents from one agent execution environment to another

d. Run time registration and invocation of agent systems

e. Run time query of a named agent execution environment, by agents, about services that can be invoked by the environment

f. Run time security of agents

Optionally, the Agent Facility may also address:

g. Identification and location of agents

h. Starting, stopping, and suspending the execution of agents

i. Run time discovery and monitoring of agent execution environments and agents by name, or by their characteristics, or by their capabilities, by other agent execution environments or agents

In addition, the Request for Proposal raises a number of technical issues that a submission should or may address:

a. Agent execution

   Agents are named objects, can arrive unexpectedly at a location to perform their tasks, and may be written in different languages.

b. Encoding

   The encoding should be IDL compliant, should provide sufficient syntactic and semantic information, and should allow the building of gateways to non-CORBA agent facilities.

c. Marshalling and unmarshalling

d. Run time security on resource access

e. Naming (optional)

   The naming should be location independent and globally unique.

f. Agent lifecycle (optional)

   Agent life cycle issues have to do with starting the execution of an agent, pausing the execution of an agent, stopping the execution of an agent, and moving or copying an executing agent.

g. Query and discovery (optional)

   These include: location of agent execution environments by name, by properties or by capabilities, and location of agents by name.

h. Asynchrony (optional)

   Agents may be forwarded from one execution environment to another. This may be done through broadcast or multicast.

3. The Joint Submission

The joint submission was originally based on the technology of Aglets Workbench [7, 11], a Java mobile agent system developed at IBM. The co-submitting companies GMD FOKUS and The Open Group had also developed Mobile Agent technologies [8] at the time of the submission preparation. These served as the starting points for defining the interfaces to be provided by the Agent Facility. Major changes (revisions, deletions, additions) have been made to the initial interfaces to:

- remove any Java specific features or dependencies,
- address the need of the CORBA world, and
- accommodate the feedback from co-submitting companies and from other companies (General Magic, Crystaliz).

The result is a specification of the Agent Facility which is based on proven technology but which applies to the CORBA environment. The joint submission meets or exceeds the technical requirements stated in the Request for Proposal and addresses the technical issues discussed there, except for areas which are covered by CORBA Services [9] and CORBA Security [10].

3.1 Design Goals

The Agent Facility exists to allow arbitrary users and objects to dispatch and retract mobile agents. In order to accomplish this goal, it may need to fetch the latter's execution code. The major design goals for the Agentare:

- It is independent of any specific agent system and it can accommodate future agent systems.
  Agent systems may be implemented in different programming languages and may provide different capabilities.
- It is independent of any specific agent transfer protocol and it can accommodate future agent transfer protocols.
  The OMG and/or IETF (Internet Engineering Task Force) may decide at a future time to standardize on a common agent transfer protocol, which will facilitate interoperability between different agent systems.
- It is consistent with the concepts and approaches used in the World Wide Web (WWW).
  With the rapid proliferation of Web browsers, Web servers and Java virtual machines, the WWW has become the most wide-spread and potent platform for mobile agents.
- It provides a mechanism to facilitate the security of host environments.
- It provides a mechanism to facilitate the security of mobile agents.
- It supports flexibility in implementation and extensions.

3.2 Architecture Overview

The Agent Facility provides an architecture which is open with respect to agent systems and agent transfer protocols and which provides mechanisms to facilitate both host environment security and agent security. It also providses essential mechanisms for the subsequent development of an Agent control and management architecture.

3.2.1 Agents

An agent is autonomous and asynchronous. It is autonomous in that it is self contained and knows what to do and where to go at any instance in time. It is asynchronous in that it has its own thread of execution, independent of that of the creator or dispatcher. An agent can move. As such, it performs its tasks by visiting the host where the tasks need to be performed and doing the tasks locally. When an agent is created, it is assigned an identifier which is globally unique and which stays immutable throughout the lifetime of the agent. An agent can have an itinerary which specifies its travel plan.

Each agent is "insulated" by an agent proxy that protects it from other malicious agents and hostile hosts. When interaction with the agents takes place through their proxies, this can only be done by exchange of messages, either synchronously or asynchronously. They cannot interact through method invocation since they have no access to each other's object reference. If security permits such direct access, agents can interact through method invocation. The agent proxy provides the "hooks" for the agent control / management architecture.

Agents and their proxies execute within an agent context that protects the host from malicious agents. The agent context is the conduit through which agents are actually executed by their agent system(s). Therefore, effectively most of the operations on an agent or its proxy, such as dispatch, retract and dispose, are carried out through the agent context.

The architecture for agents is illustrated in the following:

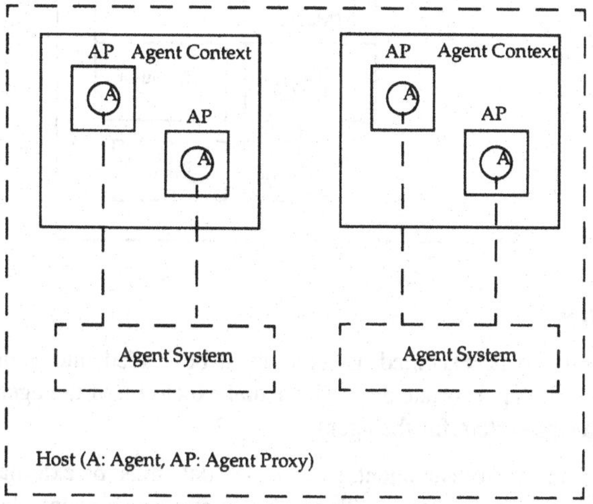

3.2.2 Agent Transfer

Agents can be transferred between named hosts or agent contexts in a computer network. Each host or agent context is associated with a globally unique name known e.g. as its URL. The transfer vehicle for agents is a bidirectional connection established through CORBA between the sending host and the receiving host.

At the sending host the transfer request is made through the local agent transfer manager. Agent transfer is performed by sending the request to an appropriate target agent transfer manager and then receiving the corresponding response.

At the receiving host, once the target agent transfer manager receives the request, it calls the appropriate agent transfer request handler to handle the request and to generate a corresponding response. The choice of the handler depends on the agent system that the agent belongs to.

The architecture for agent transfer is illustrated in the following:

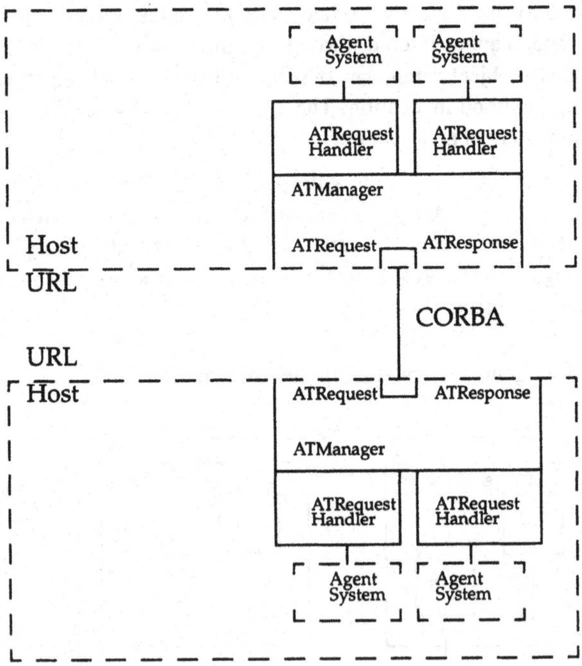

3.2.3 Agent Execution

Before an agent can be executed, its code must be loaded into memory and it must be instantiated with appropriate data. The actual execution of the agent is carried out by the specific agent system for the agent.

In order to transfer or store an agent, its code and data must be externalized into a form appropriate for transfer or storage. To receive or restore an agent, these must be correspondingly internalized. The actual externalization and internalization of the agent is again carried out by the specific agent system.

3.3 Interface Overview

The Agent Facility defines three sets of facilities. The specification is organized around these sets:

- Agent Framework

  The users of the Agent Framework include: agent application developers, agent developers, and Agent Facility developers.

- Agent Transfer Framework

  The users of the Agent Transfer Framework include agent application developers, agent developers, and Agent Facility developers.

- Agent Execution Framework

  The users of the Agent Execution Framework are Agent Facility developers.

Table 1 through Table 3 give high level summaries of the Agent Facility interfaces. The notation used in the comment column is as follows:

- AS: interfaces which require *agent-system* specific implementation.
- E: *external* interfaces which can be accessed outside the Agent Facility.
- I: interfaces which can be accessed between *interoperable* implementations of the Agent Facility.
- P: interfaces which are *pseudo IDLs* and used only within the Agent Facility.

Table 1 Interfaces defined in the *CfAgent* module

Interface	Purpose	Comment
Agent	To initialize, execute, dispatch, and dispose an Agent	AS, E
AgentProxy	To control the Agents via messages and insulate direct access of Agents methods.	E
AgentIdentifierFactory	To create an AgentIdentifier	AS, E
AgentIdentifier	To provide unique identification for an Agent	AS, E
Itinerary	To represent an Agent's itinerary	E
SimpleItinerary	To provide a default Itinerary specification	E
Message	To allow Agents to exchange messages, both synchronous and asynchronous	E
SimpleMessageFactory	To create a SimpleMessage	E
SimpleMessage	To provide a default Message specification	E
FutureReply	To represent replies of asynchronous messages	E
AgentContext	To provide the execution context for Agents	AS, E

Table 2 Interfaces defined in the *CfAgentTransfer* module

Interface	Purpose	Comment
URLFactory	To create an URL	E
URL	To represent uniform resource locators	E
ATManager	To manage agent transfer	I
ATRequestHandler	To handle agent transfer requests and to generate responses	AS, P
ATRequestFactory	To create an ATRequest	I
ATRequest	To represent an agent transfer request	I
ATResponseFactory	To create ATResponse	I

Table 2 Interfaces defined in the *CfAgentTransfer* module

Interface	Purpose	Comment
ATResponse	To represent the response to an agent transfer request	I
InputStream	To represent the input stream of an agent transfer request or response	I
OutputStream	To represent the output stream of an agent transfer request or response	I

Table 3 Interfaces defined in the *CfAgentExecution* module

Interface	Purpose	Comment
AgentClass	To denote an Agent's execution code	AS, P
AgentClassManager	To manage AgentClassLoaders	P
AgentClassLoader	To load in and get/save an Agent's execution code	AS, P
AgentReaderFactory	To create an AgentReader	AS, P
AgentReader	To read in Agents from input streams	AS, P
AgentWriterFactory	To create an AgentWriter	AS, P
AgentWriter	To write out Agents to output streams	AS, P
AgentInputStreamFactory	To create an AgentInputStream	AS, P
AgentInputStream	To represent Agent-specific input streams	AS, P
AgentOutputStreamFactory	To create an AgentOutputStream	AS, P
AgentOutputStream	To represent Agent-specific output streams	AS, P

3.4 Interface Descriptions

In the following we give brief descriptions of the major interfaces. For descriptions of the operations contained in each interface, please see [10].

3.4.1 The Agent Framework

The Agent Framework interfaces provide an extensible framework for specifying and implementing mobile agents, their identities, itineraries, and interactions through the exchange of messages. It also provides constructs for the protection of host environments against malicious agents and of agents against hostile hosts.

The major interfaces provided by the Agent Framework include:

- Agent

  An Agent has an AgentIdentifier and a code base which identifies the location of its execution code. It executes within an AgentContext and can be dispatched, deactivated, disposed, or cloned. An Agent may possess an Itinerary which defines its travel plan. It can execute tasks or handle Messages. Every Agent is managed by an AgentProxy when it executes in an AgentContext.

- AgentProxy

  The AgentProxy insulates an Agent from direct access and protects it against hostile hosts and malicious agents. Every Agent is managed by an AgentProxy which may be the only way through which one can interact with the Agent. When one interacts with an Agent through its AgentProxy, one can only send Messages to the Agent, either synchronously or asynchronously, and cannot directly invoke its operations. An Agent can move, but its AgentProxy is stationary.

- AgentIdentifier

  Every Agent has an identifier which is globally unique within a given agent system. As an Agent moves from site to site, its identifier remains unchanged. The Agent's identifier uniquely identifies the Agent throughout its lifetime.

- Itinerary

  An Itinerary defines an Agent's travel plan. It provides a single and convenient interface for one to dispatch the Agent and to manipulate the content of the Itinerary.

- Message and FutureReply

  A Message may be sent either synchronously or asynchronously. When it is sent synchronously, the sender waits for the result until it is returned. When it is sent asynchronously, the sender gets back a FutureReply, from which the sender may obtain the result when it becomes available or wait for the result unless a time-out has occurred.

- AgentContext

  The AgentContext provides a common context or environment in which agents execute. It protects the underlying host environment against malicious agents and it interacts with the appropriate agent system to accomplish its tasks of creating, retracting and activating, as well as dispatching, deactivating, disposing, receiving, and reverting an Agent. There can be more than one AgentContext on a given host or for a given agent system. Each AgentContext, however, corresponds to only one agent system.

3.4.2 The Agent Transfer Framework

The Agent Transfer Framework interfaces provide an open framework for handling agent transfer requests and responses. This is accomplished through the provision of (1) a generic ATManager interface for handling the sending and receiving of agent transfer requests and responses and (2) generic ATRequest and ATResponse interfaces for representing agent transfer requests and responses.

Conceptually, an agent transfer protocol is the means by which agents and related information are transferred across a network. It defines the syntax, format and semantics of such transfer. Different agent systems can interoperate with each other if they use the same agent transfer protocol to transfer agents. Currently no standards exist on the agent transfer protocol. Each agent system uses its own proprietary agent transfer protocol to transfer agents and related information. Therefore, different agent systems can work with each other only through hard-wired protocol translators, if they exist.

The Agent Transfer Framework provides the mechanism for different agent systems to plug and play, but not interoperate with each other, without having a standard on the agent transfer protocol. This is accomplished through the specification of a standard set of interfaces and by requiring all agent transfer protocols to support the transfer of the following types of messages:

- dispatch request

  Dispatch an agent.

- retract request

  Retract an agent

- fetch request

  Fetch the execution code of an agent.

- response

  Send a response to any of the above requests.

The major interfaces provided by the Agent Transfer Framework include:

- URL

  The URL provides a uniform mechanism to represent the location or identification of the following types of resources:

  - host and, optionally, port and/or AgentContext
  - Agent
  - an Agent's execution code
  - an Agent's principal

  It allows the specification of the protocol to be used for accessing a resource.

- ATManager

  The ATManager provides a generic mechanism for sending agent transfer requests and receiving the corresponding responses on the sending host, as well a generic mechanism for receiving agent transfer requests and returning the corresponding responses on the receiving host.

  At least one ATManager must be running on each of the hosts that an Agent may visit. The ATManager calls the appropriate ATRequestHandler to handle each request and generate the corresponding response.

- ATRequestHandler

  Each ATRequestHandler is associated with a specific agent system. It can handle the following three types of requests:

  - dispatch
  - retract
  - fetch

  and generate the appropriate response for each.

- ATRequest and ATResponse

  ATRequest and ATResponse provide a generic mechanism for representing agent transfer requests and responses, respectively.

- InputStream and OutputStream

  InputStream and OutputStream represent generic streams which, respectively, allow one to read in data transferred through a ATRequest or ATResponse and write out data for transferring through a ATRequest or ATResponse.

3.4.3 The Agent Execution Framework

The Agent Execution Framework interfaces provide an extensible framework for handling an agent's execution code and its data, including serialization and deserialization for the purpose of agent transfer and storage. This is accomplished through the provision of (1) a generic AgentClass interface to denote an agent's execution code, (2) generic AgentClassManager and AgentClassLoader interfaces to handle the loading of an agent's execute code, and (3) generic AgentReader, AgentWriter, AgentInputStream, and AgentOutputStream interfaces to handle serialization and deserialization of an agent's execution code and data.

The major interfaces provided by the Agent Execution Framework include:

- AgentClass

  The AgentClass encapsulates and denotes an Agent's execution code. It has a name and an associated AgentClassLoader. It also serves as the Agent's factory.

- AgentClassManager and AgentClassLoader

  The AgentClassManager manages AgentClassLoaders. It allows one to obtain an AgentClassLoader or to look up the code base for an Agent's execution code. An AgentClassLoader can load in an Agent's execution code, and obtain or save an Agent's execution code as a sequence of octets.

- AgentReader and AgentWriter

  AgentReader provides the mechanism to read in an Agent from an InputStream. AgentWriter provides the mechanism to write out an Agent to an OutputStream.

- AgentInputStream and AgentOutputStream

  AgentInputStream and AgentOutputStream represent Agent (and agent system)-specific streams. They allow one to read from and write to the stream, respectively, an Agent's execution code and data.

4. Summary and Conclusion

The design goals have led to an Agent Facility specification which facilitates:

- Portability of agent applications

  Agent applications which are built using the Agent Facility remain unchanged when the implementation of the Agent Facility changes or when the underlying agent system(s) changes.

- Plug-and-play of agent systems

  New agent systems can be plugged into the Agent Facility by implementing those interfaces which require agent-system specific implementation.

- Interoperability of Agent Facilities

  Different implementations of the Agent Facility can interoperate with each other if they follow the Interoperability Guide outlined in the joint submission.

The OMG Mobile Agent Facility is an important step toward standardizing the APIs for developing mobile agents and their applications, particularly in the CORBA environment. CORBA also extends the WWW platform to include intranets, as well as provides many valuable Services and Facilities which mobile agents can utilize.

Acknowledgment

The joint submission on the OMG Mobile Agent Facility is a team effort. The team consists of: Ingo Basse and Stefan Covaci from GMD FOKUS, Daniel T. Chang (editor) and Danny B. Lange from IBM, and Kathy Guo and Dejan S. Milojicic from The Open Group.

References

1. OMG, *The Common Object Request Broker: Architecture and Specification*, Revision 2.0, July 1995.

2. R. Orfali, D. Harkey, and J. Edwards, *The Essential Distributed Objects Survival Guide*, John Wiley & Sons, Inc., New York, 1996.

3. OMG, *Common Facilities RFP 3*, OMG TC Document 95-11-3, November 3, 1995.

4. OMG, *ORB and Object Services RFP 1*, OMG TC Document orbos/96-03-16, March 16, 1996.

5. OMG, *ORB and Object Services RFP 2*, OMG TC Document orbos/96-06-14, June 14, 1996.

6. Joint Submission, *Mobile Agent Facility Specification*, OMG TC Document cf/96-12-01, December 15, 1996.

7. Aglets Workbench (http://www.trl.ibm.co.jp/aglets).

8. GMD FOKUS, *Java of Fokus*, 1996

9. OMG, *CORBA Services: Common Object Services Specification*, Revised Edition, March 31, 1995.

10. OMG, *CORBA Security*, OMG TC Document 95-12-1, December, 1995.

11. D. T. Chang and D. B. Lange, *Mobile Agents: A New Paradigm for Distributed Object Computing on the WWW*, OOPSLA'96 Workshop on Toward the Integration of WWW and Distributed Object Technologies, October 6, 1996.

Mobile Agents - Smart Messages*

Leon Hurst, Pádraig Cunningham
Computer Science Department,
Trinity College Dublin,
Dublin 2, Ireland.

Fergal Somers,
Broadcom Éireann Ltd.
Kestral House, Clanwilliam Place,
Dublin 2, Ireland.

Abstract. Wireless communication with Mobile Computing devices is known to be problematic. It is very different in character from conventional communication over wired networks. Since many distributed applications make assumptions about network characteristics, they may not be used in a hostile mobile environment.

We are proposing a new kind of messaging system which incorporates adaptive behaviour *into the messages themselves*. We call these 'Smart Messages', and implement them using Mobile Agents. They are transported between machines via Agent Airports. The metaphor we use is of a message being delivered by a courier (Mobile Agent), through Agent Airports, on a potentially unresolved route. The 'intelligence' is in the messages (couriers in our metaphor) themselves rather than in the network.

The approach taken expands on the self-routing capabilities of current Mobile Agent systems such as Aglets or Telescript. We aim to provide structured support for handling the particular problems associated with wireless communications. These include very limited, variable and asymmetric bandwidth, frequent and prolonged disconnections, geographical mobility and high usage costs. We argue that this offers an *efficient, adaptable* and *robust* solution to many of the problems associated with this hostile communications environment.

1 Introduction

The Mobile Computing environment of today is characterised by very limited, variable and asymmetric bandwidth, frequent and prolonged disconnections, geographical mobility, severe resource restrictions and complex data management issues [6, 11]. In addition to these familiar issues there is also the crucial element of *dynamism*. Agent technology has already been proposed [4, 8] as a possible solution to many of these problems.

In addressing some of these problems we advocate the use of Mobile Agents as a replacement for conventional data packets. These agents manage their own routing, recovery and filtering behaviour rather than relying on "smart" [7, 9, 17] or "dumb networks". The dynamism issue is addressed by allowing these 'Smart Messages' to 'stay alive' until transmission time, when they are suspended and serialised. When 'alive' they can receive information regarding local events and *adapt to them dynamically*. This is the crux of our approach. This behaviour is encoded in State Machines with the ability to survive transmission between machines. Actions can be effected through named functions, supplied functions and external services.

1.1 Related work

Much work has been done in the area of Mobile Computing & Communications. The following paragraphs discuss some related work.

---

* The authors can be contacted at `leon.hurst@cs.tcd.ie`. This work is funded by Broadcom Éireann Ltd.

Rover and WitII are toolkits for building mobile applications. Rover [12] uses queued RPC and Relocatable Dynamic Objects to maximise use of the wireless communications medium at an application partitioning level. WitII [18] uses intelligent caching and pre-fetching based on hyper-object information.

Work at Columbia University [1, 7] proposes the creation of Proxy Servers (on the edge of the wired network) and the placement of message filters at these proxies. Messages sent to a Mobile Terminal are passed through these filters before they are dispatched over the hostile wireless connection to the mobile. A currently unresolved limitation of the proxy server is its inability to dynamically accept filters. This might adversely affect its ability to adapt to change as it cannot update its filters.

Work on Agent Tcl [13, 14] approaches the problem from an application partitioning point of view. IBM is engaged in research into Mobile Computing [5]. They take an Agent based approach where Intelligent Mobile Agents meet at Agent Meeting Points in order to acquire services. They use a Travel Reservation scenario to describe their system.

Finally the Telemedia Group, MIT, have been doing some work on incorporating interpreted code into IP packets [17, 19]. Code is piggy-backed onto the Options field of an IP packet. Such code might be executed at routers capable of interpreting the supplied code.

We have observed that a Mobile Terminal spends most of its time in a disconnected state. Hence outbound messages, usually requests, are queued at the Mobile Terminal until a connection is established [5, 12]. Furthermore inbound messages to a Mobile Host is typically *sent as a result* of requests made by the mobile. If the *originating requests can be filtered at the source* (given that they spend most of their life queued at the mobile anyway), then this would efficiently remove a significant amount of outbound traffic, inbound traffic and the associated server load needed to generate this traffic. The reason this works is due to the fact that such requests can become redundant while queued for so long. For instance map segments and traffic or weather information are only useful if they arrive on time.

To the best of our knowledge there is no system which empowers *transmitted messages* with the ability to dynamically adapt to environmental events, in a coherent, structured yet refinable manner.

In the remainder of this paper we present the context of our work (Section 2), a view of Mobile Agents as 'Smart Messages' routed by Agent Airports (Section 3), the dynamic adaptability of our 'Smart Messages' (Section 4), and conclude with a summation (Section 5).

2 The TNET system

TNET stands for "Tourist Network" [10]. The project proposes the creation of a country-wide online and interactive tourist network. The aim is to provide tourists with a single system through which they can access *all* relevant computerised services. The most interesting aspect from our point of view is that of the mobile tourist. Such a tourist might be touring the country in a coach, caravan or hire-car. Useful services for a mobile tourist would include: Route Guidance, Traffic Service, Weather Service, Emergency Notification, Inter-tourist Communications and Online Hotel Booking.

The Network Architecture we have adopted is shown in Figure 1. The inner core represents a network of servers. The outer layer consists of a network of Mobile Support Stations which acts as a gateway between the Mobile Terminals and the servers in the inner core. Finally, Mobile Terminals exist beyond the wired network and connect intermittently to the MSS layer using GSM.

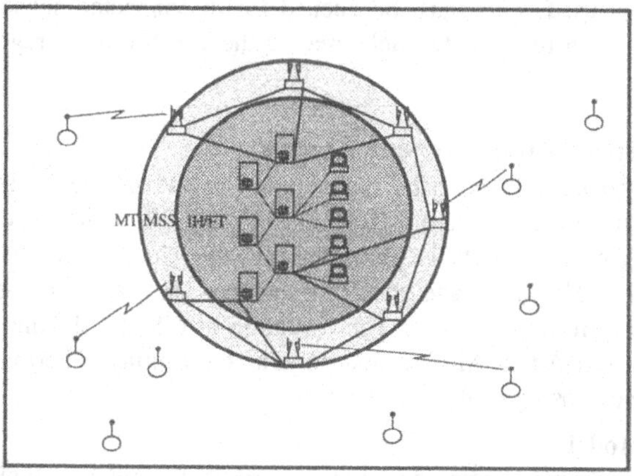

Figure 1. Network structure of **TNET**.

2.1 Limitations of Current Technologies

A Distributed Mobile System consists of several elements including the following:

- Communications
- Resource (data) management
- Application partitioning
- Colossal and increasing volumes of information

The communications issue is possibly the most prominent in a Mobile Computing environment, given its effect on other systems and the severe limitations which it incurs. For the purpose of this paper we focus on this issue alone[1]. Current communications protocols, such as streams and RPC, have been shown to be unsuitable [4]. The duration of communication must be short and packet-based, since disconnections are frequent. This makes streams unsuitable as they are long lived in nature. The volume of traffic is also important as our bandwidth is limited, hence RPC has been specifically identified as being inadequate [4]. These protocols are rather unintelligent with little or no recovery, defaulting to re-sends. Both streams and RPC have unfortunate failure characteristics which can leave both communicating entities in an inconsistent state.

There are many services which require one-to-many communication where the sender and the receiver are loosely coupled. We are essentially speaking of event based communication. Most current event systems are built for use on fixed networks, for example CMIP [2] or the new CORBA Event service [16]. These events are used for static entities (servers), are not queued, and are announced via centralised Event Managers. These solutions are used for tightly coupled, but geographically dispersed

[1] The other issues are discussed in [10].

systems. Additionally, the range of events, their routing, and filtering are hard-coded into the system and cannot be extended dynamically. What happens to events when Mobile Hosts (sending or receiving) are disconnected? Are they queued, re-routed or discarded? How do we improve handle event distribution, propagation and filtering?

In **TNET** we require a decentralised event system. It must allow the dynamic registration of events. Events must be queued for disconnected subscribers (Mobile Terminals), and when reconnected delivered to those subscribers regardless of their new location.

3 Mobile Agents and the Agent Airport

In this section we initially describe our solution to the problems described in the preceding section. This includes our Reference Model. Next, the structure of Mobile Agents and of Agent Airports is presented. Finally we explain the structure and operation of State Machines and their Processors. They are the means by which 'Smart Messages' are implemented. The operation of a State Machine occurs within the context of a host Agent Airport, and governs the routing, filtering, and recovery behaviour of the enclosing Mobile Agent.

3.1 Reference Model

A Reference Model for our agent based framework is illustrated in Figure 2. We have identified four issues in Mobile Computing that have not been adequately resolved by current technologies and methodologies for very large Mobile Distributed Systems. In each case we offer a standardised, agent based service which addresses the associated problems.

- *Communications* - Agent Airport and Distributed Events.
- *Data Management* - Proxy Agents.
- *Increasing Data Volumes* - RPA Agents.
- *Application Partitioning* - AMA Agents[2].

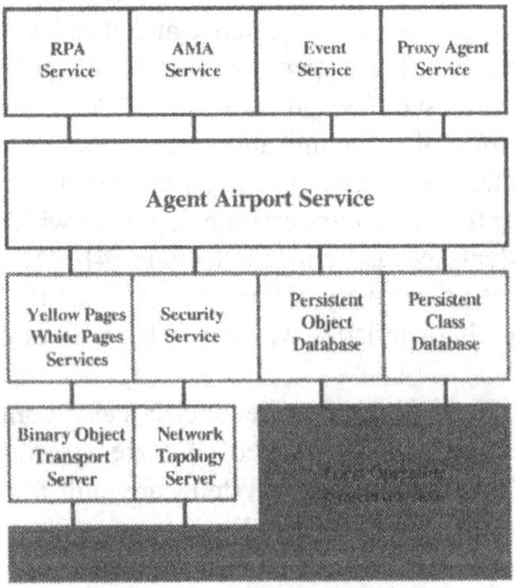

Figure 2. Reference Model.

[2] Abbreviations are AMA for Autonomous Mobile Agent and RPA for Record Playback Agent.

The basic agent service which addresses the issue of communications directly is the Agent Airport and its 'Smart Messages'. The Agent Airport is the central metaphor and is useful in understanding the other services. These services will be the subject of later papers. However, it should be noted that the Distributed Events service is used to perform actions such as announcing Mobile Terminal reconnection.

3.2 Mobile Agents

A Mobile Agent has three main components. The first is a Passport which contains information about the Mobile Agent itself. This includes:

- Globally Unique Identifier (GUID) for itself,
- GUID for its creator Service Instance and Service Type[3],
- Date of Creation,
- Set of Visas governing access to secure resources.

The second, payload component, contains the application-level message. The last component is a set of Behavioural State Machines and State Machine Processors which allow it to perform its own filtering, routing and recovery, independent of the sending or receiving application. An empty messages with minimal behaviour will be of the order of 256 bytes in size.

The Passport is used primarily to identify the Mobile Agent to the host Agent Airport and its support services. It also includes the identity of its creator and its capabilities (Visas). A Visa is an authenticated stream of bits representing a public key, capability, or digital signature. The payload can be any transportable entity from a simple byte array or complex object hierarchy to an application task. Entities that may not be transported include local system resources (running GUIs or open file handles) and secure resources such as Visas and Agent Airport Services.

The behavioural State Machines are the component that distinguishes 'Smart Messages' from more inert messages found in conventional protocols like TCP/IP. They constitute a form of primitive Reactive Planning and are implemented as *persistent* State Machines which are triggered by events. The State Machines, which represent Goals and Sub-goals, are named and maintained in a pool. The pool can be added to as the result of processing a State Machine. This occurs when a Sub-goal in the current State Machine is encountered.

For each of the three tasks (filtering, routing and recovery) there is a State Machine Processor on which the State Machines execute (see Figure 3). The processors are akin to a conventional CPU, operating on State Machines rather than on subroutines. This gives the 'Smart Messages' a "fire-and-forget" behaviour. Their performance depends on how well the behavioural State Machines are exploited. See Section 4. The execution model is that of re-entrant finite state machines. Within each state of a state machine there is a block of code which is executed on entry to the state. Finally both the states and their enclosing state machines can be interrupted by events. The synchronisation of agents is facilitated by their behaviours and the Event system.

The Mobile Agent definition is dynamically extensible so that services and applications may specialise it for their own purposes. AMAs and RPAs, mentioned in

[3] The relationship between a Service Type and a Service Instance is similar to that of a Banking Group and an office of that Group at a particular address.

Section 2, are examples of such a specialisation. Instances of the resulting specialisation would be submitted to the Agent Airport in the same manner as the submission of basic Mobile Agents. Automatic distribution of newly specialised classes is catered for in our prototype.

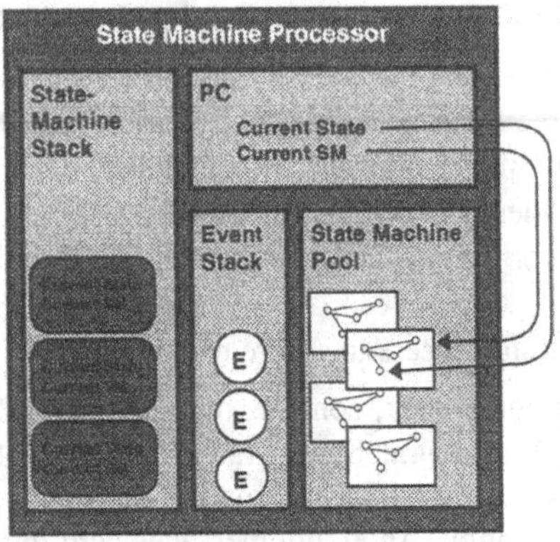

Figure 3. State Machine Processor (SMP)

3.3 Agent Airport

The structure of an Agent Airport is illustrated in Figure 4. The first role of the Airport is to accept Mobile Agents at the Check-In and to route them to the next Airport. Secondly, it receives Mobile Agents on its Inbound gates and hands them to the Arrivals. There they must choose a service or application to be delivered to. If no suitable service can be found, an alternative Airport must be chosen to which they might be transferred.

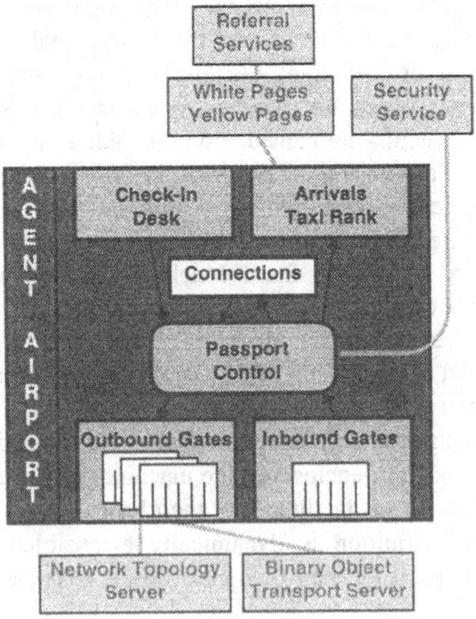

Figure 4. Agent Airport and associated services.

The two major points of interest in the Agent Airport are the Outbound gates and the Arrivals. We describe each in turn.

When Mobile Agents are passed to the Outbound gates they are handed a reference to the Agent Airport and their behavioural State Machines are (re)activated. The routing behaviour chooses a route and submits itself for transport to the first destination Agent Airport. It may use the Network Topology, Yellow and White pages services in choosing its route. It is then queued at the appropriate gate for transport. While queued a Mobile Agent may receive events which can trigger its filtering behaviour to kill, delay, resubmit or modify itself. An example might be a request that becomes outdated or redundant.

At the other end of the Airport we have Mobile Agents trying to contact destination service instances or applications. To do this they use a combination of the Yellow and White page services, and other referral services. If a service cannot be located the Mobile Agent has the option of routing to another Agent Airport that might support the service.

We handle four levels of routing in a hierarchical fashion: Content, Service, Service Instance and Agent Airport. A plan to route between two entities at one level will result in a route possibly involving several hops at a lower level. For example, requesting a routing between two service instances could result in a Agent Airport level route, which in turn could involve several hops. Finally, services and applications intending to be the destination of Mobile Agents have to implement a standard interface so that they may receive these agents from the Agent Airport as they arrive.

3.4 State Machines and their Processors

'Smart Messages' are responsible for their own filtering, routing and recovery. These are three orthogonal aspects of a 'Smart Message' which operate independent of each other. We will initially look at how a Reactive Planning system [15] is implemented using State Machines, and then examine some classes of events that affect the planning system as it executes.

3.4.1 Reactive Planning and State Machines

A Mobile Agent is alive and responsive to events at two particular times. The first is between the time it is submitted to an Agent Airport and the time it leaves that Airport. The second is from the time the Mobile Agent is received by a destination Airport and the time it leaves that Agent Airport.

Reactive Planning systems consist of Goals, Tasks and Actions. A State Machine represents a Goal to be achieved and consists of a network of States (Tasks) representing a well-structured plan to achieve that Goal. See Figure 5. States can be blocking, in which case the immediate processing of the State Machine is blocked pending an event matching the out transition arcs for that State. States contain Tasks to be performed which are Blocks of Actions. The first type of Action is a Primitive, that is an operation which can be directly called upon and results in success, failure or an error condition. The second type of Action is a Sub-goal. This Goal will cause a new State Machine to be created and popped onto the State Machine Stack. This goal subsumption leads to the creation of Goal hierarchies.

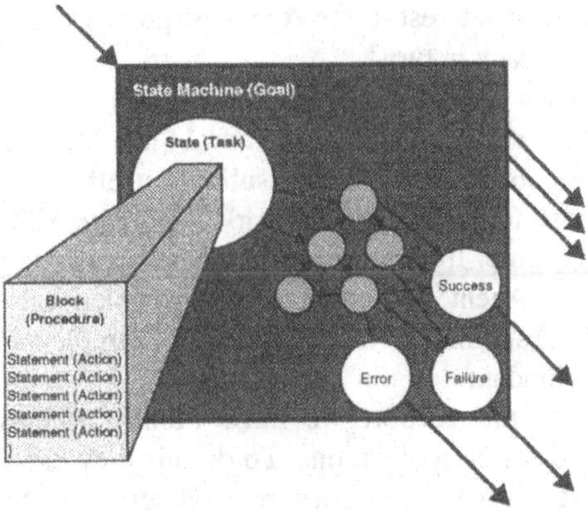

Figure 5. Hierarchy of State Machines representation of a Reactive Planning System.

The Reactive Planning system determines how interruptions to the normal deliberative execution of the State Machine Processor, are to be treated. External events must be reacted to. These external events can be directed to any of the State Machines on the stack and are processed like normal arc transitions. At the finest granularity they are handled in the current State of the State Machine. The State Machine as a whole can also subscribe to handle external events. If the State does not explicitly handle the incoming event, then it is passed to the State Machine. If that in turn does not handle the event, then the event propagates down through the State Machine stack till it arrives at the original Goal State Machine. This allows the Mobile Agent to specify reactive behaviour.

Some important aspects of the system are as follows:

1. Higher Goals should be insulated from the propagation of errors generated by Sub-goals
2. Sub-goals (plans) can be supplied by the Agent Airport and its support services. This means that Mobile Agents do not have to have completely specified plan hierarchies bundled with them at dispatch time. The Mobile Agent can obtain plans on an "as needs" basis as it progresses through the path of Agent Airports.
3. Goals are modelled as State Machines which make transitions based on Goal-level events (for example `cost_too_high`), events which are the result of executing Primitive Actions, and on external events. The external events allow the planning system to react to incidents that occur outside the Mobile Agent.
4. Goals (State Machines) are linked hierarchically in a Goal–Sub-goal relationship.
5. Finally, a Procedure can either be interruptible or non-interruptible. This means that pending events will be examined after the execution of each Action in an interruptible Procedure.

The Procedure which implements a Task is represented by a Block. Blocks have Statements which are interpreted. These Statements can result in Primitive actions being invoked, such as `GoAgentAirport` and `GoServiceInstance`. Alternatively a Statement may result in the calling of a new State Machine (Sub-goal).

3.4.2 Classes of Events

During the time a Mobile Agent is activated it can listen for events which affects its planning. These events fall under several categories:

- *External events* which include events raised by entities outside of the Agent Airport. Typically this would be an application or service.
- *Timer events* are raised by the Agent Airport at a given interval.
- *Gate (queue) events* reflect a change in the nature of the Gate. For example '`time to next connection`' and '`number of agents ahead of you`'.
- *System events* announce changes in the operating conditions of the local host such as '`Battery Low`' warnings.
- *Transport events* announce the open/closed status of Gates.
- *Agent events* are directed at a specific agent and would include '`die`' and '`new resources`'.

The above events relate directly to the Mobile Agents and their behavioural State Machines. However their are three more events which are not received by Mobile Agents but relate to their transport status. These are `MA_XPORT_SUCCESS`, `MA_XPORT_FAIL(condition)`, and `MA_XPORT_ABORT(user data)`. The Agent Airport is normally the recipient of these events.

4 Mobile Agents - Smart Messages

In this section we construct a practical example of a 'Smart Message'. The example is taken from the **TNET** system. A tourist arrives in a new city and decides to look for accommodation. The tourist generates an Accommodation Enquiry using his Personal Tourist application. The application takes this request and deploys it in a 'Smart Message'. The first two parts of a Smart Message contain data presented in Table 1.

Table 1. Passport and Payload components of a 'Smart Message'

Passport	
Self	-randomly generated GUID-
Service Instance	Application instance GUID
Service	Application type GUID
Datestamp	13:00 17 June 1997
Visas	Transport capabilities; Tourist's personal digital signature.
Payload	
Type	"An Accommodation Enquiry"
Content	The Accommodation Enquiry

The intelligence of the Smart Message is encoded in the State Machines. The next two sections cover the Filtering and Routing machines. The third machine, Recovery, is the simplest and handles exceptional circumstances such as a low battery.

4.1 Source Filtering

The generated request is specified as becoming redundant five hours after its creation and should kill itself. If the 'Smart Message' observes the queuing of another 'Smart

Message', of the same type and origin as itself, it should retire itself as it is being superseded. The State Machine for this is presented in Figure 6.

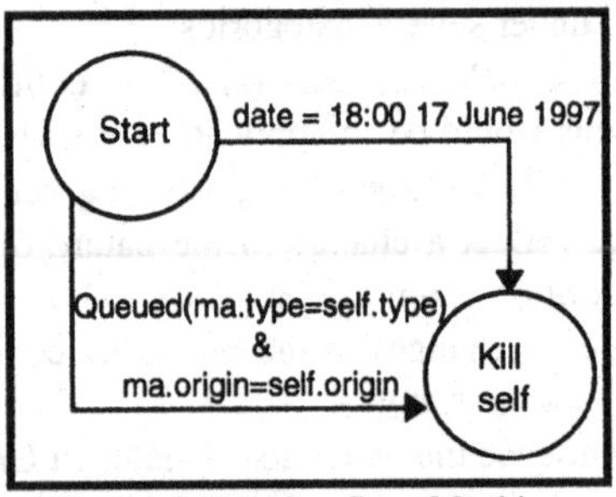

Figure 6. Filtering State Machine.

This State Machine handles some simple source filtering. It is termed "source" filtering as the behaviour is provided by the source application. It is also possible that the destinations of such 'Smart Messages' would like to kill them at their source. This is termed "destination" filtering and is implemented with Annihilator and Terminator Agents. It is beyond the scope of this paper to examine these.

4.2 Routing

Routing occurs at four different levels: Content, Service, Service Instance and Agent Airport. Each level will potentially have its own routing plan. It is often the case that a 'Smart Message' does not know its exact destination. It must therefore be learned from an Agent Airport or other Service. This is the case for Content and Service level routing which have no specified destination. Routing plans come from three sources:

1. Requests to the Agent Airport return routing plans devised by the Airport.
2. Requests to Services above the Agent Airport, known as Referral Services, result in plans devised by those Services.
3. Finally a routing plan can be supplied by the creating application or service. This would involve manual lookups of the local Yellow & White Page services.

It is also possible to have a mixture of the above methods. Hence one could try an application supplied routing plan. If it fails, default to an Agent Airport supplied route.

For this simple example we will use a fictitious Referral Service, named WiseMan, to find a Service Type which matches our Content Type. See Figure 7. This is done by invoking the `GetService` operation on the WiseMan referral service.

If WiseMan returns a Service Type we can request a routing plan from the local Agent Airport (AA prefix in Figure 7). This is done by invoking the `GoService` operation on the Agent Airport. If however, the WiseMan service cannot match a Service to the specified Content Type, or the resulting Service is unreachable, we must use the basic Agent Airport referral services. We do this by invoking `GetService` on the Agent Airport instead of WiseMan.

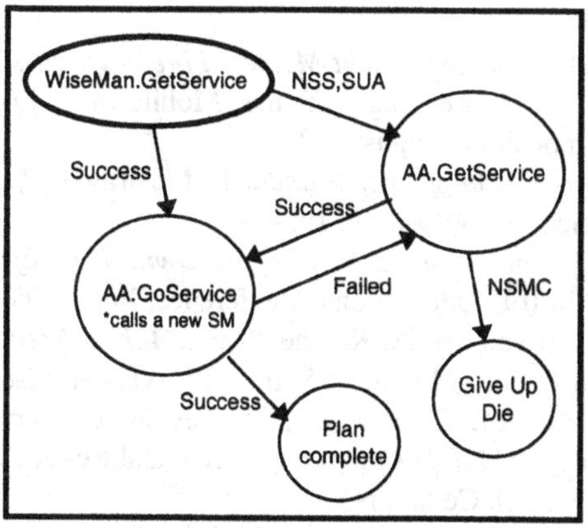

NSS = No Such Service
SUA = Service Unavailable
NSMC = No Service Matches Content

Figure 7. Simple Routing State Machine.

When a suitable Service is found the 'Smart Message' requests a routing plan from the Agent Airport (AA.GoService). This plan is supplied in the form of a set of new State Machines. Finally, the 'Smart Message' will either be routed to a Service Instance which can process its content, or it will run out of suitable Service Types that support such content.

5 Conclusions and Future Work

We believe that the advantages of 'Smart Messages' are as follows:

1. Filtering redundant requests queued to leave a Mobile Terminal. This in turn removes the needless consumption of resources in processing and replying to those requests.
2. Routing of 'Smart Messages' can be altered dynamically as the network changes.
3. A 'Smart Message' can be routed based on its Content Type or Service Type. In these cases it is the Agent Airport which constructs the routing plans.
4. 'Smart Messages' operate independent of the sending application, therefore removing any dependencies with the application.

We believe that the Agent Airport will have advantages over RPC under the following conditions:

1. When the Remote server contains large volumes of data to be processed;
2. There are hard real-time constraints;
3. Communication is costly;
4. The recipient of the mobile agent is itself located on another mobile terminal;
5. The processing capability of an Agent Airport Server is a limited.

Current prototyping is taking place using the Smalltalk language. Initial results are positive. However further work is required to fully evaluate the state machine model, to address the security issues including passports, and finally to determine the most common cases where the use of Smart Messages adds value.

References

1. Athan A. and D. Duchamp, *Agent-Mediated Message Passing for Constrained Environments.* In Proceedings of the Mobile and Location-Independent Computing Symposium, August 1993.
2. Black U., *Network Management Standards*, McGraw-Hill Series on Computer Communications, second edition, 1994.
3. Borenstein N., *Email with a Mind of its Own: The Safe-Tcl Language for Enabled Mail.* In IFIP International Conference, June 1995, Spain.
4. Chess D., C. Harrison and A. Kershenbaum, *Mobile Agents: Are they a good idea.* Technical Report, March 1995, IBM TJ. Watson Research Center, NY.
5. Chess D., B. Grosof, C. Harrison, D. Levine, C. Parris and G. Tsudik, *Itinerant Agents for Mobile Computing.* Technical Report, October 1995, IBM T.J. Watson Research Center, NY.
6. Duchamp D., *Issues in Wireless Mobile Computing,* Internal Report, Computer Science Department, University of Columbia, NY.
7. Duchamp D. and B. Zenel, *Intelligent Communication Filtering for Limited Bandwidth Environments.* In Proceedings of the 5th Workshop on Hot Topics in Operating Systems, IEEE, May 1995, Rosario WA.
8. Gosling J. and H McGilton, *The Java Language Environment: A White Paper.* Sun Microsystems, 1995.
9. Harrison G., *Smart Networks and Intelligent Agents.* In Mediacom'95, April 1995, Southampton, UK.
10. Hurst L., *TNET: Executive Summary.* Internal Report available from `http://www.cs.tcd.ie/~lahurst/currentwork/execsum.html`
11. Imielinski T. and B. Badrinath, *Wireless Computing,* In Communications of the ACM, October 1994/Vol.37, No.10.
12. Joseph A., A. deLespinasse, J. Tauber, D. Gifford and M. Kaashoek. *Rover: A Toolkit for Mobile Information Access.* In Proceedings of the 5th Symposium on Operating Systems Principles, December 1995.
13. Kotz D., R. Gray and D. Rus, *Transportable Agents Support Worldwide Applications.* In Proceedings of the 7th ACM SIGOPS European Workshop, September 1996, Connemara, Ireland.
14. Kotz D., R. Gray, D. Rus, S. Nog and G. Cybenko, *Mobile Agents for Mobile Computing.* In Technical Report PCS-TR96-285, May 1996, Computer Science Department, Dartmouth College.
15. Pryor L., *Adaptive Execution in Complex Dynamic Worlds.* Technical Report No. 53, 1994, Institute for Learning Sciences, North Western University, IL.
16. Siegel J., *Common Object Services Specification, Volume I.* OMG Document No. 94-1-1
17. Tennenhouse D. and D. Wetherall, *Towards an Active Network Architecture.* In Proc of Multimedia Computing and Networking, January 1996, CA.
18. Watson T., *Efficient Wireless Communication Through Application Partitioning.* In Proceedings of the 5th Workshop on Hot Topics in Operating Systems, IEEE, May 1995, Rosario WA.
19. Wetherall D. and D. Tennenhouse, *The ACTIVE Option.* In Proc of the 7th ACM SIGOPS European Workshop, September 1996, Connemara, Ireland.

Communication Concepts for Mobile Agent Systems[1]

Joachim Baumann, Fritz Hohl, Nikolaos Radouniklis,
Kurt Rothermel, Markus Straßer

Institute of Parallel and Distributed High-Performance Systems (IPVR),
University of Stuttgart, Germany

{baumann, hohlfz, nsradoun, rothermel, strasser}@informatik.uni-stuttgart.de

Abstract. Driven by the question how to identify potential communication partners and the need for well-suited communication schemes in agent-based systems, we discuss two communication concepts: sessions and global event management.

Sessions establish either actively or passively a context for inter-agent interactions. Communication partners are addressed by globally unique agent identifiers or via badges. Communication in sessions is based on RPC or message mechanisms.

Global event management addresses the need for anonymous communication. Event managers are employed as a synchronization means within agent groups. Based on this approach, we introduce synchronization objects, – active components that offer various synchronization services. The presented model is finally mapped onto OMG event services.

1 Introduction

Mobile agents are often described as a promising technology, moving towards the vision of usable distributed systems in widely distributed heterogeneous open networks. Particularly, its promise to offer an appropriate framework for a unified and scalable electronic market has led in the past years to a great deal of attention. Since the deployment of mobile agent systems in a large scale is crucial for the success of this technology, the emerging problems and needs have to be well understood.

Though first prototype systems (e.g, see [IBM96]) and even products (e.g., see [GM96]) exist, the architecture of mobile agent systems is not well understood today and hence needs more investigation. In our paper, we will address two issues, communication and synchronization in agent-based systems.

A fundamental question tightly related to communication is how mobile agents are identified. On the one hand, there is certainly a need for globally unique agentIds. Identifier schemes that provide for migration transparency are well-understood today. However, such a scheme might be too inflexible in agent-based systems. Assume for example, that a group of agents cooperatively perform a user-defined task. Assume further that one group member wants to meet another member of this group at a particular place for the purpose of cooperation. In this case, the member should be identified by a (placeId, groupId) pair. If the agent to be met additionally is expected to play a

1. This work was funded by Tandem Computers Inc., Cupertino (CA) and the German Research Community (DFG)

particular role in this group, the identifier would have the form (placeId, groupId, roleId). For supporting those application-specific naming schemes we propose the concept of badges.

For the purpose of cooperation mobile agents must 'meet' and establish communication relationships from time to time. For this purpose, we propose the concept of a session, which is an extension of Telescript's meeting metaphor. Numerous existing agent systems are purely based on an RPC-style communication. While this type of communication is mainly appropriate for interactions with service agents, i.e. those agents that represent services in the agents' world, it has its limitations if agents interact like peers. Therefore, we propose to support both message passing and remote method invocations.

In the general case, a group of agents performing a common task may be arbitrarily structured and highly dynamic. In those environments, one can not assume that an agent that wants to synchronize on an event (e.g. the completion of some subtask this agent depends upon) knows a prior which agent or agent subgroup is responsible for generating this event. Therefore, we suggest to use the concept of anonymous communication, allowing agents to generate events and register for the events they are interested in, as a foundation for agent synchronization.

The remainder of the paper is structured as follows. In Section 2, we present an overview of the employed agent model. Various agent communication types and their need for well-suited communication schemes are then discussed in Section 3. Section 4 examines one of these schemes, the session-oriented communication and its benefit for mobile agent systems. Section 5 focuses on global event management as a vital infrastructural component. A brief overview of Mole, our current agent system is presented then. The paper concludes with a list of related work and a summary of the article's key issues and future work.

2 An Agent System: A Collection of Agents and Places

Our model of an agent-based system – as various other models – is mainly based on the concepts of agents and places. An agent system consists of a number of (abstract) places, being the home of various services. Agents are active entities, which may move from place to place to meet other agents and access the places' services. In our model, agents may be multi-threaded entities, whose state and code is transferred to the new place when agent migration takes place. Places provide the environment for safely executing local as well as visiting agents.

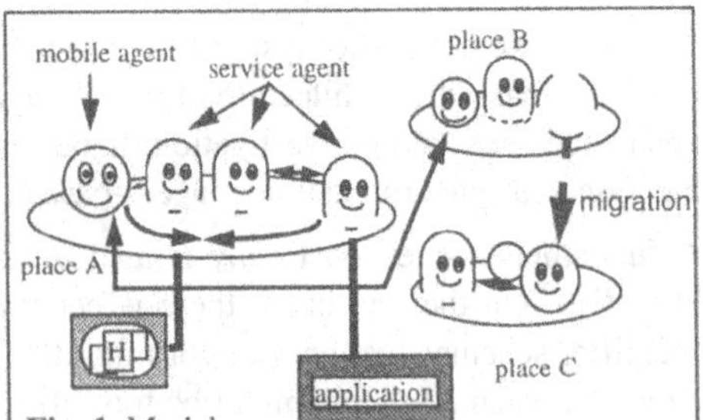

Fig. 1. Model

Our model distinguishes between mobile agents and so-called service agents. Service agents are stationary and interface the services available at places. Those services may include system services, such as a file or directory access, as well as application-level services, such as a hotel reservation or flower delivery service. Service agents encapsulate arbitrary services and represent them in the agent world. From a technical point of view, service agents map the service request expressed in the „agent language" to the individual service interface. This mechanism allows legacy systems to be incorporated. Moreover, service agents will be the place, where access control mechanisms are located. In contrast to service agents, mobile agents may migrate from node to node.

Each agent, whether mobile or stationary, is identified by a globally unique agent identifier. An agent's identifier is generated by the system at agent creation time. It is independent of the agent's (current) location, i.e. it does not change when the agent moves to a new location. In other words, the applied identifier scheme provides location transparency.

A place is entirely located at a single node of the underlying network, i.e. all service agents associated with a place reside on the same node. Conversely, multiple places may be implemented on a given node. For example, a node may provide a number of places, each one assigned to a certain agent community, allowing access to a certain set of services, implementing a certain prizing policy, and so on.

The requirement of having places being realized on a single node does not mean that all service implementations have to be located at the place's node also. It is well conceivable that the place's service agents provide access not only to local but also to remote services, typically accessible via a LAN. Single node places lead to well defined properties in terms of communication: Intra-place communication between an agent and a service agent is always local an hence is (in general) cheaper than inter-place communication. Moreover, single node places are much simpler to implement than distributed places.

3 Types of Agent Communication

In this section, we will address the various types of communication. Considering inter-agent interaction, we have to distinguish between following types of communication:

1. Agent/service agent interaction
   Since service agents are the representatives of services in the agent world, the style of interaction is typically client/server. Consequently, services are requested by issuing requests, results are reported by responses. To simplify the development of agent software, an RPC-like communication mechanism should be provided.
2. Mobile Agent/Mobile Agent Interaction
   This type of interaction significantly differs from the previous one. The role of the communication partners are peer-to-peer rather than client/server. Each mobile agent has its own agenda and hence initiates and controls its interactions according to its needs and goals. The communication patterns that may occur in this type of interaction might not be limited to request/response only. The required degree of flexibility is provided by a message passing scheme. Even higher-layer cooperation protocols, such as KQML/KIF [FMM94], are based on message passing.
3. Anonymous agent group interaction
   In the previous two types, we have assumed that the communication partners know each other, i.e. the sender of a message or RPC is able to identify the recipient(s).

However, there are situations, where a sender does not know the identities of the agents that are interested in the sent message. Assume, for example, a given task is performed by a group of agents, each agent taking over a subtask. In order to perform their subtasks, agents itself may dynamically create subgroups of agents. In other words, the member set of the agent group responsible for performing the original task is highly dynamic. Of course, the same holds for each of the subgroups involved in this task. Now assume that some agent wants to terminate the entire group or some subgroup. In general, the agent that has to send out the terminate request does not know the individual members of the group to be terminated. Therefore, communication has to be anonymous, i.e., the sender does not identify the recipients. This type of communication is supported by group communication protocols (e.g., see [BvR94]), the concept of tupel spaces [CG89], as well as sophisticated event managers. In the latter approach, senders send out event messages anonymously, and receivers explicitly register for those events they are interested in.

4. User/Agent Interaction
   Although a very interesting area of research, the interaction between human users and software agents is beyond the scope of this paper. For a discussion of this type of communication the reader is referred to e.g. [Mae94].

Let us briefly summarize our findings. Different types of communication schemes are needed in agent-based systems. Besides anonymous communication for group interactions, message passing and an RPC-style of communication is suggested. In our model, message passing and RPC is session-oriented, which means that agents that want to communicate have to establish a session before they can send and receive data. In the remainder of the paper, we discuss the concept of session-oriented communication in the context of agent-based systems and investigate event managers for anonymous communication.

4 Session-Oriented Communication

As will be seen below, a session between agents can be established only if the agents can identify each other. In our model, there are basically two ways how agents can be identified, the agent_Ids introduced in Section 1 and so-called badges.

In the case of mobile agents the concept of agent_Ids is not always sufficient. Assume for example, that an agent wants to meet some other agent participating in the same task at a given place. If only agent_Ids were available, both agents would have to know each others ids. Actually, for identification it would be sufficient to say „At place XYZ I would like to meet an agent participating in task ABC“. This type of identification is supported by the concept of badges. A badge is an application-generated identifier, such as „task ABC“, which agents can „pin on“ and „pin off“. An agent may have several badges pinned on at the same time. Badges may be copied and passed on from agent to agent, and hence multiple agents can wear the same badge. For example, all agents participating in a subtask may wear a badge for the subtask and another one for the overall task. The agent that carries the result of the subtask may have an additional badge saying „CarryResult“.

Using badges, an agent is identified by a (placeId, badge predicate)-pair, which identifies all agents fulfilling the *badge predicate* at the place identified by placeId). A badge predicate is a logical expression, such as („task ABC“ AND („CarryResult“ OR „Coordinator“)). Obviously, this is a very flexible naming scheme, which allows to assign any number of application-specific names to agents. To change the name assignments two functions are provided, PinOnbadge(badge) and PinOffbadge(badge).

Now let us have a closer look to sessions. A session defines a communication relationship between a pair of agents. Agents that want to communicate with each other, must establish a session before the actual communication can be started. After session setup, the agents can interact by remote method invocation or by message passing. When all information has been communicated, the session is terminated. Sessions have the following characteristics:

- Sessions may be intra-place as well as inter-place communication relationships, i.e., two agents participating in a session are not required to reside at the same place. Limiting sessions to intra-place relationships seems to be too restrictive. There are many situations, where it is more efficient to communicate from place to place (i.e., generally over the network) than migrating the caller to the place where the callee lives. Consequently, we feel that the mobility of agents cannot replace the remote communication in all cases.
- In order to preserve the autonomy of agents, each session peer must explicitly agree to participate in the session. Further, an agent may unilaterally terminate the sessions it is involved in at any point in time. Consequently, agents cannot be "trapped" in sessions.
- While an agent is involved in a session, it is not supposed to move to another place. However, if it decides to move anyway, the session is terminated implicitly. The main reason for this property is to simplify the underlying communication mechanism, e.g., to avoid the need for message forwarding.

The question may arise, why sessions are needed at all. There are basically two reasons: First, the concept of a session used to synchronize agents that want to 'meet' for cooperation. Note that the first property stated above allows agents to 'meet' even if they stay at different places. The concept of a session is introduced to allow agents to specify designated agents they are interested to meet at designated places. Furthermore, it allows agents to wait until the desired cooperation partner arrives at the place and indicates its willingness to participate.

Secondly, we intend to support both "stateless" and "stateful" interactions. In contrast to the first, the latter maintain state information for a sequence of requests. Obviously, if they encapsulate "stateful" servers, service agents have to be "stateful" also. A prerequisite for building "stateful" entities are explicit communication relationships, such as sessions.

Session Establishment

In order to set up sessions two operations are offered, *PassiveSetUp* and *ActiveSetUp*. (see Fig. 3). The first operation is non-blocking and is used by agents to express that they are willing to participate in a session. In contrast, *ActiveSetUp* is used to issue a synchronous setup request, i.e., the caller is blocked until either the session is successfully established or a timeout occurs.

```
PassiveSetUp({PeerQualifier}, {PlaceId})-> nil
ActiveSetUp(PeerQualifier, PlaceId, Timeout) -> SessionObject
Terminate(SessionObject) -> nil
SetUp(SessionObject)
```

Fig. 3. session methods

In the case *ActiveSetUp* succeeds, it returns the reference of the newly created session object to the caller. Input parameter *PlaceId* identifies the place, where the desired session peer is expected, and *PeerQualifier* qualifies the peer at the specified place. A *PeerQualifier* is either an agent_Id or a badge predicate. Note that at most one agent qualifies in the case of a single agent_Id, while several agents may qualify if a single badge predicate is specified. To avoid infinite blocking, parameter *TimeOut* can be used to specify a timeout interval. The operation blocks until the session is established or a timeout occurs, whatever happens first.

Parameters *PeerQualifier* and *PlaceId* of operation *PassiveSetUp* are optional. If neither of both parameters is specified, the caller expresses its willingness to establish a session with any agent residing at any place. By specifying *PlaceId* and/or *PeerQualifier* the calling agent may limit the group of potential peers. For example, this group may be limited to all agents wearing the badge "Stuttgart University" and/or that are located at the caller's place.

As pointed out above, before a session is established both participants must agree explicitly. An agreement for session setup is achieved if both agents issue matching setup requests. Two setup requests, say R_A and R_B of agents A respectively B, match if

- *PlaceId* in R_A and R_B identifies the current location of B and A, respectively, and
- *PeerQualifier* in R_A and R_B qualifies B and A, respectively.

If a setup request issued by an agent matches more than one setup request, one request is chosen randomly and a session is established with the corresponding agent.

A combination of PassiveSetUp and ActiveSetup allows a client/server style of communication (see Fig. 4). The agent playing the server role once issues PassiveSetUp when it is ready to receive requests. When an agent playing the client role invokes ActiveSetup, this causes the SetUp method of the server side to be invoked implicitly. SetUp implicitly establishes a session with the caller and assigns a thread for handling this session. Therefore, once the server agent has called PassiveSetup, any number of sessions can be established in parallel, where session establishment is purely client driven.

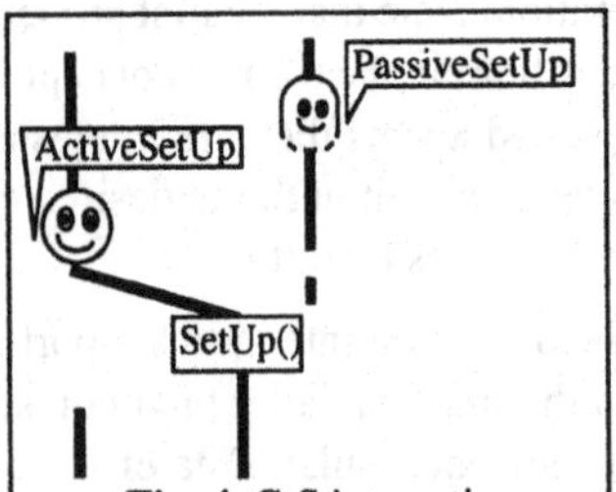

Fig. 4. C-S interaction

If both agents issue (matching) ActiveSetUp requests this corresponds to a rendezvous, both requestors are blocked until the session is established or timeout occurs (see Fig. 5). This type of session establishment is suited for agents that want to establish peer-to-peer communication relationships with other agents. Communication between agents is peer-to-peer if both have their own "agenda" in terms of communication, i.e., both decide - depending on their individual goals - when they want to interact with whom in which way.

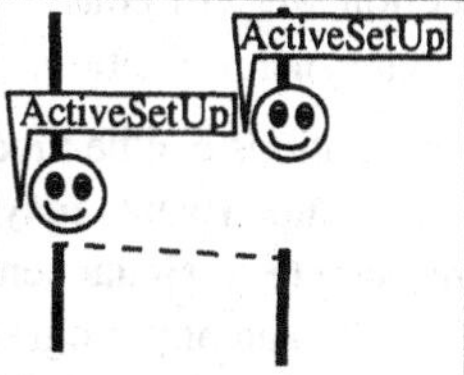

Fig. 5. P-P interaction

Communication

As pointed out above, Remote Method Invocation (RMI), the object-oriented equivalent to RPC, seems to be the most appropriate communication paradigm for a client/server style of interaction, while message passing is required to support peer-to-peer communication patterns. The available communication mechanisms are realized by so-called *com* objects. Currently, there are two types of com objects, RMI objects and Messaging objects.

Com objects are associated with sessions. Each session may have an RMI object, a Messaging object, or both. Each session object offers a method for creating com objects associated with this session. With the *RMI object* the methods exported by the session peer can be invoked. It can be compared with a proxy object known from distributed object-oriented systems. With the *Messaging object*, messages can be conveyed asynchronously between the participants of a session. Messages are sent by calling the send method. For receiving messages the receive and subscribe methods are provided. The receive method blocks until a message is received or timeout occurs, whatever happens first. If the *subscribe* method is invoked instead, the incoming messages are handed over by calling the *message* method of the recipient and passing the message as method parameter.

The advantage of having the concept of com objects is twofold. First, only those communication mechanisms have to be initiated that are actually needed during a session, and secondly, additional mechanisms, such as streams, can be added to the system. The latter advantage enhances the extensibility of the system.

Session Termination

At any time, a session can be terminated unilaterally by both session participants, either explicitly or implicitly. A session is terminated explicitly by calling *Terminate* (see Fig. 3), and implicitly when a session participant moves to another place. When a session is terminated, this is indicated by calling the SessionTerminated method exported by agents. Moreover, all resources associated with the terminated session are released.

5 Anonymous Communication by agent synchronization

Two widely deployed concepts for anonymous communication are tuple spaces and sophisticated event managers. In contrast to the blackboard concept, tuple spaces provide additional access control mechanisms. Agents employ tuple spaces to leave messages without having any knowledge who will actually read them. In the remainder of this section we will concentrate on event mechanisms as a well-suited concept for inter-agent synchronization.

Applications can be modeled as a sequence of reactions to events, that in turn generate new events. Events may be user- (e.g. reaction to a message), application-, or system-initiated (e.g. signal sent by a process). An event-based view maps quite closely onto real life, and any programming primitives that support event-based concepts tend to be more flexible in modeling a given problem.

The event model is particularly well-suited for distributed communication since it abstracts from the receiver's identity. As a consequence, it enables the specification of complex interactions without the need to know the communication partners in advance. With regard to agent systems, the event model simplifies application – as well as system-level communication. On the application level, events are employed as a general communication means. On the system level, events can be used to design and implement protocols that encompass agent synchronization, termination, and orphan detection.

5.1 Events

In our notion, events are objects of a specific type, containing some information. Events are generated by so-called producers and are transferred to the consumer by the event service. Consumers (and, depending on the concrete implementation of the event service, also producers) have to register at the event service for the type of events they want to receive or send.

As consumers and producers may only interact if both know which events to produce or to consume, they necessarily have to share common knowledge of the used event types in an interaction group. For this, there exist two alternatives: either the event types are negotiated at startup time, then this information configures the agents before a migration, or the event types have to be communicated to the members of the interaction group.

5.2 Synchronization objects

Synchronization objects are defined as active components responsible for the synchronization of an entire application or only parts of it. Synchronization objects monitor specific input events. Depending on these events, internal rules, state information and timeout intervals, output events are generated, that in turn may be the input for other synchronization objects.

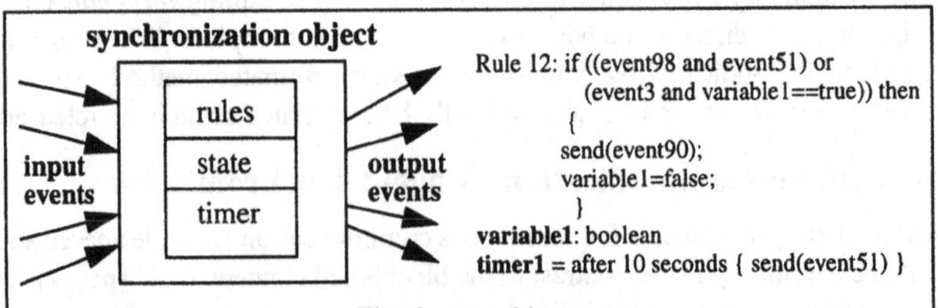

Fig. 6. sync. object

Rules are arbitrarily complex expressions triggered through input events. They consist of a condition and an action part. The condition part is a logical expression composed of event types and state information of the synchronization object. If the logical condition becomes true, the action part is triggered. The action part itself consists of simple commands (e.g. send output events, change internal state, stop the synchronization object to process events). The state consists of a set of variables. Timers are special rules with no input events that trigger actions after a specified amount of time.

An agent group comprises logically related agents. Synchronization objects are well-suited to model dependencies within agent groups. Relationships between agents are expressed by the synchronization object's internal rules and can be defined in terms of success (i.e. a group is only successful if a well defined set of the group members have succeeded). Agents participating in such groups send success events after they have accomplished their task. The synchronization object receives success events and processes this input through its internal rules. As a result, output events are generated. In case a generated event is a success event it can be used to nest groups (i.e. an output event of one group is used as input event for another group).

Example: OR and AND groups

Two agent group types of particular interest are the OR-group and the AND-group. AND-groups succeed only if all agents have accomplished their task. For the OR-group's success it is sufficient if at least one group agent accomplishes its task. OR-groups are eligible for parallel searching in a set of information sources. As soon as one agent has found the required information the group has succeeded in its task.

A simple OR group (Fig. 7) includes only three event types. The input event *agentsuccess*, signaling the success of an agent, and the output events *successful* and *not_successful*, signaling the group's success. The OR group employs only one rule and one timer. The rule causes the synchronization object to send an event signaling the group's success (*successful*) and to disable itself afterwards. If the timer fires first (e.g. caused by application specific timeouts or processing failures like deadlocks or crashes), the synchronization object signals *not_successful* and stops the processing.

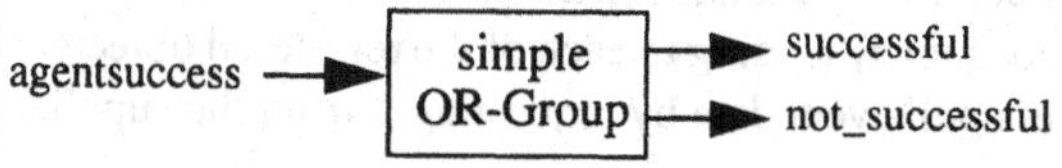


```
if (agentsuccess) then{
  send(successful); stop;}
timer1 = after (30min){
  send(not_successful); stop;}
```

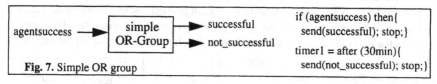

Fig. 7. Simple OR group

The presented model is not very efficient: if one group member succeeds, all other group members are obsolete and, if all group members detect that they are not able to complete their task, the group fails. The definition of the OR-group illustrated by Fig. 8 takes these cases into account. Agents detecting that they cannot succeed, generate the *giveup* event. If all group members signal a *giveup*, the group fails.

For this, the group has to know its members – either by keeping them in mind at the group's creation time or by registering group agents through the *register* event. In the latter case the number of members potentially being able to succeed is counted and stored in the state variable *members* (more sophisticated approaches could maintain an agentId list, transmitted via the events and ensuring that only events from subscribed agents are accepted). If *members* becomes zero, the event *not_successful* is instantly generated. The *terminate* event (to terminate the group members) is generated if the group either succeeds or fails.

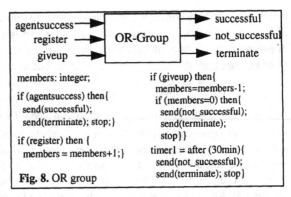

```
members: integer;

if (agentsuccess) then{
  send(successful);
  send(terminate); stop;}

if (register) then {
  members = members+1;}

if (giveup) then{
  members=members-1;
  if (members=0) then{
    send(not_successful);
    send(terminate);
    stop}}
timer1 = after (30min){
  send(not_successful);
  send(terminate); stop}
```

Fig. 8. OR group

5.3 The OMG event model

The Object Management Group event services specification ([OMG94]) defines the Event Service in terms of suppliers and consumers. Suppliers are objects that produce event data and provide them via the event service, consumers process the event data provided by the event service. If a consumer is interested in receiving specific events, it has to register for them. This means a supplier of events knows who the recipients are (this does not exactly conform to the original definition of event mechanisms). Two communication models are supported between suppliers and consumers, the *push* model and the *pull* model. In both models all communication is synchronous. In the push model, a supplier pushes event data to the consumer, sending to each of the registered objects the event. In the pull model, consumers pull event data by requesting it from the supplier.

What makes this event service flexible and powerful, is the notion of the event channel. To a supplier, an event channel looks like a consumer. To a consumer on the other hand, the event channel seems to be a supplier. Furthermore, the communication model between the different participants can be chosen freely. By using an event channel, suppliers and consumers are decoupled and can communicate without knowing each other's identity. Suppliers and consumers communicate synchronously with the event channel but the semantics of the delivery are up to the designer of the specific event channel. Two types of channels are defined, typed and untyped channels. How these event channels are implemented is not defined in the OMG specification. By not imposing any restrictions on the semantics, the specification allows implementations to provide additional functionality in the event channel implementation. Persistent events (events that are logged) or reliable event delivery mechanisms come to mind. Because the event channel interface complies to the definition of the consumer's interface and to the definition of the sup-

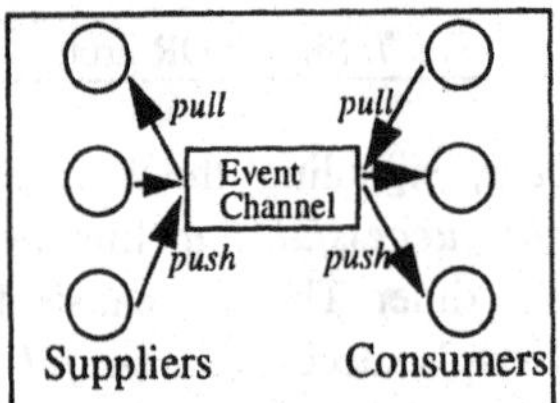

Fig. 9. Event Channels

plier's interface, they can be chained without problems. This allows to build arbitrarily complex event channel hierarchies with a broad functionality.

Products following the OMG specification are commercially available (e.g. Iona OrbixTalk[ION96], or Sunsofts NEO [Sun96]).

5.4 Synchronization using the OMG model

This section tries to map the presented group model onto OMG event services. Hereby, it is assumed that, in contrast to current implementations, event services support mobile participants. Support of mobile participants will be subject of future work.

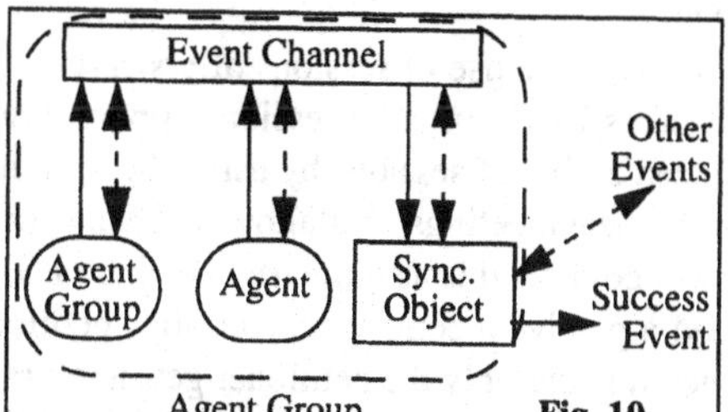

Fig. 10.

With the employment of an untyped event channel for group communication, OR and AND-groups can be implemented. The channel is untyped because different event types are transmitted through it. As the information about success is of foremost importance to the synchronization object, agents and synchronization object implement the push model. The synchronization object contains a reference to the event channel. The agent that creates the group has access to its synchronization object and thus the ability to forward the event channel reference to other agents, e.g. at creation time. The group members subscribe to the event channel as suppliers (e.g. for *agentsuccess* event) as well as consumers (e.g. for *termination* event). The communication to non group entities is handled by the synchronization object, either by sending the events directly to an agent (e.g. the parent agent creating the group) or by using another event channel (e.g. an event channel of a higher-level group).

6 Mole

In order to allow research in the field of mobile agent systems, Mole [SBH96] was developed at the University of Stuttgart. Mole is a platform for mobile agents which uses Java as the agent programming and as the implementation language. Therefore, Mole is a pure Java application and can be started at every computer platform for which a Java Development Kit is available. Agents in Mole may use multiple threads, have globally unique names and can provide or request services, which can be looked up locally. A service is currently the implementation of one or more methods with specified names and parameters (which are called interfaces in Java), services are requested by calling those methods by using a kind of remote method invocation (a Java object RPC). When it comes to communication, Mole currently supports the (global) exchange of messages and the mentioned RMI. Both are addressed by using a direct addressing scheme. The only way to obtain the needed referencing addresses is the use of the local service lookup mechanism which associates a list of agent names to service names. A mechanism which is able to associate current location to agent names is in the implementation stage. Mole will be used, among other things, as the infrastructure for an electronic documents system [KMV96] and in a distributed variant of a Multi-User Dungeon (MUD), in which players can use mobile agents as artificial team-mates.

Mole is available as source code; the first public version was released in June 1996. Further informations about the Mole project can be found at *http://www.informatik.uni-stuttgart.de/ipvr/vs/projekte/mole.html.*

7 Related Work

Current mobile agent systems employ many communication mechanisms such as messages, local and remote procedure calls or sockets, but, at our knowledge, no system uses a global event management for communication and synchronization. There are "events" in AgentTcl [GCK96], but they are simply (local) messages plus a numerical tag.

Although the use of sessions offers certain advantages as shown above, existing agent systems barely provide session support. Telescript [GM96], for example, which introduced a kind of sessions by using the term meeting for mobile agent processing, offers only local meetings, that allow the agents only to exchange local agent references. The meet command is asymmetric, i.e. there is an active meeting requester, the "petitioner" and a passive meeting accepter, the "petitionee". The petitionee can accept or reject a meeting, but only the petitioner gets a reference to the petitionee. Agents communicate after opening a meeting by calling procedures of each other (i.e. the petitioner can call procedures of the petitionee). As there is no possibility during the execution of a procedure to obtain information about an enclosing meeting, agents cannot access session context data. Thus, according to our definition the Telescript meeting is not a session.

There are also "meetings" in ARA[Pei96] and in AgentTcl. Meetings in ARA build up communication relations between two agents over which (string) messages can be exchanged, meetings are local and the only supported "specification method" is anonymous addressing via meeting names. Meetings in AgentTcl are just a mechanism that opens a socket between two agents.

8 Summary and Future Work

Driven by the question how to identify potential communication partners and the need for well-suited communication schemes with regard to different types of agent interaction, we discussed two communication concepts in the context of Mobile Agent systems: sessions and the use of a global event management for infrastructural purposes.

After presenting a brief description of our agent model, we identified different types of communication schemes that please the requirements of agent based systems. Sessions establish either actively or passively a context for interactions. The communication partners are addressed either by globally unique agent identifiers or via badges. Agents can build several sessions simultaneously - even with the same communication partner. Communication in sessions is based on RPC or message mechanisms.

To bypass the problems arising from the need to communicate to potentially unknown group members performing the same task, we proposed the use of a global event management. The employment of events for the realization of a general synchronization was shown. Therefore, we introduced the notion of synchronization objects, active components that offer different synchronization services. Using timers and state information, synchronization objects consumed, processed and produced events as input for other synchronization objects or other components. After a short overview of the OMG event model, the presented group model is mapped onto the OMG event services.

Existing implementations of event services already provide persistency (NEO and IONA OrbixTalk). But none of the existing implementations can cope with mobile participants. In order to support particular requirements imposed by mobile agents, appropriate event channel designs are required. While distributed event services with stationary participants are well understood, additional questions are raised by the mobility issue. The further exploration of this promising research field comprises the design and implementation of such distributed event services that support – apart from different channel semantics – also mobility of participants. The proposed mechanisms are not implemented in our Mole system yet (see Section 6). Future work will encompass the integration of the session concept and a distributed event service into Mole.

9 Literature

[BvR94] Birman, K.P.; van Renesse, R.: Reliable Distributed Computing with the ISIS Toolkit, IEEE Computer Society Press, 1994

[CG89] Carriero, N.; Gelernter, D.: Linda in Context, CACM 32(4), April 1989

[FMM94] Finin, T.; McKay, D.; McEntire, R.: KQML as an Agent Communication Language, in: Proc. Third Int. Conf. Information and Knowledge Management, ACM Press, November 1994

[GCK96] Gray, R.; Cybenko, G.; Kotz, D.; Rus, D.: Agent Tcl. To appear in: Itinerant Agents: Explanations and Examples with CD-ROM, Manning Publishing, 1996.

[GM96] General Magic, Inc: The Telescript Language Reference, 1996. http://www.genmagic.com/Telescript/TDE/TDEDOCS_HTML/telescript.html

[IBM96] IBM Tokyo Research Labs: Aglets Workbench: Programming Mobile Agents in Java, 1996. http://www.trl.ibm.co.jp/aglets

[ION96] IONA Technologies Ltd: OrbixTalk Programming Guide, April 1996

[KMV96] Konstantas, D.; Morin, J.; Vitek, J.: MEDIA: A Platform for the Commercialization of Electronic Documents, in: Object Applications, ed. Dennis Tsichritzis, University of Geneva, 1996

[Mae94] Maes, P.: Agents that Reduce Work and Information Overload, in: CACM 37(7), July 1994

[OMG94] Common Object Services Specification, Volume 1, OMG Document Number 94-1-1, March 1994

[Pei96] Peine, H: Ara: Agents for Remote Action. To appear in: Itinerant Agents: Explanations and Examples with CD-ROM, Manning Publishing, 1996.

[SBH96] Straßer, M.; Baumann, J.; Hohl, F.: Mole: A Java based mobile agent system, in: Baumann;Tschudin;Vitek(editors): Proceedings of the 2nd ECOOP Workshop on Mobile Object Systems, dpunkt, 1996

[Sun96] Sun Microsystems: Solaris NEO: Operating Environment Product Overview, March 1996. http://www.sun.com/solaris/neo/whitepapers/SolarisNEO.front1.html

Mobile Agent Interaction in Heterogeneous Environments

Peter Dömel Anselm Lingnau Oswald Drobnik
E-Mail: {doemel,lingnau,drobnik}@tm.informatik.uni-frankfurt.de

Dept. of Computer Science
J.W. Goethe–Universität Frankfurt/Main

Abstract An open problem in mobile agent research is the interaction between agents in different 'worlds'. In this paper, we survey various approaches to agent interaction and discuss the interoperation between Telescript and `ffMAIN` agents through the use of the Hypertext Transfer Protocol (HTTP) and the shared information space provided by `ffMAIN`.

Keywords: mobile agents, interaction, HTTP, Telescript, `ffMAIN`, KQML

1 Introduction

Mobile agents—programs that can move around in a computer network on behalf of their users—are attracting more and more attention. Various research efforts take place in this area, for example TACOMA (Tromsø and Cornell, [1]), Ara (Universität Kaiserslautern, [2]), Mole (Universität Stuttgart, [3]), and the projects InAMoS and InAVAS of the DAI Laboratory/TU Berlin [4]. Several interpreted languages are suitable for the programming of mobile code. Among them Java [5], Tcl (with extensions like `[incr tcl]` or AgentTcl) [6], Python [7], and Perl [8]. Commercially available systems include Telescript [9] and CyberAgents [10]. Operating systems like Inferno [11] are also likely to support mobile agents in the future, because much of the necessary infrastructure is already provided.

With so many infrastructures available, an obvious question to ask is how one could try to make different kinds of mobile agents interoperate. Since it is unlikely that a common standard for 'doing' mobile agents will emerge anytime soon, it seems worthwhile to examine how different agent systems handle interaction 'internally', and how one might establish 'interfaces' that let information cross the border between different mobile agent 'worlds'.

To begin with, a coarse distinction may be drawn between *direct* and *indirect interaction*. With direct interaction, agents can directly call code within other agents—this is usually approached from an object-oriented point of view, with agents advertising *interfaces*, i.e., sets of methods that other agents may access. For example, this style of interaction is used within Telescript. Indirect interaction means that the agent system mediates interaction between agents without letting them contact one another directly—either by having agents send *messages* to others which are forwarded by the agent infrastructure, or by interposing an *information space* where agents can deposit items. These approaches are surveyed more closely in the first part of the paper.

A protocol which is widely used, albeit not only in the context of mobile agents, is the *Hypertext Transport Protocol* (HTTP, [12]). This is the standard protocol for information access on the World-Wide Web [13]; since many agent systems allow agents to retrieve WWW resources or even to provide such resources themselves, it turns out that the necessary mechanisms for HTTP access are already in place for many mobile agent systems. The second part of the paper examines two such systems—Telescript and the authors' own `ffMAIN` (short for *FrankFurt Mobile Agent INfrastructure*)—in more detail, and in the final part of the paper we argue that HTTP is a useful protocol for enabling information exchange and cooperation across different agent 'worlds'. This is exemplified by an experiment linking Telescript and `ffMAIN` agents in the context of an electronic marketplace.

2 Mobile Agent Interaction: An Overview

2.1 Direct Agent Interaction

In some of the systems, agents are implemented as active objects (objects which represent running threads or processes). The natural way for an agent in such an environment to interact with another agent is by simply calling that agent's methods. To be able to do this, agents need references to one another. By carefully controlling which agent obtains what references to other agents, the privacy of agents can be assured.

To give an example of a system with very tightly coupled object-oriented agent interaction, we look at the Telescript platform. However, it is imaginable that Java-based mobile agent platforms could use a similar way for agents to communicate, because the basic language concepts of Java and Telescript are very similar.

Telescript is a proprietary programming language developed at General Magic [14]. Its goal is to make it possible to program computer networks like Postscript allows to program printers. Mobile agents seem to be ideally suited to provide offline support for small portable devices like PDA's (Personal Digital Assistants), PICs (Personal Intelligent Communicators) and computerized cellular phones.

Telescript can be briefly characterized like this: There are three simple concepts to the language: agents, places and 'go'. Agents 'go' to places, where they interact with other agents to get work done on a user's behalf. Agents are, in fact, mobile programs capable of transporting themselves between places in a Telescript network. The language is implemented through a multitasking interpreter, called the *Telescript engine*.

The use of direct method calls is one of the central agent interaction mechanisms in Telescript. In order to be able to call another agent's methods an agent must first meet the other agent, which is only possible if both agents are visiting the same place. A meeting is initiated by executing the `meet` operation of this place, which returns a reference to the agent to be met. This operation takes a *petition object* as its argument. An agent can only successfully meet another agent if it possesses a valid petition.

When an agent calls another agent's methods, it usually passes some objects as arguments and often receives one or more objects as the result of the method calls. But what happens when two agents have references to the same objects and one agent decides to go to another place (which might be located on another machine)? This conflict is resolved in Telescript by the *object ownership concept*. The default behaviour is that an object is owned by the thread under whose control it was created. This means that when an agent creates an object, it owns that object. Whenever an agent migrates itself to another place, it takes with it all the objects it owns. To do this, the engine collects all the objects owned by this agent and voids the references other agents or the place may have to these objects. In case an agent does not recognize that its partner has left and tries to use the reference an exception will be thrown.

Other ways for agents to interact asynchronously in Telescript are through thread synchronization mechanisms like events and resource-protection.

A system which extends the direct interaction paradigm is the Common Object Request Broker Architecture (CORBA, [15]). This architecture allows the remote invocation of objects in a distributed environment via an RPC mechanism. An object request broker (ORB) allows the interaction of objects written in different languages but not the mobility of code.

2.2 Indirect Interaction

The `ffMAIN` Infrastructure Many mobile-agent systems (e. g., Telescript) can be considered closed and proprietary: They prescribe a given language for agent development and use custom protocols for agent mobility and interaction. In contrast, the `ffMAIN` infrastructure [16] developed by the authors is not tied to any particular programming language and effects agent interaction and movement through the *Hypertext Transport Protocol* (HTTP), an Internet standard [12]. Agents are controlled by *agent servers* (typically one per host) which help agents communicate among themselves and with users as well as move between servers. Users can take advantage of common World-Wide Web browsers to submit agents to the system as well as to interact with the agents or retrieve results; the agent servers function as HTTP servers in order to present information to users via pages and forms using the Hypertext Markup Language (HTML) [17].

With a language-independent system like `ffMAIN`, a direct-interaction approach such as the one discussed in the previous section is not feasible, since differences in the languages concerned will preclude the direct invocation of one agent's methods by another. (This could be worked around to a certain extent by concepts like CORBA.) Therefore, the abstraction used in `ffMAIN` is similar to that put forward in *LINDA* [18]: Each agent server maintains a local *information space* that agents can use to publish interesting pieces of information for perusal and manipulation by other agents. Items in the information space are identified through unique *keys* and endowed with a set of *access rights* detailing which agents are allowed what operations. The basic operations defined on information space items include *put* (insert an item), *get* (read an item) and *dget* ('destructive get'—read and remove an item). All these operations are performed atomically; their implementation is based on HTTP with several (small) extensions[1]. The information space is also used by the agent server to publish interesting data. This lets agents find out about other agents as well as the services offered by the agent infrastructure on the host in question.—It is possible to develop more refined interaction schemes such as RPC, broadcast, blackboard systems, ... based on these basic operations (see [19]). While agents currently use custom protocols to interoperate—they can find out what other agents support by looking at the agent list published by the server—it would also be possible to implement KQML-based agent interaction (see next section) via the information space.

KQML and its Infrastructure KQML, the *Knowledge Query and Manipulation Language* [20], is a language and protocol for exchanging information. Its purpose is to facilitate the cooperation of very different intelligent agents, by providing a framework to support them in identifying, connecting with and finally exchanging information with each other. It does so by defining an extensible set of message types (*performatives* or *speech acts*) and their meanings. KQML consists of a *communication layer* (dealing with the identity and addresses of agents), a *message layer* (defining the performatives) and a *content layer* (dealing with the actual content); it does not attempt to standardize the format of the information being exchanged, nor does it specify exactly how this information is to be moved.

Figure 1 shows the conceptual architecture used in the KQML specification by the External Interfaces Group, a working group of the ARPA Knowledge Sharing Effort. This architecture serves as another example for indirect agent interaction, whereas the language KQML itself can well be used in other architectures (like `ffMAIN`) as an abstraction for describing and encapsulating agent operation invocations. In contrast to direct object-oriented agent interaction, it does not require mobility of the interacting agents, although agent mobility could improve the efficiency of the system.

Each software agent has a separate router process (K-router), which handles all KQML messages sent and received by its agent. When a K-router is unable to find the recipient for a message, it consults *facilitator agents* which provide network services like content-based routing, brokering between suppliers and consumers, recruiting suppliers to deal directly with consumers, and smart multicasting. The KRIL (KQML Router Interface Library) is an API to the external K-router process which is embedded in the agent application itself. Two common KRIL operations are `send-kqml-message` and `declare-message-handler` for submission and reception of KQML messages.

KQML represents a framework for agent communication rather than something which is directly useful. It can serve as a conceptual *middleware* between agents by

[1] Making extensions to HTTP is explicitly condoned by the protocol definition.

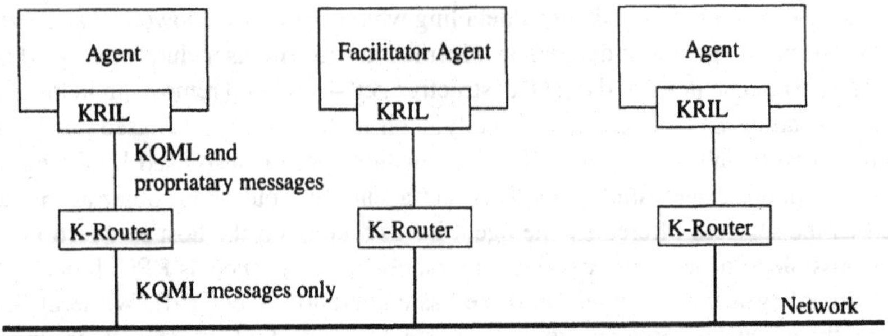

Figure1. Conceptual KQML infrastructure

introducing a common set of operations (the performatives) that various agents can support. KQML by itself cannot guarantee that the agents will actually be able to do something useful with the information they exchange.

3 Interfacing Mobile Agents and the Web

3.1 Telescript Agents and the Web

The Telescript runtime environment was originally designed for the use in big network servers, operated by service providers. A set of tools [21] allows users to create, control and interact with Telescript agents via ordinary Web browsers. Moreover, these tools enable Telescript agents to access the WWW and support them in using its services by filling out forms and parsing the resulting HTML pages.

Using these tools, Agents may be used to build value added Web services. Agents can, e.g., be used to search information in the Internet, monitor changes of Web pages or build meta services[2]. The mobility of agents can help to do this more efficiently by avoiding network traffic whenever great amounts of data have to be processed.

In figure 2 we give a rough overview of how a Telescript engine is connected to the WWW via the *Telescript Web Tools* resp. *TabrizWare*.

Users (and administrators) can create and control their personal agents by selecting special URLs in their Web browsers. Another way to communicate is by filling out HTML forms generated by their agents. Such a URL may, e.g., look like:

`http://deneb:3000/login/telescript/CDShoppingAgent/findCD?title=Equinoxe`

The browser requests the resource bound to this URL from an ordinary Web server running on host `deneb` using port 3000. This server was configured such, that the `login` part of the URL causes it to perfom HTTP-based authentication. By requiring users to log in, the system can bind identities of agents to identities of users. The URL part `telescript` refers to a CGI process, `webtots`, which takes all the

[2] Hide several similar services behind one common user interface.

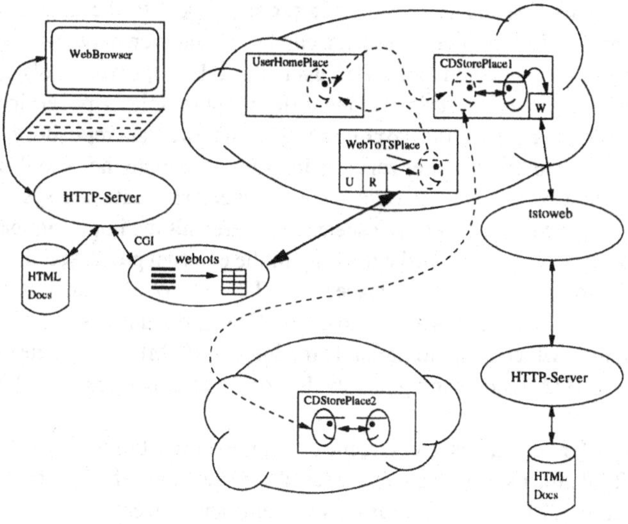

Figure2. Telescript Web Tools (Tabriz)

CGI variables provided by the Web server and the user and creates a Telescript datastructure out of it. Then `webtots` connects to the Telescript engine (represented by a cloud) where the rest of the URL is processed.

Because the user has not created a `CDShoppingAgent` earlier in our example, by default such an agent will be created by the `webtots` place, which also contains a registry of services ('R' in figure 2) and information about registered users ('U' in figure 2). From this service registry the agent gets the addresses (represented by `ticket` objects) of two places offering CDs as well as a ticket to the `UserHomePlace`. First the agent 'goes' to the `UserHomePlace` where it makes a note (enters its URL) in the user's personal HTML pages, so that the user can contact it, if necessary.

The part `findCD?title=Equinoxe` of the URL invokes the agent's `findCD` method. Because the agent owns the associative array (created by the `webtots` process) which contains all the necessary CGI variables, it knows that the user is interested in CDs with the title *Equinoxe*. First it visits the `CDStorePlace1` where it `meets` the shop's service agent and asks it about availability and price of CD's with the title *Equinoxe*. This service agent, however, is only a front-end to a normal WWW CD store service. With the help of a Web access API ('W' in figure 2) it communicates with the external process `tstoweb`, which uses the HTTP client library `libwww` [22] to access a HTML form based WWW CD store service. The service agent of the `CDStorePlace1` simply fills out the appropriate forms and parses the resulting Web pages. From this information it generates the result to the `CDShoppingAgent`'s question.

After it got its first result, `CDShoppingAgent` 'goes' to the `CDStorePlace2` which is provided by another Telescript engine on another network server. This engine may also be connected to the Web using the Telescript Web Tools, but it may as well be a standalone Telescript engine, offering pure Telescript services. In our example the service agent of `CDStorePlace2` has its own data repository inside the place and no need to access other services in order to operate the 'shop'. However, this agent could as well be an interface agent to an external database system.

This little electronic marketplace scenario covered all the important parts of the Telescript Web Tools, which consist not only of the external processes, the `webtots` place and the so-called mix-in interfaces 'R', 'U' and 'W', but also of an HTML API which on one hand allows agents to create HTML documents as a hierarchy of Telescript objects which are automatically rendered to HTML, and on the other hand is able to parse HTML code and generate the corresponding hierarchy of Telescript objects.

A library of superclasses gives agents, e.g., the ability to interactively 'talk' to users via HTML forms. These superclasses also provide all of the necessary infrastructure to hide HTTP-specific issues from agents and places.

3.2 Controlling Agents in `ffMAIN`

As explained in section 2.2, the `ffMAIN` infrastructure is completely based on HTTP. In principle, a user can create an agent simply by submitting an appropriately formatted file containing its source code and initial state through a WWW browser (or even a TELNET connection). For convenience, this is usually done via an auxiliary 'launching' program. As a matter of fact, this program can be invoked from the Web; this makes it straightforward for information providers to add mobile agents to their offerings. Another advantage of this approach is that agents can be conveniently configured through a HTML form which is constructed dynamically by the launching software from a specification embedded within the agent's source code (see fig. 3).

Once an agent has been submitted, the launching software returns to the user a URL which can be used for subsequent queries about the agent, to fetch its results or to kill or revoke the agent. This URL leads to a HTML page maintained by the agent server the agent was initially submitted to (its *home server*); the agent servers keep track of agents moving among one another in order to keep the information about an agent's whereabouts up-to-date. HTTP 'redirect' messages are used to point an inquiring user's WWW browser to the correct server. Agents, in turn, can send partial results to their home servers to be made available to users as HTML pages.

This focus on HTTP for agent mobility and control allows users to view mobile agents as a seamless extension to their usual World-Wide Web environment. They do not have to get familiar with yet another user interface in order to take advantage of mobile agents.

In `ffMAIN`, agents can also interact with other resources on the World-Wide Web. In order to effect a separation of concerns and to keep generic mobile agents operating on a basis of least-privilege, WWW access would usually be through a

```
#Desc: Find cheapest supplier of product \
#  and order it
  ...
# Product: STR
set product %%PRODUCT%%
# Amount to order: STR
set amount %%AMOUNT%%
# Disposal: ALT [Buy outright|Just reserve]
set disposal %%DISP%%
```

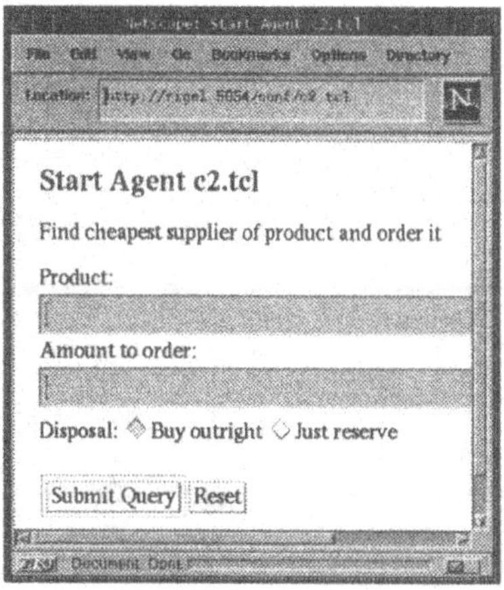

Figure3. Agent configuration in `ffMAIN`: Specification and presentation

trusted stationary agent accepting URL requests via the information space, possibly vetting these to avoid costly requests (e. g., non-local or international), and returning the data addressed by the URL in question to the requesting agent, again via the information space. While there is no problem in principle with allowing every mobile agent to access the WWW at will, this approach lets the maintainer of an agent server retain maximum control over the site's security and resource usage. `ffMAIN` does not offer in-built methods for parsing and generating HTML by agents; it is believed that this can be safely left to the relevant support available in the various agent implementation languages. Tcl and Perl, for example, contain sophisticated extensions for HTML management; it appears more worthwhile to offer safe methods of accessing these rather than re-invent the wheel.

4 Interaction Between Agent Systems Through HTTP

4.1 Direct Agent Interaction

If users can control and interact with agents through WWW browsers by using an HTTP-based remote control mechanism (as in section 3.1) and agents can act on behalf of their users by issuing HTTP requests, it follows that agents can interact with one another using HTTP. In the case of direct interaction, HTTP represents a simple RPC mechanism. Every URL corresponds to a remote method invocation; arguments can be wrapped up in the URL, and results are returned just like WWW pages. Thus, agents have the option to decide whether they want to 'go' to another agent, or whether it is cheaper or faster to remotely invoke its methods. This decision is a trade-off between the costs of agent migration (depending on its code and data size and the costs for encryption and encoding of the agent) and the amount of data to be exchanged between service and agent (plus the RPC-overhead).

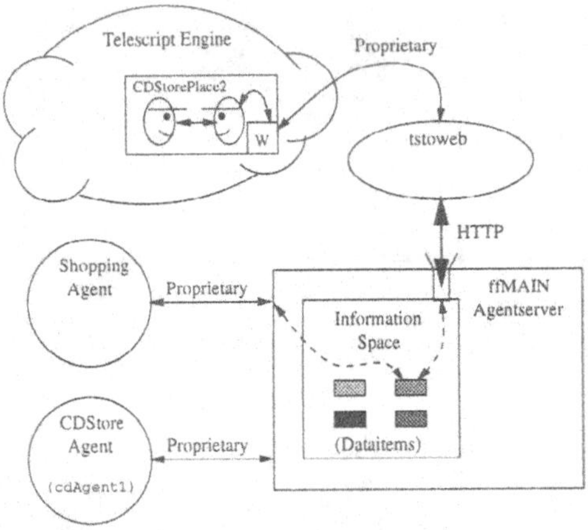

Figure4. Telescript agents access information space via HTTP

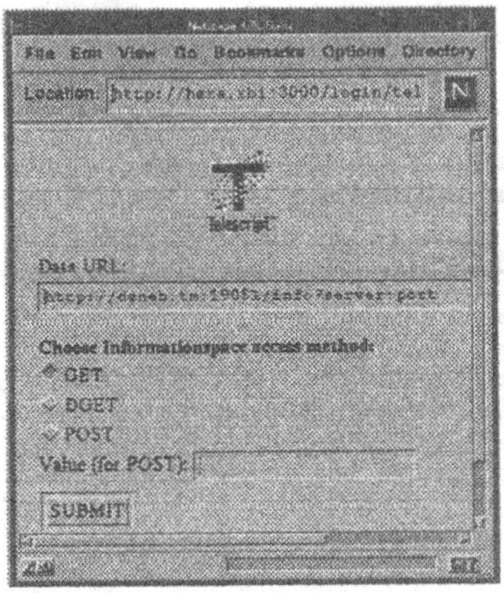

Figure5. Access form generated by a Telescript agent

As already mentioned in section 2.1, CORBA could be considered for language independent remote interaction between agents. But although CORBA allows programs written in different languages to interact, usually different platform/language-dependant APIs are used (e.g. DSOM for IBM UNIX workstations and DCOM / ActiveX for environments based on Microsoft Windows). This does not represent a problem for non-mobile distributed software, but for *mobile* agents this is more of an issue because the CORBA libraries needed for the remote method invocations may differ from server to server. It could be necessary to have the agent platform provide some additional middleware as a common agent CORBA API. This 'glue' code would likely be language-dependant as well as platform dependant. Moreover, the runtime environment needed by CORBA-based applications is relatively heavy-weight and would require service providers to buy and run CORBA support software, whereas HTTP is, by comparison, such a lightweight protocol that every agent can easily carry its own protocol implementation. Also, there is no need to define and compile CORBA IDL specifications in order to remotely invoke methods offered by other agents or services. It is sufficient to create simple URL strings containing the parameters. A more practical reason why we decided to experiment with the HTTP approach is that currently CORBA support by online service providers is not very common, but most services already are HTTP-based.

Another simple example of HTTP usage, this time for agent/user interaction, is shown in figure 5. The HTML form was generated by a Telescript agent which takes the input from the user to access the information space and reads the `prices` value stored by the `cdAgent1`.

Telescript agents may use the existing `WebAccessing` mix-in class to issue HTTP requests. This mix-in also uses a proprietary protocol to communicate with the external `tstoweb` process which, e.g., translates Telescript objects into C++ objects. This interaction can be considered similar to the KRIL/K-Router connection mentioned in section 2.2. In this case, the `WebAccessing` mix-in corresponds to the KRIL and the target of the HTTP requests—e. g., an `ffMAIN` information space—to the set of interconnected K-Routers.

Furthermore, as we have seen in section 3.1, it is also straightforward to construct an HTTP interface that will accept requests from an outside source and translate them into the appropriate native calls. Therefore, HTTP can play the role of a 'common denominator' for communication between many different platforms.

4.2 Indirect Agent Interaction

The *agent servers* in the `ffMAIN` infrastructure communicate via HTTP. Their HTTP interface also allows authenticated access to their information spaces from outside. Not only does this enable management tools to connect to agent servers, e.g., to display and edit the content of the information space, but it also provides a simple way for other agent systems to read, write and remove data items with ease. Figure 4 shows how, e.g., Telescript agents may interact with `ffMAIN` agents by exchanging data via the information space. Other systems could be connected in the same fashion. (Actually, native `ffMAIN` agents use a compressed protocol based on HTTP to interact with the `ffMAIN` agent servers and to access the information space. This saves overhead and allows for more advanced features – native agents can, e.g., request to be asynchronously notified by the information space, whenever a certain data item has changed. This does not detract from the general accessibility of the information space through the usual HTTP operations.)

Table 1 shows some examples for the protocol data exchanged with an agent server to communicate to the information space. The `GET` example reads the server's port number (made available by the server itself in `server:port`). The `POST` example creates a new data item `prices` which is owned by the agent `cdAgent1`. The `DGET` example reads and removes the entry `cdAgent1:prices`.

Figure 6 gives a few examples of how an `ffMAIN` agent would interact remotely with a Telescript agent using the information space. Of course, two Telescript agents could also interact this way, which might be useful to save the overhead of two go and one `meet` operation when only a few bytes of information have to be exchanged.

In the 'electronic marketplace' example, `ffMAIN` and Telescript agents can coexist and work together through the information space. 'Shops' based on both `ffMAIN` and Telescript agents can publish catalogues and prices in the information space or accept requests for further information through an HTTP-based remote call mechanism. This means that `ffMAIN` users can take advantage of information available in the Telescript 'world' and vice-versa.

4.3 High-Level Interaction

Enabling different agent infrastructures to interact through a mechanism like the `ffMAIN` information space does not solve the problem that agent developers still have to know a lot about the other agents with whom 'their' agents are going to

```
GET /info?server:port HTTP/1.0
Authorization: Infospace-1 wizard xyzzy
```

```
HTTP/1.0 200 Request fulfilled, document follows
Server: ffMAIN/1.0 Perl/5.003
Date: Thu, 20 Nov 1996 14:11:48 GMT
Content-Type: application/octet-stream
Content-Length: 5
Content-Transfer-Encoding: binary

19051
```

```
POST /info?cdAgent1:prices HTTP/1.0
Authorization: Infospace-1 wizard xyzzy
Content-Type: application/octet-stream
Content-Transfer-Encoding: 8bit
Content-Length: 4

7.95
```

```
DGET /info?cdAgent1:prices HTTP/1.0
Authorization: Infospace-1 wizard xyzzy
```

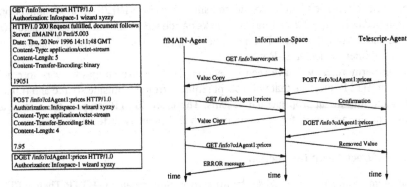

Table1. HTTP protocol data exchanged in information space access

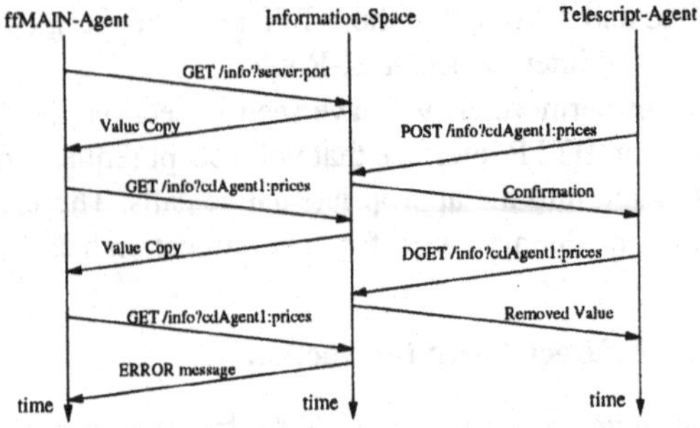

Figure6. Accessing the Information Space.

interact. They need to know the other agent's interfaces (operation signatures, protocols and data formats) in order to communicate effectively. Moreover, the agents will need support to find other agents which provide a certain service or possess certain information.

By encapsulating the data written into the information space inside KQML perfomatives, all the higher-level agent support mechanisms offered by KQML—like facilitator agents and other mediators—come within the compass of mobile agents. HTTP to access to the information space plus the information space itself would provide a possible implementation of the communications infrastructure consisting of KRILs and K-Routers shown in section 2.2.

Another advantage of KQML is that it facilitates the integration of mobile agents with stationary agents and other knowledge-based systems. Using KQML, however, requires a translation between KQML performatives and an agent's internal programming-language-dependant mechanisms (usually methods or functions) which implement the actual service. Mobile agents could contain an KQML parser and operation dispatcher. However, it would probably be sufficient to have one dedicated agent per host and agent platform to provide a KQML translation service. This agent would interact with other agents in its environment by using the interaction mechanism native to this platform (in Telescript, e.g., it would meet other agents and invoke their methods).

5 Conclusion and Further Work

In this paper we demonstrated that it is feasible to interconnect very different agent systems—Telescript and `ffMAIN`—using HTTP, letting agents within one system communicate with agents inside the other. HTTP is an obvious choice because it is likely to be supported in some way or other by most agent infrastructures.

We have implemented a prototype system resembling the one shown in Figure 4. We plan to proceed in the direction described in the previous section in order to provide 'our' agents with support for a subset of KQML. Of course there are still many problems to be solved, e.g., how to define the right 'ontologies' to ensure that different communicating agents actually 'understand' one another. However, the same problem also exists in homogeneous systems. This falls in the realm of AI research. The biggest challenge remains, however: Now that we can get information across the boundary between agent worlds, what about the agents themselves?

References

1. Dag Johansen, Robert van Renesse, and Fred B. Schneider. *An Introduction to the TACOMA Distributed System*. Computer Science Technical Report 95-23, Universitet Tromsø, Institute of Mathematical and Physical Sciences, Department of Computer Science, University of Tromsø, N-9037 Tromsø, Norway, June 1995.
2. Holger Peine, Torsten Stolpmann, and Jürgen Nehmer. Ara: Agents for Remote Actions. See `http://www.uni-kl.de/AG-Nehmer/Ara`.
3. Fritz Hohl. Konzeption eines einfachen Agentensystems und Implementation eines Prototyps. Diplomarbeit, Universität Stuttgart, August 1995.
4. Sahin Albayrak, Siegfried Ballmann, Indra Gunawan Harijono, and Többen Hermann. InAMoS: Intelligent Agents for Mobile Services; InAVAS: Intelligent Agents for Value Added Services. See `http://dai.cs.tu-berlin.de/e/projekte`.
5. James Gosling and Henry McGilton. *The Java Language Environment: A White Paper*. Technical Report, Sun Microsystems, 1995.
6. John K. Ousterhout. *Tcl and the Tk Toolkit*. Addison-Wesley, Reading, MA, 1994.
7. Mark Lutz. *Programming Python*. Nutshell Handbook. O'Reilly & Associates, Sebastopol, CA., 1996.
8. Larry Wall and Randal L. Schwartz. *Programming Perl*. O'Reilly & Associates, Sebastopol, CA, 1990.
9. General Magic, Inc. *Telescript Language Reference*. 420 North Mary Avenue, Sunnyvale, CA 94086, 1995.
10. FTP Software. CyberAgents. See `http://www.ftp.com/cyberagents`.
11. Lucent Technologies. Inferno. See `http://www.lucent.com/inferno`.
12. T. Berners-Lee, R. Fielding, and H. Frystyk. *Hypertext Transfer Protocol—HTTP/1.0*. RFC 1945, Network Working Group, May 1996.
13. T. Berners-Lee, R. Cailliau, A. Luotonen, H. Frystyk Nielsen, and A. Secret. The World-Wide Web. *Communications of the ACM*, 37(8):76–82, August 1994.
14. James E. White. *Telescript Technology: The Foundation for the Electronic Marketplace*. General Magic White Paper GM-M-TSWP1-1293-V1, General Magic, Inc., 420 North Mary Avenue, Sunnyvale, CA 94086, 1994.
15. Object Management Group. *Common Object Request Broker Architecture and Specifications (Document no. 91.12.1)*, 1991.
16. Anselm Lingnau, Oswald Drobnik, and Peter Dömel. An HTTP-based Infrastructure for Mobile Agents. In *Fourth International World Wide Web Conference Proceedings*, number 1 in World Wide Web Journal, pages 461–471, Boston, MA., December 1995. W3C, O'Reilly and Associates.
17. T. Berners-Lee and D. Connolly. *Hypertext Markup Language—2.0*. RFC 1866, Network Working Group, November 1995.
18. D. Gelernter. Generative Communication in Linda. *ACM Transactions on Programming Languages and Systems*, 7(1):80–112, January 1985.

19. Anselm Lingnau and Oswald Drobnik. Making Mobile Agents Communicate: A Flexible Approach. In *The First Annual Conference on Emerging Technologies and Applications in Communications (etaCOM'96)*, pages 180–183. IEEE, May 1996.
20. T. Finin, R. Fritzson, D. McKay, and R. McEntire. KQML as an Agent Communication Language. In *Proc. of the 3rd International Conference on Information and Knowledge Management (CIKM '94)*. ACM Press, November 1994.
21. General Magic, Inc. Tabriz. See `http://www.genmagic.com/Tabriz/`.
22. Henrik Frystyk Nielsen, Tim Berners-Lee, Håkon Lie, Anselm Baird-Smith, José Kahan, and Jean-François Groff. *Libwww—The W3C Reference Library*. World-Wide Web Consortium. Available from `http://www.w3.org/pub/WWW/Library/`.

Strategically Mobile Agents

Teck-How Chia
Department of Computer Science
Cornell University
Ithaca, New York

Srikanth Kannapan
Xerox Corporation
Design Research Institute
Cornell University
Ithaca, New York

Abstract

To realize its promise of providing scaleable and optimal use of network resources, mobile agent technology must be integrated with non-mobile architectures (e.g., client-server) while taking into account the specific needs of applications. This paper introduces a general characterization of mobile agent applications that provides a framework for reasoning about such optimization issues. This framework is refined to enable analysis of alternative mobility policies, and the development of a new *strategic mobility* policy that uses the application characterization to intelligently decide on mobility. The analysis shows that the extreme cases of 'always mobile' and 'always stationary' are sub-optimal with respect to *strategic mobility*. Strategic mobility has been implemented in a software prototype called *MobileAgentX* and successfully tested in an application of concurrent engineering of Micro-Electro-Mechanical Systems (MEMS).

1. Introduction

Mobile agents are intelligent programs that can migrate on computer networks. The concept of having mobile agents carrying out tasks for their owners is creating a new paradigm for network-enabled distributed computing. Mobile agents not only enable more efficient utilization of network resources, but provide a more scaleable model for implementing distributed applications on wide-area networks.

Among the more compelling advantages that mobile agents can provide over traditional client-server computing are overall network traffic reduction, reduction in connectivity requirements and enabling control of remote operations with real-time constraints [Harrison and Chess, 1995]. Enabling technologies for implementing mobile agents are maturing [Gray, 1995] [Clark and McCabe, 1994] [Telescript, 1996] [Bharat and Cardelli, 1995] [Johansen, van Renesse, Schneider, 1995] [Straßer, Baumann, and Hohl, 1996]. Prototype applications using various mobile agent systems are emerging in workflow management [Cai, Gloor and Nog, 1996], mobile computing [Chess et al, 1995], information retrieval [Rus, Gray and Kotz, 1996], electronic commerce [Telescript, 1996] and Internet chat applications [Ranganathan et al, 1996]. However, the major challenge for wider use of mobile agents is the proper integration of this technology with non-mobile (e.g., client-server) concepts, while taking into account the specific needs of applications. [Carzaniga, Picco and Vigna, 1997] describes a classification of different mobile and non-mobile architectures, viz. client-server, remote evaluation, code-on-demand, and mobile agent. Our focus in this paper is on client-server and mobile agent architectures. (Another barrier to widespread deployment of mobile agents is the security of executing mobile programs [Harrison and Chess, 1995] -- this issue is not addressed in this paper.)

To fully exploit the advantages that mobile agents provide, they must be designed in the context of the application domain. A mobile agent should utilize knowledge about the problem that it is assigned to solve to make optimal decisions about its mobility, which naturally translates to the optimal use of computing and network resources. In current mobile agent architectures agents are mobile all the time independent of the characteristics of the application. This might not be optimal, since in some situations, it might save resources if a stationary agent communicates with a remote program through a network similar to client-server or other non-mobile agent architectures. In order for mobile agents to make intelligent decisions about mobility, we need to extract relevant characteristics of mobile agent applications and use them to design strategies for agent mobility. Based on these characteristics, agents should be able to dynamically change between mobile and non-mobile modes of operation to best satisfy the objectives of the application - we call this notion *strategic mobility*. The rest of this paper describes a means of designing, implementing and applying strategically mobile agents: Section 2 identifies application characteristics that affect mobility decision-making; Section 3 describes how application characteristics can be obtained and used; Section 4 and Section 5 design and analyze mechanisms for strategic mobility; Section 6 describes an architecture and implementation of strategic mobility (*Mobile-AgentX*); Section 7 describes the application of Mobile-AgentX for distributed Micro-Electro-Mechanical Systems (MEMS) design; and Section 8 provides a summary and conclusion.

2. Characterization of Mobile Agent Applications

Mobile agent applications, though implemented differently, share common features. In terms of purpose, mobile agent applications seek to utilize a network of distributed resources (e.g., specialized software or knowledge, robots) in a planned or opportunistic way to solve a problem for a client (or end-user). In terms of architecture, a mobile agent is usually deployed on a network by a *Service Provider* application. The mobile agent migrates to distributed resources with a static or dynamically-generated visit plan to request information from and provide information to the distributed resources in order to solve the problem. In this paper, we call the mobile agent *Task Agent,* and the distributed resources *Consultants*. (Note that this terminology is introduced to help define a slightly higher level of application abstraction, namely that of distributed problem solving, in comparison to existing mobile agent terminology at the distributed systems level of abstraction such as places, meetings and movement ('go') [Telescript 1996] [Straβer, Baumann, and Hohl, 1996].) Figure 1 shows a generic mobile agent framework, where a mobile Task Agent migrates to various Consultants distributed in a computer network and returns with a solution. As a simple example, if this framework is used to design a house, then there might be a materials consultant, a structure consultant, a piping consultant and an architectural consultant among others. As another example, to design a micro-electromechanical device there are consultants for design optimization, fabrication process selection and

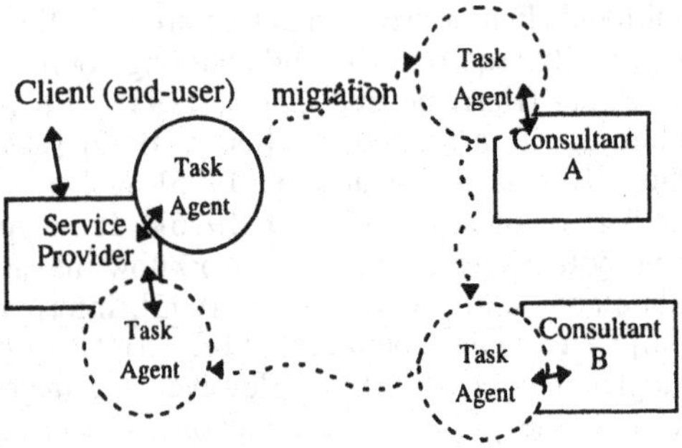

Figure 1: Mobile Agent framework.

mask layout, geometric modeling and fabrication simulation, and performance analysis - see Section 7 of this paper.

Figure 2 shows mobile agent applications characterized in three layers of abstraction, viz., problem, application framework, and infrastructure. The topmost layer represents the requirements of the problem to be solved. The bottom two layers represent the capabilities of the mobile agent application. In each layer, the figure shows common features relevant to agent mobility in boldface (e.g., Problem Objectives). Each feature is further characterized by a set of parameters (e.g., migration size of Task Agent). A variety of applications can be characterized by the parameters shown in Fig. 2. For example, at the level of the problem layer in Fig. 2, a mobile agent application for collecting stock quotes from different exchanges around the world for a specific set of companies may have the characteristics of low volumes of interaction, number of interactions, and total interaction time between the Task Agent and the Consultants that provide the stock information - since the interactions are likely to take the form of simple database queries. There are no serious security requirements since stock quotes are public. The problem solving objectives might be strongly weighted by speed and reliability of problem solution since timely and accurate stock information may enable significant buy/sell financial decisions.

Problem Layer

TaskAgent-Consultant Interaction
- *Volume of interaction* - *Number of interactions*
- Total interaction time - Security of transactions
- Real-time requirements of interactions

Problem Objectives
- *Cost/Budget* - Speed of problem solution
- Reliability of solution - Quality of solution

Application Framework Layer

Task Agent
- *Migration Size* (size of Task Agent when it migrates from one host to another.)

Consultant
- Consulting fee - Quality of results - *Result size*
- Speed of solution - Reliability of results

Infrastructure Layer

Computer Network
- Load/Latency - Reliability
- Security - *Cost of using network*

Computing Resources
- Cost of usage - Speed of computation
- Reliability of computation
- Resource access (e.g. storage, robot arm)

Figure 2: Abstraction Layers and Features Characterizing Mobile Agent Applications.

In contrast, consider a distributed engineering design application for mobile agent technology. Again, at the problem layer, a Task Agent assigned to design the piping layout for a house is likely to have large volumes of interactions and total interaction times with Consultants capable of constructing 3D geometric information of the house, transforming piping specifications to layout plans, assessing conformance with building codes, developing cost estimates etc. If the piping design process requires substantial iteration, there can be a large number of interactions between Task Agents and Consultants. There is a requirement for secure transactions since they involve information proprietary between the customer and builder of the house.

For an individual house builder and its customer who may view piping as basic infrastructure for the house, the problem solving objectives might be strongly weighted by the cost of the problem solving process as well as the quality and cost of the piping layout solution.

Distinctive characteristics are also apparent at the application framework layer and infrastructure layers for the two examples described above. Briefly, for the stock quote application, migration sizes and result sizes may be smaller due to simpler logic and data requirements, but with greater demands on speed and reliability which translate to less tolerance for network latency and failure. The application and infrastructure layer characteristics of the distributed piping layout design application are quite the opposite.

Often the problem solving objective is to have the problem solved optimally with respect to certain constraints like time or cost. The parameters of each feature can affect the problem objectives as well as one or more of the constraints. By identifying the relevant parameters and modeling their interrelationships, the Task Agent can use these models to make intelligent decisions in the problem solving process such that the objectives are optimized. For example, if the objective were to solve the problem with high reliability, a Task Agent may decide on a one-time migration to a consultant node at a greater cost rather than take the risk of a network failure during many interactions with the consultant. In the next section, we suggest various ways that parameter values can be obtained or approximated. Then, we will show how a subset of the parameters in Fig. 2 (shown italicized) can be used by a Task Agent to make decisions about its mobility. (Another example of such an approach applied to the dynamic location of Internet chat servers, is described in [Ranganathan et al, 1996].)

In our discussion, we distinguish between three types of Consultants in terms of what services they provide: (a) *process consultant*, a server which provides the Task Agent with information regarding decomposition of the problem into subproblems and the inter-dependencies between them; (b) *problem consultant,* domain-specific server that solves a specific class of problem or subproblem; and (c) *'Yellow Pages' consultant*, a directory of process consultants and problem consultants, their services, locations, fees, reliability, interaction characteristics and other parameters that might be helpful for strategic decision-making by the Task Agent.

3. Obtaining Parameters for Application Characterization

One of the key issues in using the characterization described above is in obtaining good estimates of the parameters for different applications. Parameters and their values that characterize an application can either be static, i.e., parameter values such as code size for a task agent, that are known before actual problem solving; or dynamic, i.e., parameter values such as network latency between two hosts, that are known during or after specific instances of problem solving. Static parameter values specific to applications are appropriately modeled as attributes of the Task Agent and can be implemented as such. Dynamic parameter values are problematic; they can only be estimated. Two approaches can potentially be used for estimation: (1) infer parameter values inductively using historical data and statistical analysis, and (2) model specific application classes and specify estimated values of parameters. A combination of the two approaches may also be used to enable a 'predictor-corrector' mechanism - and in fact such an approach might be preferable. Such an integrated approach would first provide a mechanism for specific Task Agents (which are expected to represent some class structure of applications) to begin problem solving with some predicted values for parameters based on historical data or deeper models of the application (as described in the examples of the previous section). During or at the end of a problem solving session, the parameter statistics associated with that session will be analyzed and the results stored for future use by the same or other instances of the Task Agent.

To implement such an integrated approach, a mobile agent framework will have to provide mechanisms to collect and analyze parameter statistics and to maintain this information. Instead of approximating a single function to estimate a certain parameter value, the statistics are grouped under different application classes and in each class, a function will be approximated with the statistics of that class. As a result, each application class will have different estimation functions for the same set of parameters. Maintaining the application context of an estimation function in this manner provides a more accurate estimate of a parameter value that can then be reused by other Task Agents of the same application.

In the *Mobile-AgentX* architecture, we delegate the task of collecting and analyzing statistics to the Problem Consultant and Task Agent. The Problem Consultant is responsible for collecting and analyzing parameter statistics related to itself (e.g. volume of interaction, result size) and the Task Agent is responsible for parameters that it is capable of obtaining (e.g. migration size, network latency). The analysis involves determining the estimation functions from the statistics in each of the application classes. If the newly determined functions are significantly different from previously obtained ones, they are reported to the Yellow Pages Consultant for update. The Yellow Pages Consultant acts as a database where Task Agents can query for these estimation functions.

Usually, the Task Agent will be given all the relevant estimating functions before the problem solving session begins. However, changes in the visit plan which may be due to unavailability of a certain Problem Consultant will necessitate selecting a new Problem Consultant and asking the Yellow Pages Consultant for the relevant parameters and estimation functions.

4. Strategic Mobility

To illustrate the concept of strategic mobility, let us consider a simple problem which requires only two Consultants and that the (static) visit plan is Consultant C_j followed by Consultant C_k as shown in Figure 3. Let us say that the Task Agent carries its initial data and subproblem solutions in a *backpack*. Furthermore, the input to the Consultant at each step is the result returned from the previous Consultant in the visit plan. So, the input to Consultant C_j will be the backpack with just the initial data, and the input to Consultant C_k will be the backpack with the results returned by Consultant C_j. The results at each Consultant replaces the previous backpack contents. This is just a simplifying assumption. Typically, there will be additional data in the backpack that is not used as input to the next Consultant.

Let us explore the above problem situation with the following assumptions. The objective is to have the problem solved at the lowest cost. The network fee is charged according to the volume of bytes transmitted through the network. The consulting fees are fixed, so the only variable cost here is the network cost. Thus, to minimize cost in this example would be to minimize network usage.

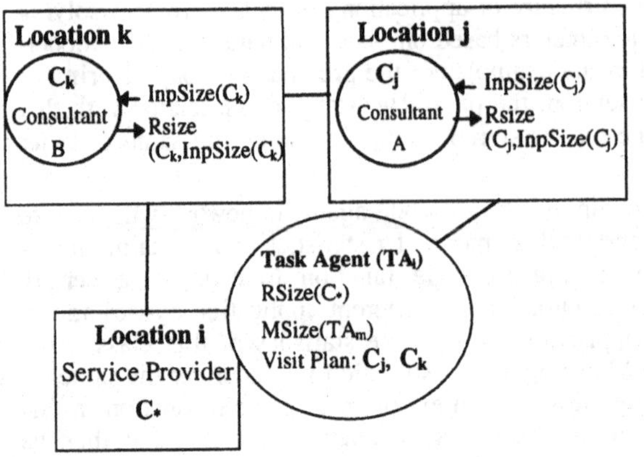

LEGEND

TA_m denotes the Task Agent at location m.

C_m denotes the Consultant at location m.

C_* is the service provider.

MSize(TA_m) is the migration size of the *Task Agent*, which is the actual number of bytes transmitted when it migrates through the network.

InpSize(C_m) denotes the size of the input to consultant at location m.

RSize(C_m, InpSize(C_m)) denotes the size of the results returned by the Consultant at location m.

RSize(C_*) denotes the initial size of the backpack for the Task Agent

Figure 3: A Parametric Characterization of a Mobile Agent Application.

The problem solving process begins with the Task Agent carrying a backpack containing the initial data provided by the Service Provider C_*. The Task Agent has the ability to either migrate and co-locate with a consultant, or consult remotely with the consultant from a different node.

The nature of the interaction between the Task Agent and a Consultant is such that there will be one or more iterations of input-output message-passing between them corresponding to an iterative solution process between the Task Agent and the Consultant. In this case, one iteration of interaction refers to the Task Agent sending the input values to the Consultant and the Consultant returning the result to the Task Agent. Once the result from C_j is obtained, this result is added to the backpack, and the Task Agent interacts with C_k by providing the contents of the backpack as input. When the problem is solved the final result is sent back to the Service Provider C_*.

We will show that making intelligent decisions about mobility of the Task Agent can lead to better achievement of the problem objective, which in this case reduces to minimizing network traffic.

Let us consider a specific illustrative example as follows. As shown in Figure 3, MSize(TA_m) is the size of the code controlling the behavior of the Task Agent and assumed to be constant throughout its lifetime (say 120kb). RSize(C*) is the size of the initial backpack (say 2 kb). Table 1 gives the parameter values for interactions between the Task Agent and the Consultants. We also define n(TA,C_m) as the number of interactions and ISize(TA,C_m) as the total volume of interaction between the Task Agent (TA) and a Consultant (C_m).

Msize (TA_m)	Consultant C_m	a = InpSize(C_m)	b = RSize(C_m,InpSize(C_m))	n (TA, C_m)	ISize(TA, C_m) = n*(a+b)
120 kb	C_j	2 kb	18 kb	12	240 kb
120 kb	C_k	18 kb	22 kb	1	40 kb

Table 1: An Illustrative Example of Mobile Agent Application Characterization.

Strategic mobility involves making a deliberate decision on whether to migrate to the next consultant on the visit plan located at a different node. Most mobile agent applications today require that the mobile client agent always migrate to the consultant's node. In contrast, non-mobile agents and client-server architectures have no notion of mobility. Client-server computing can be thought of as a mobile agent application that has its mobile feature turned off. We will show that both policies of being mobile all the time, and not allowing mobility at all are not optimal when compared to a one where the Task Agent have a choice of being mobile or stationary during the problem solving process.

5. Comparison of Three Mobility Policies

Let's consider three cases, the first where the Task Agent is always mobile, the second where it is always stationary and the third where it is *strategically mobile.* In each case, we analyze how many bytes are actually transmitted through the network.

Case 1: Task Agent always mobile

In this case, the Task Agent migrates to both consultants C_j and C_k, one after the other, and at C_k the agent sends the results back to C_* and kills itself (see Fig. 4). The total bytes transmitted will include the size of the Task Agent itself, the data it carries at each step and the size of the final result which is sent back from location k. Since the Task Agent is always co-located with the Consultant, the volume of interaction is not included in the calculation of network traffic. Total bytes due to migration is 2*MSize(TA_m) since the agent migrates twice. While migrating from location i to j it carries RSize(C_*) bytes. From j to k, the agent carries the result of size RSize(C_j,InpSize(C_j)) and finally sends back the result of size RSize(C_k,InpSize(C_k)).

Therefore, total bytes transmitted through the network = $T_{always\text{-}mobile}$ = MSize(TA_i) + MSize(TA_j) + RSize(C_*) + RSize(C_j, InpSize(C_j)) + RSize(C_k, InpSize(C_k)). Using the values in Table 1, $T_{always\text{-}mobile}$ = 120 + 120 + 2 + 18 + 22 = 282 kb.

Case 2: Task Agent always stationary

In this case, (Fig. 5) the Task Agent stays at location i and consults with the Consultants remotely by passing messages. Thus, only the interaction messages are transmitted through the network.

Total bytes transmitted through network = $T_{always\text{-}stationary}$ = ISize(TA,C_j) + ISize(TA,C_k). Again, using the values in Table 1, $T_{always\text{-}stationary}$ = 240 + 40 = 280 kb.

Case 3: Task Agent strategically mobile

Now, let us consider the case when the Task Agent migrates to C_j, but doesn't migrate to C_k (see Fig. 6). This means MSize(TA_i) bytes is transmitted through the network when it migrates from location i to j. And when the Task Agent communicates remotely with C_k, only ISize(TA,C_k) bytes are transmitted through the network. After Consultant B is done, the final result of size RSize(C_k, InpSize(C_k)) is sent back to the Service Provider C_*. Therefore, the total number of bytes transmitted through network, $T_{strategically\text{-}mobile}$ = MSize(TA_i) + RSize(C_*) + ISize(TA,C_k) + RSize(C_k, InpSize(C_k)). Using the values in Table 1, $T_{strategically\text{-}mobile}$ = 120 + 2 + 40 + 22 = 184 kb.

Comparing the three cases, we see that the Task Agent with strategic mobility uses the network most sparingly in terms of total bytes transferred. Network traffic for the strategically mobile agent is 96 kb less than if it is always stationary and 98 kb less than if it is always mobile. It can be seen that if mobile agents were aware of even a subset of the characterizing parameters of applications shown in Fig. 2, they would be able to perform analysis similar to the above analysis and be able to make better mobility decisions that satisfy the objectives of the end-user. Besides reducing network traffic, mobility can be strategically used for intelligent network routing or reducing connectivity requirements in an unreliable network by using the relevant characteristics as mobility decision factors. For this example, since the objective is to minimize network traffic, only parameters concerned with sizes of data are considered. More subtle uses of the various parameters will be required for more demanding problem objectives.

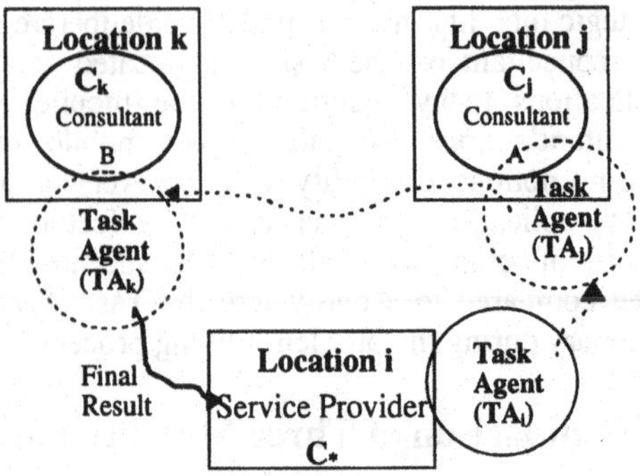

Figure 4: Always Mobile Policy

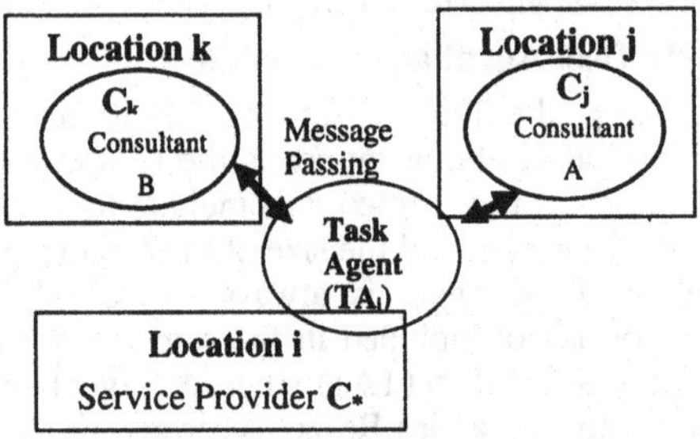

Figure 5: Always Stationary Policy

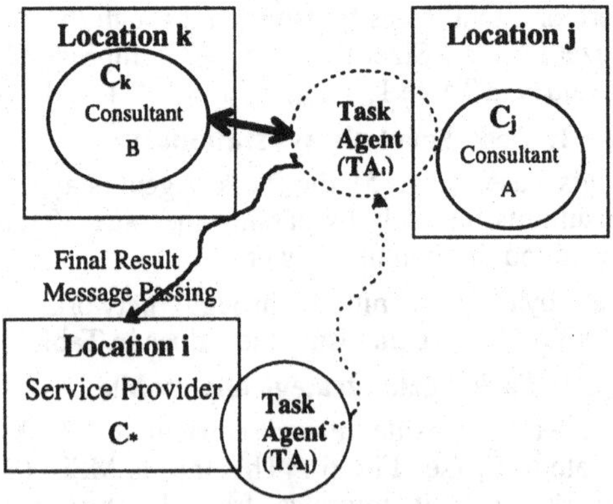

Figure 6: Strategic Mobility Policy

6. Architecture and Implementation of Mobile-AgentX

Figure 7 shows the architecture of a prototype implementation of a mobile agent framework called *Mobile-AgentX* which is able to support strategically mobile agents. The framework is not specific to any domain, yet the application characterization and evaluation of mobility policy described in earlier sections enables strategic mobility decisions consistent with application requirements and infrastructure capabilities. The architecture is scaleable to problems with large number of distributed components since additional Problem Consultants and Process Consultants can be added by registering them in the Yellow Pages Consultant. The distinction made between Problem Consultants and Process Consultants is a division of labor that enables further flexibility and scalability since the same Process Consultant can propose alternative plans involving the use of different sets of Problem Consultants. Conversely, Process Consultants can be specialized by application (e.g., different Process Consultants for collecting stock quotes and solving a kind of engineering design problem) and yet use the same Problem Consultant (say for statistical processing and data visualization of stock prices and engineering simulation).

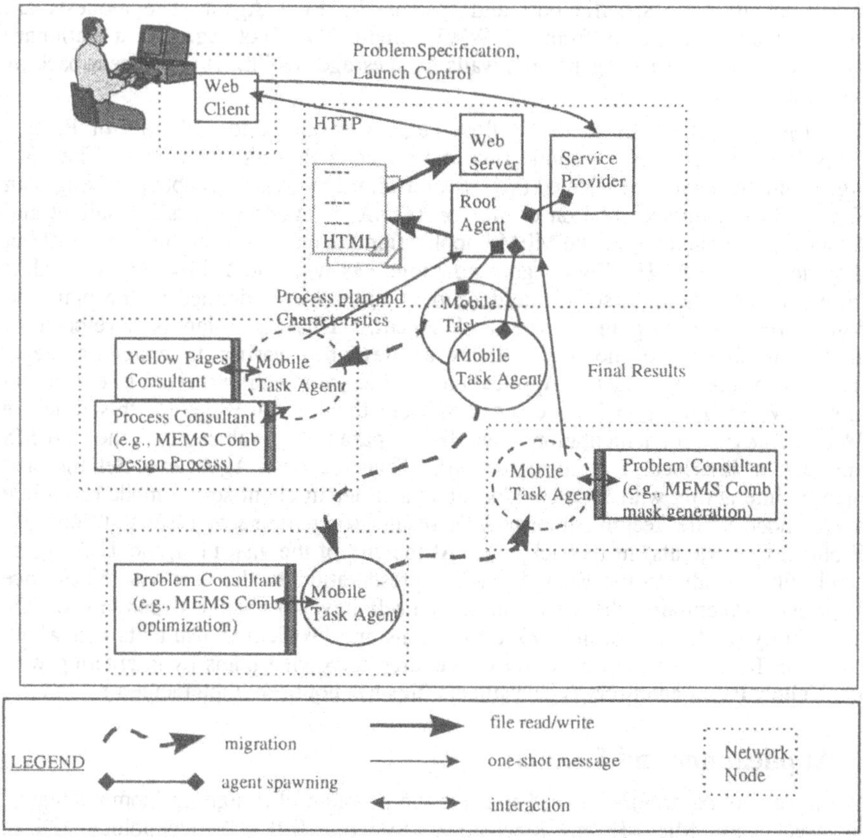

Figure 7: Architecture of Mobile-AgentX Implementation of Strategic Mobility.

The analysis of the previous section illustrates the advantages of strategic mobility with an example using only a limited subset of the set of features described in Section 2 and Figure 2. The use of the full set of features characterizing mobile agent applications can potentially provide further improvement in satisfying the problem objectives while optimizing the use of computing and network resources. The research approach taken in this paper is to first implement and apply the limited subset of application features in the *Mobile-AgentX* architecture to gain some practical experience of the use of strategic mobility. The strategies that the Task Agent uses must be explicitly programmed into its control code. The relevance of each parameter depends on the problem objectives and it is the responsibility of the agent programmer to decide which parameter should be used to decide mobility.

Mobile-AgentX is implemented using AgentTcl [Gray, 1995] and uses the World-Wide-Web (WWW) as the interface to the system extending the models and architecture described in [Davis and Kannapan, 1993][Kannapan and Taylor, 1994]. The operation of Mobile-AgentX is as follows. As shown in Fig. 7, the Service Provider is a dedicated server that listens to problem-specific requests from the WWW client on a specific port and spawns the Root Agent. The requests are produced by Java applets from the WWW client. The Root Agent is a stationary agent that spawns Task Agents and waits for messages (solutions) to be sent back by the Task Agent.

The Task Agent moves to the Yellow Pages Consultant for referrals of Process Consultants for its class of application and selects a Process Consultant. The Task Agent interacts with the selected Process Consultant to create a problem solving plan (in the current implementation of *Mobile-AgentX* the Yellow Pages Consultant and the Process Consultant for the MEMS application are co-located on the same host but they need not be.) The Task Agent now interacts with the Yellow Pages to select Problem Consultants to solve interdependent subproblems defined in the plan and hence create a visit plan for the Task Agent. This visit plan is developed by analyzing alternative mobility policies as described earlier to enable strategic mobility for the Task Agent. Application specific parameters involved in evaluating alternative mobility policies are obtained from the Yellow Pages (at this time the *Mobile-AgentX* implementation has fixed parameter values for the MEMS application described in the next section). Then the Task Agent executes the visit plan by interacting with Problem Consultants either in client-server mode or mobile agent mode while keeping intermediate results (or pointers to results stored with Problem Consultants) in its backpack. At the end of the visit plan, the Task Agent sends final results to the Root Agent for presentation to the user via the Service Provider. Potentially, the visit plan may itself have to change depending on the availability (or failure) of network connections and Problem Consultants - in which case, the Task Agent will have to explore alternative visit plans by interacting with the Yellow Pages and Process Consultants (this has not been implemented.)

7. Applications and Results

We have applied *Mobile-AgentX* to solve the problem of designing 'comb actuator' devices using Micro-Electro-Mechanical Systems (MEMS) technology [Dixit, Taylor, Kannapan, 1996] [Dixit, Kannapan, Taylor, 1997]. Figure 8 shows the WWW interface to *Mobile-AgentX*. This application problem has two Consultants, the design optimization consultant, and a fabrication process selection and mask layout consultant. The window on the top left of the screen snap in Fig. 8 shows the input form for specification of the comb actuator design problem. The window on the right in Fig. 8 shows the results from the design optimization consultant which consists of optimized values for a set of design parameters. The window on the bottom left in Fig. 8 shows a view of the mask layout generated by the mask layout consultant.

We experimented with using the three different mobility policies for the *Task Agent* in this problem. For each case, we captured the byte volume that is transmitted through the network throughout the entire problem-solving process. Figure 9 shows the traffic volume plotted against time. Each time instant represents the start time for an event that represents a step in the problem-solving process. Since the size of messages transmitted through the network in this context is small enough that latency is negligible, we represent them by vertical spikes at the time that they are transmitted on the network. This representation includes the migration of the Task Agent as well. The problem solving process has three major steps. In the first step, time T1-T2, the Task Agent interacts with the "Yellow Pages" consultant. In the second step (T3-T4) and third step (T5-T6), the Task Agent interacts with the design optimization consultant and the mask layout consultant respectively. The interaction with the design optimization consultant involves several iterations of message passing - shown in the second graph in Fig. 9 as a series of spikes in the interval T3-T4. On the other hand, interaction with the mask layout consultant involves only one iteration. For the strategic mobility case, the Task Agent interacts remotely with the Yellow Pages consultant (client-server mode), migrates to the design optimization consultant for local interaction, and subsequently, interacts remotely with the fabrication process selection and mask layout consultant (client-server mode).

A careful examination of Fig. 9 shows that neither an 'always mobile' or 'always stationary' policy is optimal. Indeed, if we sum up the total bytes transmitted through the network, for always mobile it is 91,796 bytes, for always stationary it is

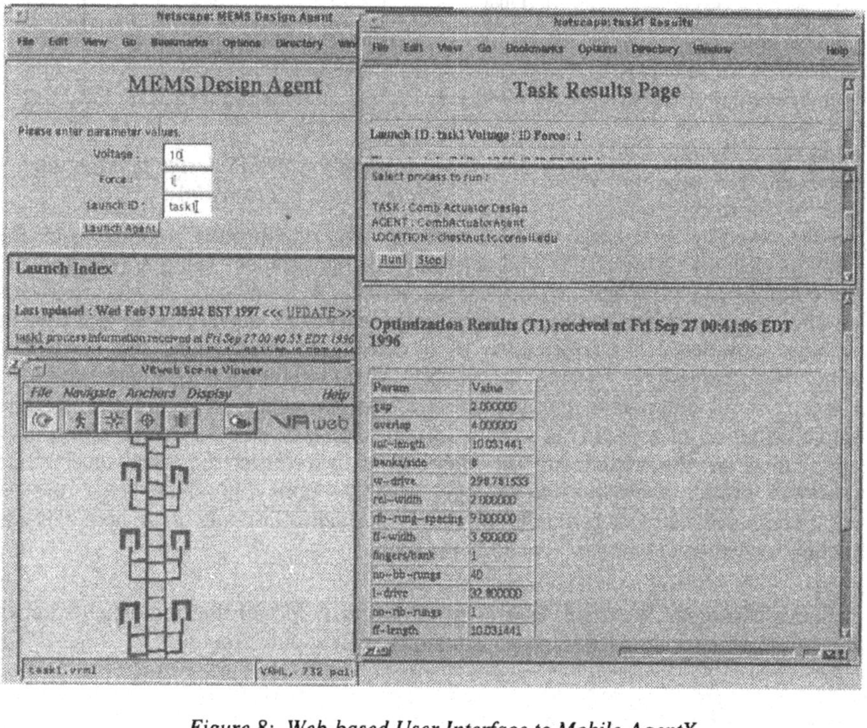

Figure 8: Web-based User Interface to Mobile-AgentX.

90,553 bytes, and for strategically mobile it is 88,454 bytes. The advantage provided by strategic mobility is even more apparent when the final result size (which is significantly larger than the other results and the same for all three cases) is subtracted from this calculation. In this case, network traffic for 'always mobile' is 5,796 bytes, for 'always stationary' it is 4,553 bytes, and for 'strategically mobile' it is 2,454 bytes. Thus 'strategic mobility' reduces network traffic by 58% compared to 'always mobile', and 46% compared to 'always stationary'.

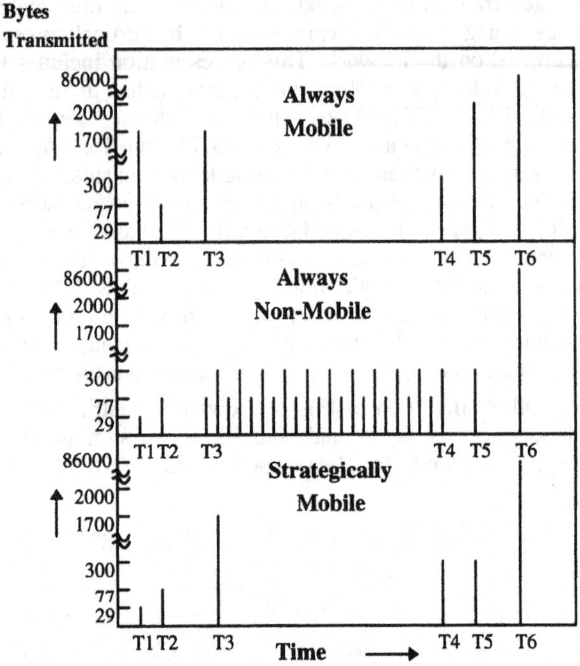

Figure 9: Traffic Graph for MEMS design application (Note: Y-axis not to scale)

8. Conclusion

This paper showed that *strategic mobility* can better leverage the use of mobile agents. In contrast, the policies in current agent technologies and applications can be characterized as 'always mobile' or 'always stationary'. A strategic mobility policy seeks to achieve the objectives of the application domain by deciding to migrate over a network to a needed resource, or instead to communicate with the needed resource over the network depending on certain characteristics of the problem being solved and the underlying computing and network infrastructure. A framework for characterizing an application problem and the underlying infrastructure was presented and a more detailed parametric characterization of mobile agent applications was developed using this framework. Using the mobile agent application characterization, a comparison of alternative mobility policies was presented. The architecture and implementation of a prototype system (*Mobile-AgentX*) was described. Results of application of the system in the domain of Micro-Electromechanical-Systems (MEMS) design show that a strategic mobility policy provides better use of computing and network resources to satisfy problem objectives than both 'always mobile' or 'always stationary' mobility policies.

Acknowledgment: We thank Hrishikesh Dixit for help with the implementation of the consultants for the MEMS comb actuator design application.

References

[Bharat and Cardelli, 1995] Bharat, K. A., L. Cardelli, Migratory Applications, DEC Systems Research Center Tech. Report, 1995.

[Cai, Gloor and Nog, 1996] Cai, T., P.A. Gloor, S. Nog. DartFlow: A Workflow Management System on the Web using Transportable Agents. Dartmouth College, Dept. of Computer Science Tech. Report PCS-TR96-283, May 14, 1996.

[Carzaniga, Picco and Vigna, 1997] Carzaniga, G. P. Picco, and G. Vigna, "Designing Distributed Applications with Mobile Code Paradigms", to appear *Proceedings of the 19th Intl. Conference on Software Engineering*, Boston, 1997.

[Chess et al, 1995] Chess, D., B. Grosof, C. Harrison, D. Levine, C. Parris, G. Tsudik. Itinerant Agents for Mobile Computing, *IEEE Personal Communications Magazine*, October 1995.

[Clark and McCabe, 1994] McCabe, F. G., K. L. Clark, April: Agent Process Interaction Language, Department of Computing, Imperial College Technical Report, Nov. 25, 1994.

[Davis and Kannapan 1993] Davis, J., and S. Kannapan, AgentX: An Environment for Coordinating Distributed Problem Solving in Product Development, *Proceedings 2nd IEEE Workshop on Enabling Infrastructure for Collaborative Enterprises*, Morgantown, West Virginia, April 20-22, 1993.

[Dixit, Kannapan, Taylor, 1997] Dixit, H., S. Kannapan, D. L. Taylor, 3D Geometric Simulation of MEMS Fabrication Processes: A Semantic Approach, submitted to *ACM Symposium on Solid Modeling Applications*, 1997.

[Dixit, Taylor, Kannapan, 1996] Dixit, H., D. L. Taylor, S. Kannapan, Design Considerations for Manufacturability of MEMS Comb Actuators, *ASME Design for Manufacturing Conference*, Irvine, California, Aug. 18-22, 1996.

[Gray 1995] Gray, R. S., Agent Tcl: A transportable agent system. Dartmouth College, Dept. of Computer Science Technical Report, 17 November 1995.

[Harrison and Chess, 1995] Harrison, C. G., D.M. Chess, A. Kershenbaum. Mobile Agents: Are they a good idea? IBM Research Division Tech. Report. March 28 1995.

[Johansen, van Renesse, Schneider, 1995] Johansen, R. van Renesse, F.B. Schneider. Operating System Support for Mobile Agents, *Proc. 5th IEEE Workshop on Hot Topics in Operating Systems*, pp. 42-45, May 1995.

[Kannapan and Taylor 1994] Kannapan, S., and D. Taylor, The Interplay of Context, Process, and Conflict in Concurrent Engineering, *Journal of Concurrent Engineering Research and Applications*, Vol. 2, 1994, pp. 183-196.

[Ranganathan et al, 1996] Ranganathan, M., A. Acharya, S. Sharma, J. Saltz. Network-aware Mobile Programs, Dept. of Computer Science Tech. Report, University of Maryland, College Park, 1996.

[Rus, Gray and Kotz, 1996] Rus, D., R.S. Gray, D. Kotz. Autonomous and Adaptive Agents that Gather Information. Dartmouth College, Dept. of Computer Science Tech. Report, 1996.

[Straßer, Baumann, and Hohl, 1996] Straßer, M., J. Baumann, F. Hohl. MOLE - A Java Based Mobile Agent System, University of Stuttgart Tech. Report. May 1996.

[Telescript 1996] Telescript Technology: Mobile Agents, General Magic Inc. White paper, 1996.

A Novel Mobile Agent Search Algorithm

Wen-Shyen E. Chen[1] and Chun-Wu R. Leng[2]

[1] Institute of Computer Science, National Chung-Hsing University, Taichung, Taiwan 40227, ROC

[2] Department of Computer Science, National Chengchi University, Taipei, Taiwan ROC

Abstract. Intelligent Agent has been shown to be a good approach to addressing the issues of mobile computing. However, before the approach can be commercially viable, a set of management capabilities that support the controls of intelligent agents in a mobile environment need to be in place. Since controls can only be applied after the target agent is located, an effective agent search algorithm is an indispensable part of the management functions. In this paper, we propose a new algorithm, the Highest Probability First Algorithm, for locating the target agent. The approach makes use of the execution time information to reduce cost and network traffic. The execution time of the agent on a server is assumed to be binomial distributed and therefore is more realistic.

1 Introduction

Compared to the conventional computers with a fixed connection to wired networks, mobile computers have narrow, unreliable connectivity, limited processing power and battery capacity, and have to operate in a dynamic, heterogeneous environment [1, 2, 3]. As a result, to realize nomadicity – the ability to allow the user to move from place to place and retains access to a rich set of information and communications services while moving – a new paradigm for information processing and communications is needed. Intelligent Agent [4, 5, 6, 7, 8] is shown to be promising in addressing the issues of limited capacity and unreliable links of mobile computers. In this approach, an electronic message that carries a computer program, whether procedural or declarative, which can be executed by the computer system of the recipient on behalf of the client, is submitted by the client and can navigate autonomously through heterogeneous networks. The message is capable of interacting with servers or other agents at where the services are provided, moving to another machine while carrying the intermediate results, and resuming execution when it reaches the destination. After the message is submitted, the client can be disconnected from the network. The client will be notified when the agent finishes its task or is aborted.

With this approach, the mobile clients and servers are decoupled in the sense that instead of getting intermediate results many times, the client interacts with the network only when it is submitting the agent and when the agent returns with results, as depicted in Fig. 1. The asynchronous interaction between the client and the server provides robustness against frequent disconnection suffered by mobile computers. In addition, since the agent can incorporate smarter query language, less data needs to be transmitted in the network. The feasibility of this approach is evidenced by several prototypes that employ this new paradigm of computing [8, 9].

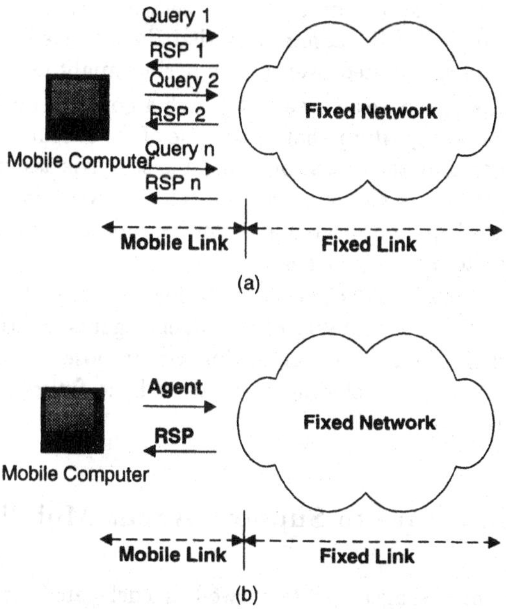

Fig. 1. The interactions between the mobile computer and the fixed network: (a) The conventional approach, (b) The Intelligent Agent approach.

Nevertheless, a complete functioning agent, whether simulated in software or implemented from a robot, needs an integrated collection of diverse but inter-related capabilities, i.e., an architecture [8, 9]. In addition, before an intelligent agent service can be accepted, a high quality and cost effective agent mobility operation, administration and maintenance (OA&M) system must be in place to guarantee a certain level of service quality. For any control to be applied to the target agent, it needs to be located first. Therefore, *agent location* is an indispensable part of the OA&M.

There are several approaches for agent location [10]: A straightforward approach, which is suitable for locating a target agent traversing the servers it will visit in a non-deterministic order, requires the dispatched agent to report its location and status to a *status holder* when it arrives at a server or when some specified events happen. The target agent can then be located by consulting the status holder. The other approach that does not require any status holder is to "blindly search" the target agent by broadcasting search agents to servers.

These approaches will generate unwanted network traffic and further complicate management functions. However, there are applications that can determined the servers and the sequence of the servers the mobile agent will traverse before it starts. In [10], the author proposed to make use of the execution time information available to search the target agent more intelligently when the sequence of the servers to traversed can be determined beforehand. The result shows that the number of the probes can be effectively reduced. Nevertheless, the complexity of the algorithm is high and the assumption that the expected execution time on a server is *uniformly* distributed over a time period might not be realistic.

In this paper, we propose a new agent search algorithm, the Highest-Probability-First search (HPFS) algorithm, that makes use of the execution time information. In the HPFS algorithm, the execution time on a server is assumed to be *binomial distributed* [11], which is closer to reality. The derived probability function is shown to be much less complicated and can be adopted by a search agent when being sent to locate the target agent.

The rest of the paper is organized as follows. Section 2 illustrates an architecture that supports the mobility of intelligent agents. Section 3 describes the Highest-Probability-First search algorithm we propose. Simulation results are presented in Section 4. Concluding remarks and the future research topics will be given in Section 5.

2 An Architecture to Support Agent Mobility

In many cases, a mobile agent can be viewed as a delegate for a client. It travels in a service network, acting on behalf of the client to request services from servers it visits. An architecture that can be used to support intelligent messaging in mobile computing is depicted in Fig. 2. Note that in the architecture, there are four types of agents: User Agent, Broker Agent, Service/Resource Agent, and Management Agent.

The User Agent is submitted by the client to the fixed network. It carries the "goals" or requests for services from the client and will first arrive at the Mobile Supporting Server (which can either be an Access Node (AN) or a Home Base Node (HBN)). The Mobile Supporting Server acts as a "proxy" for the mobile client and will be the home base for the agent being submitted. The User Agent will first consult with the Broker Agent for the servers that can fulfill its goals or provide the requested services. It then travels to the resource/service providers and interacts with their Service/Resource Agents at that location. The User Agent might have to move in between several service/resource providers to have the requested work done. When the requested services are fulfilled or when the user agent is being called back, the user agent will return to the client. If the client is not currently available, the result will be temporarily stored in the Access Node or Network Management Center (NMC) and the mobile client will be notified. The mobile client can then retrieve the stored result. When the user agent is in the service network, the client can also request management functions

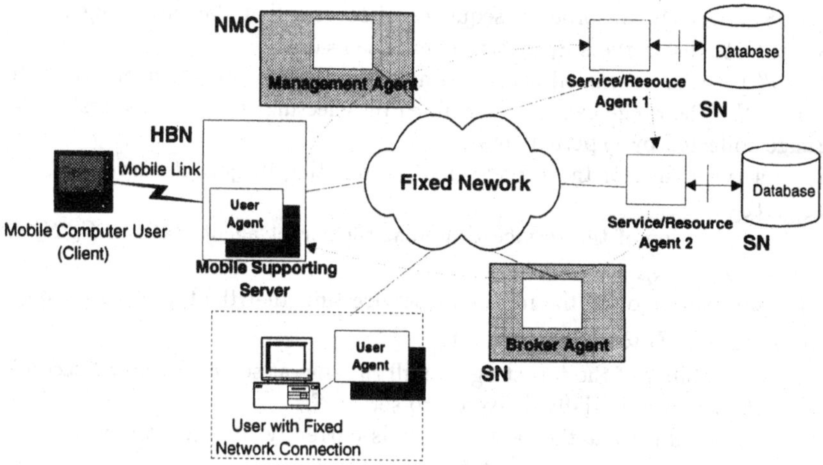

Fig. 2. An Architecture to Support Intelligent Agent in the Mobile Environment.

from the Management Agent to have the control over the target agent. Basic control functions include:

- **terminate** - terminate the execution of the target agent;
- **freeze** - postpone the forwarding of an agent until a resume message is received;
- **suspend** - suspend the execution of an agent until a resume message is received;
- **resume** - resume the execution of a suspended or frozen agent.

The same architecture can be used by both mobile clients and clients with fixed network connections, as shown in Fig. 2.

3 The Highest Probability First Search Algorithm

3.1 Location Estimation

According to the previous discussion, the performance of a search algorithm is determined by the time spent on locating the target agent, as well as the network overhead caused by the algorithm. Both evaluation criteria, in fact, are mainly resulted from the number of times that the search agent probes servers to locate the agent. Therefore, a strategy of querying to the server with the highest probability among those servers will consequently consume less search time and network overhead than blind search strategies. For instance, comparing with the Binary Search (BS) Algorithm [10], the Highest Probability First Search (HPFS) Algorithm not only reduces the network traffic when searching the target agent, but also improves search efficiency.

The following notations are used in evaluating the HPFS.

1. $(S_1, S_2, \ldots, S_n)$: an ordered sequence of servers that the target agent will visit. Note that servers S_i and S_j can be the same.
2. $[t'_{S_i}, t''_{S_i}]$: a an estimated service time range that the target agent stays in server S_i. The range can be determined by selecting the worst (widest) time range collected by experiements.
3. t_{S_i} : service time of the target agent completing its job at server S_i; i.e., $t''_{S_i} - t'_{S_i}$.
4. T_{S_i} : summation of the service time that the target agent stays in S_1, S_2 to S_i; i.e., $\sum_{\ell=1}^{i} t_{S_\ell}$.
5. T'_{S_i} : summation of all the minimum service time that the target agent stays in servers S_1, S_2 to S_i; i.e., $\sum_{\ell=1}^{i} t'_{S_\ell}$.
6. $\bar{\mathcal{F}}^t_{S_i}$: probability of the target agent still running at server S_i after t seconds since the agent is initially delivered to server S_i.
7. $P^T_{S_i}$: probability that the target agent is currently located at server S_i, T seconds after it was initiated at S_1.

Instead of blindly searching for the target agent, the HPFS algorithm sends a probe to a server with the highest probability that the agent might currently stay. If the result of probing is negative, the server with the second highest probability will be the next target. This search strategy will continue until the agent is located. Obviously, HPFS requires less number of probes to reach the agent than other blind search algorithms, and thus reduces a certain amount of search time as well as network traffic overhead. However, the essential part of the HPFS algorithm is the method to evaluate probabilities for the servers that the agent might currently stay. Conclusion of the following theorem provides an efficient way to determine the probability values.

Theorem 1 *Assume that the service time of an agent to complete its job on each server is binomial distributed over the time range $[t'_{S_i}, t''_{S_i}]$. After T seconds since the target agent is initialized in the first server S_1, the probability $P^T_{S_i}$ of the agent being located in server S_i is formulated as:*

$$P^T_{S_i} = \frac{1}{2^{T_{S_{i-1}}}} \sum_{j=0}^{t''_{S_i}} \binom{T_{S_{i-1}}}{T - T_{S'_{i-1}} - j} \cdot \left[1 - \frac{1}{2^{t_{S_i}}} \sum_{\ell=0}^{t''_{S_i}} \binom{t_{S_i}}{\ell - t'_{S_i}} \right] \quad (1)$$

To verify Theorem 1, without loss of generality, we make the assumption that the probability function, say $\mathcal{F}_{S_i}(x)$, of the service time on server S_i is a *normal-distribution-like* function over the execution time range from t'_{S_i} to t''_{S_i}. That is, the agent could spend an arbitrary length of time to finish its work in server S_i within the time range, but the highest probability of the length of time for the agent to complete its job should be around the mid-point between t'_{S_i} and t''_{S_i}. Obviously, the assumption of normal-distribution-like probability function seems to be more practical and reasonable than other distribution function, such as the uniform distribution function. Consequently, the probability function $\mathcal{F}$ can be formulated to be a binomial distribution function, which is a *discrete function* with a shape similar to that of the curvature of a normal distribution function [11].

$$\mathcal{F}_{S_i}(x) = \frac{1}{2^{t_{S_i}}} \sum_{\ell=0}^{t_{S_i}} \binom{t_{S_i}}{\ell} x^{t'_{S_i}+\ell} \tag{2}$$

Note that $x^{t'_{S_i}}$ is the lower bound of the time interval that the agent will stay in server S_i. The coefficient of a term $x^{t'_{S_i}+\ell}$ in Eq. 2 represents the probability of agent to spend $t'_{S_i} + \ell$ seconds to accomplish the work in S_i. Those which term powers are out of the summation range will be considered to have zero probability. Consequently, Eq. 2 can be simplified as:

$$\mathcal{F}_{S_i}(x) = \frac{1}{2^{t_{S_i}}} x^{t'_{S_i}} \cdot (1+x)^{t_{S_i}} \tag{3}$$

Eq. 3 is mainly used to depict the length of time that agent requires to complete its work in a server. If the time to deliver the agent from the end of a server S_i to the start of the next server S_{i+1} is negligible (or the deliver time can be treated as a part of the responsibility to server S_i), Eq. 3 is useful to analyze an agent search model which prioritizes the order of servers to be searched according to their corresponding $\mathcal{F}_{S_i}(x)$ values.

The $P^T_{S_i}$ for each server S_i not only can be used to determine which server has the highest probability that the target agent is currently located, but also to calculate the expecting number of probes to be sent to reach the target agent. Considering the probability that the target agent is in server S_i after T seconds from the client sending out the agent to the first server, the probability consists of several disjoint components. The first component is in conjunction with two probability values: the probability that the previous $i-1$ servers spend all the T seconds services time, and the probability that server S_i will not finish the job with zero second. According to the results of Eq. 3, probability function of the first $i-1$ servers is the production of each individual server probability functions because all the first $i-1$ servers can be considered as one large system, and each individual server among them is just one step of the whole procedure. Therefore, the probability function of the first $i-1$ servers as a whole can be formulated as

$$\prod_{k=1}^{i-1} \mathcal{F}_{S_k}(x) = \frac{1}{2^{T_{S_{i-1}}}} x^{T'_{S_{i-1}}} \cdot (1+x)^{T_{S_{i-1}}} \tag{4}$$

Then, the coefficient of the term x^T in Eq. 4 represents the probability that the target agent spends exactly T seconds in $i-1$ servers.

$$\text{coef. of } x^T = \frac{1}{2^{T_{S_{i-1}}}} \binom{T_{S_{i-1}}}{T - T'_{S_{i-1}}} \tag{5}$$

Next, the probability that the target agent *will not* finish the work at server S_i in t seconds is abbreviated by a notation $\bar{\mathcal{F}}^t_{S_i}$. We can describe the function $\bar{\mathcal{F}}^t_{S_i}$ from a different point of view: the probability value will be one minus each probability value that the job will be done in less than t seconds.

$$\bar{\mathcal{F}}^t_{S_i} = 1 - \frac{1}{2^{t_{S_i}}} \sum_{\ell=0}^{t} \binom{t_{S_i}}{\ell - t'_{S_i}} \tag{6}$$

Concluding from the the discussion above, as well as Eqs. 5 and 6, Theorem 1 can be verified from the following formulation.

$$\begin{aligned}
P^T_{S_i} = {} & \text{(prob. of first } i-1 \text{ servers spend } T \text{ seconds} \times \\
& \text{prob. of server } S_i \text{ spends over 0 second)} + \\
& \text{(prob. of first } i-1 \text{ servers spend } T-1 \text{ seconds} \times \\
& \text{prob. of server } S_i \text{ spends over 1 second)} + \\
& \text{(prob. of first } i-1 \text{ servers spend } T-2 \text{ seconds} \times \\
& \text{prob. of server } S_i \text{ spends over 2 seconds)} + \\
& \cdots + \\
& \text{(prob. of first } i-1 \text{ servers spend } T - t''_{S_i} \text{ seconds} \times \\
& \text{prob. of server } S_i \text{ spends over } t''_{S_i} \text{ seconds)} \\
= {} & \frac{1}{2^{T_{S_{i-1}}}} \binom{T_{S_{i-1}}}{T - T'_{S_{i-1}}} \cdot \left[1 - \frac{1}{2^{t_{S_i}}} \sum_{\ell=0}^{0} \binom{t_{S_i}}{\ell - t'_{S_i}} \right] + \\
& \frac{1}{2^{T_{S_{i-1}}}} \binom{T_{S_{i-1}}}{T - 1 - T'_{S_{i-1}}} \cdot \left[1 - \frac{1}{2^{t_{S_i}}} \sum_{\ell=0}^{1} \binom{t_{S_i}}{\ell - t'_{S_i}} \right] + \\
& \cdots + \\
& \frac{1}{2^{T_{S_{i-1}}}} \binom{T_{S_{i-1}}}{T - t''_{S_i} - T'_{S_{i-1}}} \cdot \left[1 - \frac{1}{2^{t_{S_i}}} \sum_{\ell=0}^{t''_{S_i}} \binom{t_{S_i}}{\ell - t'_{S_i}} \right]
\end{aligned} \tag{7}$$

Note that Eq. 7 is the same as Eq. 1

3.2 The Highest Probability First Search Algorithm

With the results from the previous subsection, we propose to include the following Highest Probability First Search Algorithm in the search agent to locate the target agent.

Highest Probability First Search Algorithm

```
Main {
        ServerSet = {S1, S2, ..., Sn}
        PrioServerList = Sort(ServerSet)
        HPFS (target, ServerSet)
}
Procedure Sort(ServerSet){
        Sort ServerSet in decreasing order according to
        corresponding probability values
```

```
}
Procedure HPFS (target, ServerSet){
    if (ServerSet = Ø)
    then return NOT_FOUND
    S_t = First server in PrioServerList
    Move the Search Agent to S_t
    if (target found in S_t)
    then return (S_t)
    else if (S_t has been visited by the target agent)
    then PrioServerList = Sort (ServerSet - {S_1, S_2, ..., S_t})
    else PrioServerList = Sort (ServerSet - {S_t, S_{t+1}, ..., S_n})
    return (HPFS (target, PrioServerList))
}
```

Note that "ServerSet" and "PrioServerList" are global variables.

In this algorithm, if the search agent arrives at a server S_t and finds that the target agent has moved away from that server, then we should exclude all the servers that proceed S_t from the search list. This is based on the assumption that the servers will be visited in sequence. On the other hand, if the target agent has not arrived at S_t, then all the servers following S_t in the original execution order will be excluded in the future search for the same reason. The search list will then be sorted according to the servers' corresponding probability values. Since the target agent is still mobile before being located, it is possible that the target agent might "slip through" the search, i.e., the target agent might move to servers excluded from the search list in previous rounds of search. A simple solution is to leave some information at the servers that the search agents have visited and ask the target agent to report its position and status when it arrives at those servers. As can been seen, the HPFS can effectively reduce the unnecessary probes in searching the target agent.

4 Simulation Results

In this section, we present the simulations results and use "number of probes" needed to locate the target agent as a performance measure to compare the basic binary search and the HPFS.

In the simulations, we assume that the target agent will visit twenty servers, numbered form 1 to 20, in sequence. The service time ranges for the servers are as shown in Table 1. The elapsed times range from 1 to 200 in the simulations and the service time range for server 20 is chosen so that it can be a "sink", i.e., the target agent will not go beyond server 20. The values of the simulation results are obtained by taking the average of he results of 1000 runs.

Our goal is to predict with certain accuracy where the target agent is when the elapsed time and execution time ranges are given. Therefore, it is of interest to know if the Eq. 1 can show the probability of where the agent is accurately and if the the difference between the theoretical and simulations results vary

Table 1. Service Time Ranges for the Servers

Server	1	2	3	4	5	6	7	8	9	10	11	12	13	14	15	16	17	18	19	20
t'_{S_i}	3	4	6	2	3	2	8	7	4	1	8	6	3	5	9	2	4	2	7	500
t''_{S_i}	8	20	17	10	14	6	16	22	20	9	17	20	18	14	13	11	17	21	28	600

with time elapsed. Figures 3 to 5 (with elaspe time equals to 15, 85, and 145, respectively) show that the simulation results are very close to the theoretical results with differnt elapsed time, with the highest probability all pointing to the same server.

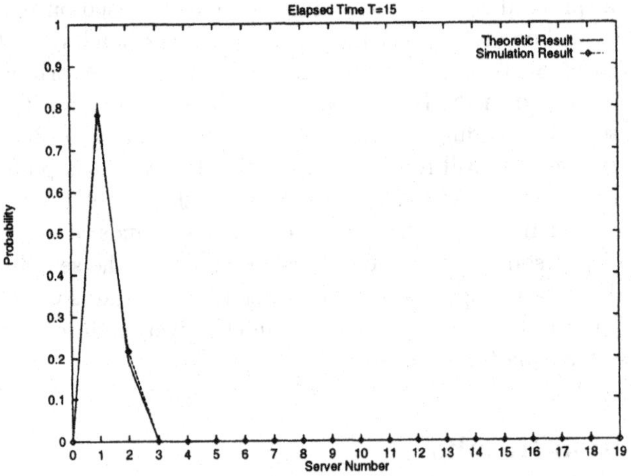

Fig. 3. Probability Distribution of Where the Agent Is (Elapsed Time = 15).

Figure 6 shows the comparison between the basic binary search and the HPFS algorithms. As illustrated in the figure, the basic binary search algorithm needs more probes to locate the target agent. In addition, the numbers of probes needed vary in a wide range with the elapsed time. On the contrary, the expected values of the probes needed for the HPFS algorithm are lower than those for basic binary search and the variation is much smaller. The simulation results match the theoretical results quite well. Consequently, the validity of Theorem 1 can be verified.

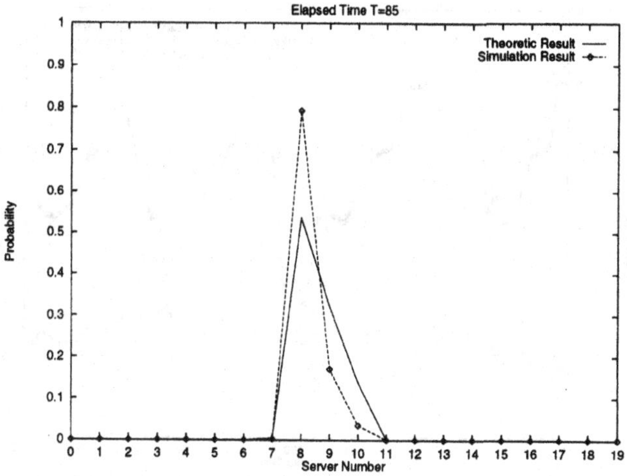

Fig. 4. Probability Distribution of Where the Agent Is (Elapsed Time = 85).

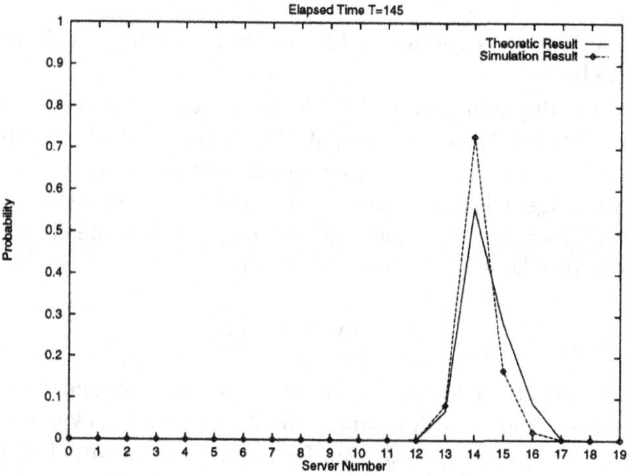

Fig. 5. Probability Distribution of Where the Agent Is ((Elapsed Time = 145).

5 Conclusion

Agent location is an indispensable part of the management functions needed to support the mobility of intelligent agents. Straightforward agent search algorithms often lead to excessive network traffic. In this paper, we have proposed a new agent search algorithm that makes use the execution time information available. The execution time is assumed to be binomial distributed, which is closer to reality. With the probability functions we came up with, the Highest Probability First Search algorithm is then formulated. It is expected to generate

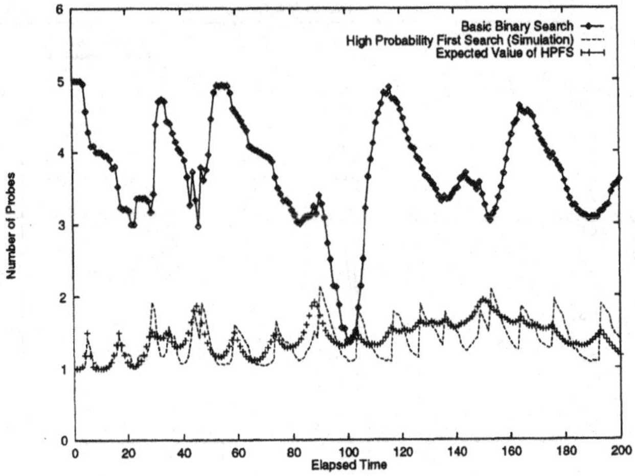

Fig. 6. Number of Probes Needed to Locate the Target Agent vs. Elapsed Time.

less probes to locate the target agent. The simulation results match the theoretical results quite well

We had made the assumption that the target agent traverse the servers in a predetermined order. However, the path the target agent takes might depend on the real time condition and could be non-deterministic. In addition, the relationship between agent location and agent control functions (how to apply the control function after the target agent is located?) needs to be clarified. We plan to resolve these problems in the future research.

Acknowledgment

We would like to thank anonymous referees, whose comments greatly improve the quality of presentation of this paper. We also gratefully acknowledge the help of C..-Y. Lin, Y.-T. Liu, and C.-J. Chu for developing the simulation programs.

References

1. M. Weiser. Some Computer Science Issues in Ubiquitous Computing. *Communications of the ACM*, 36(7):75–84, July 1993.
2. G. H. Forman and J. Zahorjan. The Challenges of Mobile Computing. *IEEE Computer*, pages 38–47, March 1994.
3. T. Imielinski and B. R. Badrinat. Mobile Wireless Computing: Challenges in Data Managemen. *Communication of the ACM*, August 1994.
4. M. Wooldridge and N. R. Jennings, editors. *Intelligent Agents: Theories, Architectures, and Languages*. Springer-Verlag Lecture Notes in AI - vol. 890, 1995.
5. M. Wooldridge and N. R. Jennings, editors. *Intelligent Agents II: Theories, Architectures, and Languages*. Springer-Verlag Lecture Notes in AI - vol. 1037, 1996.

6. N. Jennings and M. Wooldridge. Software Agent. *IEEE Personal Communications Magazine*, pages 17–20, Janurary 1996.
7. J. E. White. Telescript Technology: The Foundation of the Electronic Marketplace. White paper, General Magic, 1994.
8. W.-S. E. Chen and Y.-N. Lien. Intelligent Messaging for Mobile Computing over the World-Wide Web. In *Proceedings of the Second Workshop on Mobile Computing*, April 1995.
9. Y.-N. Lien. An Open Intelligent Messaging Network Infrastructure for Ubiquitous Information Service. In *Proceedings of the First Workshop on Mobile Computing*, April 1995.
10. Y.-N. Lien and C.-W. R. Leng. On the Search of Mobile Agents. In *Proceedings of the 7th IEEE Symp. of Personal, Indoor, and Radio Communications*, October 1996.
11. R. Jain. *The Art of Computer System Performance Analysis.* John Wiley & Sons, Inc., 1991.

Insisting on Persistent Mobile Agent Systems

M. Mira da Silva[1] and A. Rodrigues da Silva[2]

[1] University of Évora, Rua Romão Ramalho 59, 7000 Évora, Portugal
[2] INESC, Rua Alves Redol 9, 1100 Lisboa, Portugal

Abstract. In this paper we continue arguing that persistence is a fundamental requirement to support the development of next-generation agent-based applications. After a general overview of mobility and persistence to clarify the main issues discussed in the paper, we propose a tentative list of facilities that should be supported by *persistent mobile agent systems*. The main contribution of the paper is a survey of existing persistent and mobile agent systems that includes a comparison based on how well (or badly) they support the proposed list of facilities.

1 Introduction

There are now several research prototypes and even commercial products of *mobile agent systems* for building distributed applications based on mobile agents.*** We argue that many of these applications will manipulate complex, long-lived data structures and thus need persistence (see section 2.2). Unfortunately, elaborated forms of persistence are not adequately supported by existing agent systems [26]. On the other hand, current persistent systems lack modelling, security, communication and other facilities that are necessary to support mobile agents.

The next-generation of real-world agent-based distributed applications will have to be built using *persistent mobile agent systems*. These will not only support features traditionally found in both persistent and agent systems but will also be based on Java [1].

Java was chosen as the support programming language for a number of reasons. First, it is becoming ever more popular both amongst naive and expert computer users. It will probably be one of the mainstream languages in 3 or 5 years. Second, it is a much better language than what is currently available (for example, Visual Basic or C++). Third, Java has a number of interesting characteristics (e.g., easy to learn, type-safe, object-oriented) and technical features (e.g., garbage collection, native threads, dynamic loading). In addition, Java will run on most *computing environments*, including hand-held PCs, TV sets and maybe even on mobile phones.

Persistence is fundamental for the next-generation of agent-based applications because many of these will access, manipulate, carry and store large amounts of complex, inter-related data — and, as we argue, code as well.

*** We prefer the term *mobile objects* to avoid any confusion with "intelligent" agents. In this paper, however, agents will be used for coherence with the workshop title.

The requirement for persistence is supported by observing modern business applications and their development environments. It is further confirmed by a Java *database access library* [38] and Java development tools with integrated database support from Microsoft [23], Borland [11] and Symantec [39].

The paper is organized in five sections. The next section introduces mobile agent systems and persistent systems (a knowledgeable reader may opt to skip one or both). In section 3 we propose a list of facilities for mobility and persistence that are required to support next-generation agent-based applications. Section 4 presents a survey of existing systems and how they support the proposed list of facilities, always from a Java perspective. In section 5 we summarize the paper and present our planned future work.

2 Overview of Mobility and Persistence

In this section we present a brief introduction to agent systems and persistent systems. We hope it will help clarify the meaning of some words and the emphasis we put on each characteristic of both research areas. (This is not a survey paper; the interested reader should follow the references in the text for more information on a given commercial product or research prototype.)

2.1 Mobile Agents

A mobile agent is a live object that can migrate between autonomous programs. *Life* means the agent has behaviour of its own, it is not just a data object. *Mobility* separates mobile agents from that other kind of (stationary) agents based on artificial intelligence, e.g., those used to filter information. *Autonomy* makes the difference between mobile agent systems and distributed systems, an overlapping but distinct research area (see below). Many other issues are certainly relevant for mobile agents — such as openness, communication and security — but will not be discussed in this paper.

Mobile agents have been claimed to be more suitable than other approaches to design and implement certain categories of distributed applications. The word "distributed" is crucial here because it is the network — with its latency, slowness, and failures — that brings problems to traditional approaches to distributed computing [40]. More recently, the popularity of the Web and Java gave a new momentum to mobile agents [18].

However, it should be clear that mobile agents will not be better than existing distributed programming models for all and every application. For each application, or part of an application, we have to compare agents with other models and try to understand what are we gaining and what are we loosing. Other players in this contest for "best programming model for the Internet" include: centralized applications based on mainframes; client/server computing (client program accessing a remote database server); Web (local visualisation and remote application/database); and Web/Java (Web with a client/server flavour). There are also many variations of these basic approaches, typically under the "three-tier" marketing umbrella.

Following our experience from a previous workshop on mobile agents [8], in this paper we discuss only "brain less" agents (that is, without artificial intelligence) and agents that actually move and execute on *autonomous* programs. For example, although the work by Kato and others [15] is highly relevant for higher-order distributed systems, it does not address code migration between programs that are mostly disconnected. The emphasis is thus on *migratory applications* as proposed by Cardelli with Visual Obliq [9, 10] and popularized by Java applets [1].

At the implementation level, mobile agents have been typically discussed in terms of migrating programs (in the Java sense), objects (in the object-oriented sense) or threads of control (in many senses). However, as far as this paper in concerned, the actual representation of mobile agents and how they are used at the programming language are details; the important issues are that a mobile agent has: *code* to know what to do remotely and *data* to carry, collect and return with information. (Optionally the agent may contain state, although we suspect that state can always be represented by data. This will have to be confirmed by building a real agent-based application with no-state agents.)

In section 4.1 we will discuss why existing agent systems are still not adequate to implement the next-generation of agent-based applications. In order to concentrate on the important aspects, we compare only a small but representative number of systems: Telescript, Java and the Aglets Workbench.

2.2 Persistent Systems

Data needs to outlive the program that created them for at least three reasons: to be *stored* for future use; to be kept *safe and secure*; and to be *shared* amongst a number of programs. In addition, a modern database system is expected to provide a number of other features, such as: efficient access to large amounts of data; a language for querying the database, concurrency control, check-pointing mechanisms, back-up facilities, data mining and warehousing, and so on.

There are also a number of specific reasons why databases can be useful for an application based on mobile agents: to maintain the data that agents are supposed to query (e.g., a CD database); to support the agent run-time system (e.g., to know where agents are); to maintain knowledge given to the agents (e.g., the owner, what to buy, for how much); to support agents that carry data/state with them (e.g., electronic money and commodities bought); and to serve as a "home" for agents during and between jobs.

The current database technology is represented by relational database management systems (RDBMS) and the SQL standard language for querying and manipulating stored data. Programs are written in any language, Java for example, but use SQL to retrieve data from, and write data back to, the database. (In order to avoid embedding SQL directly in the host language, SQL is nowadays wrapped in a *database access library* such as JDBC [38].) This means that application programmers have to learn two different programming systems and maintain the mapping between them (from object graphs to flat records).

They are also constrained to the limitations of SQL, that has a poor type system when compared with modern object-oriented programming languages like Java.

In contrast, an *orthogonal persistent system* makes no difference between short-term (volatile) data and long-term (database) data [2, 7]. An object will be garbage collected only if it is unreachable using the normal constructs in the persistent language. Thus a persistent programming language is both a programming language and a database management system with a single programming model. Examples include Napier88 [30, 29] and PJava [5, 3].

In order to guarantee that an object can always be used later if it can be reached, the persistent system has to store not only the *data* of that object but also its *code*. This small but important point is the main difference between object-oriented database systems (OODBS) and persistent systems.

An OODBS such as ObjectStore [16] is a persistent version of an object-oriented language (typically C++) that stores the data belonging to persistent objects automatically in the database. However, C++ classes — the code to manipulate those objects — are stored separately in the file system when the program is compiled. If the file is removed, then objects of that class will become useless. There are many other problems with OODBS, e.g., deciding which objects should persist and regarding type-safety [7]. (On the other hand, OODBS generally have a better support for indexing and querying than persistent systems, not to mention a number of commercial products.)

Recently, a number of simple, cheap solutions for supporting "persistence" in Java have been proposed based on *object serialization* [31, 35]. Serialization is the act of linearizing a graph of objects into a byte array. The byte array can then be sent to another program (e.g., via sockets) or stored somewhere (e.g., in a file). Serialization is used by RMI [36], JavaSpaces [37], and Aglets [12].

For example, Sun claims that JavaSpaces support persistence in Java. However, all mechanisms based on object serialization have the same basic limitation: the relationships that link objects together in the program are not maintained between serializations. In particular, sharing relationships are destroyed when objects are re-built. It is also not clear whether JavaSpaces are persistent at all: in the JavaSpace specification (revision 0.1) [37] is written "Unfortunately, in Java 1.1, the only kind of server type available is not persistent". There are other problems with serialization as a persistence mechanism [3].

3 List of Facilities

In this section we propose a set of facilities that should be supported by a *Persistent Mobile Agent System* in order to implement the next-generation of agent-based applications. A short sentence identifies the facility which is then briefly discussed to avoid any doubts by what we mean with that sentence. (In section 4.2 we will use this list as a basis to compare existing mobile agent systems and persistent systems.)

1. *Migrate complex data* — Migration of arbitrary data structures, including shared and cyclic graphs of objects of any type available in the programming

language. Parameterized and abstract data types are optional because they pose especial problems for migration. In addition, even though threads are just a normal type in many modern languages, we keep thread migration as a separate facility here (see below).

2. *Migrate complex code*—Migration of arbitrary graphs of functions, procedures, classes or whatever represents code in the programming language. Dynamic loading is included as part of the facility, since in this context it is useless to migrate code that cannot be executed immediately when it arrives. (The format in which code is stored and transmitted is not discussed in this paper, although highly relevant for building agent systems.)
3. *Migrate together*—Migration of data and code closely bound together in the same transmit operation, e.g., if a function refers to a free variable.
4. *Migrate threads*—A thread is suspended and copied to another program where it resumes execution. The original thread is killed after the copy has arrived in the other program and before it starts executing. (Fault-tolerance is optional but desirable.) Thread migration poses a number of interesting problems because threads are strongly bound to the run-time system.
5. *Store complex data*—Storage and retrieval of arbitrary data structures, including shared and cyclic graphs of objects of any type. Furthermore, this should be achieved without requiring extensive knowledge on databases or extra effort when compared with non-persistent programming.
6. *Store complex code*—Storage and retrieval of complex, inter-related graphs of code. Dynamic loading of programs is required to bind persistent code to the current execution on demand, since it is not realistic to assume that all code in the database will be fetched on start-up. (The format in which the code is stored is not relevant here, but typically several formats are required.)
7. *Store together*—Storage and retrieval of complex data and code together. (Persistent systems are specifically designed to support this facility.)
8. *Store threads*—Storage and retrieval of (running) threads in the database. If execution of the whole program is suspended, then all running threads are automatically suspended and stored in the database. When the program resumes execution, all threads will be fetched and re-started again.
9. *Same syntax as Java*—The agent system offers a programming language with exactly the same syntax of Java (although the semantics may differ in a very small sub-set of the language). This facility is especially useful if the application is already written in Java.
10. *JDK-compatible*—The applications developed with the agent system run on top of any Java virtual machine. The facility is required if the system aims at being "open" (that is, compatible with standard operating systems, Web browsers, and so on). Optionally, the agent system itself can run on top of the Java virtual machine as well.

In order to clarify the list above, we now discuss some of the many relationships that exist between these facilities and show why Java and other well-known agent systems do not support all of them.

Facilities 1 and 2 are a "must have" for every programming system candidate to support mobile agents. Java applets support only half of facility 1 because data communication is very low-level (bytes via sockets) and half of facility 2 since an applet is just a byte array stored in a file. (Java fully supports 1 if we include RMI [36] as being part of Java, and it will probably be in the next release.) Visual Obliq [9, 10] supports 1 and 2, as well as many agent systems.

Facility 3 is highly desirable because it guarantees that an agent arrives as a "whole" and not in pieces that have to be assembled by the run-time system. The Aglets Workbench [12] not only supports 3 but also supports 10 (see section 4.1) thus making it more suitable for developing Java-based agent applications than Java itself. Facility 4 is interesting, but it may be difficult to implement (e.g., threads are one of the few Java types not supported by RMI [36]). On the other hand, it does not seem to exist any clear use for facility 4 that cannot be solved by facilities 1 and 2, or 3 (after all, a thread is ultimately code and data) so we will pursue more research on this topic to understand better the advantages of migrating threads.

Facility 7 is clearly desirable in general, although facilities 5 and 6 may replace 7 adequately in many applications. An OODBS supports 5 but not 6, and this limitation can be very restrictive if the application makes extensive use of complex persistent code. File systems and relational databases support only a small part of 5 and 6, although they are still proposed by most agent programming systems. Facility 8 has been implemented in a number of persistent systems and being used in practice, so this facility is clearly required.

Facility 9 is also important, not the least for marketing purposes (like Netscape's JavaScript). However, the full potential of 9 can only be explored together with facility 10, since a Java-like program is useless if browsers and operating systems only support Java byte-code. This has been recognized as a crucial issue for the acceptance of an agent system [18].

Not all facilities are possible or even desirable together. For example, facility 10 makes more difficult or even impossible to support facilities 8, 7, and 6 (possibly 5 as well). But facility 9 seems to be compatible with all others due to the initial good design of Java.

In addition, mobility and persistence also have a difficult co-existence — see for example, the work on Tycoon [20, 21, 22] and Napier88 [24, 28, 27, 25]. Facilities 3 and 7 are particularly difficult to achieve together, while 4 and 8 have been achieved only by Tycoon to our knowledge.

4 Survey of Existing Systems

We have argued in a previous paper that the combination of mobility and persistence leads to new opportunities and challenges [26]. In this section we present examples of existing systems in each of these research areas and discuss how much they support facilities traditionally belonging to the other area. The section includes a table summarizing the support given by each system to the facilities proposed in the previous section.

4.1 Mobile Agent Systems with Persistence

The large majority of mobile agent systems was not designed to handle persistent agents or agents that deal with persistent objects. Examples include Facile [14], Java [1] and MOLE [34]. The usual argument is that persistence can always be added to the application by means of another, separate mechanism. In particular, using a database access library such as Java's JDBC [38] is a popular solution because it is easy to use from Java and (via ODBC) supported by all leading database vendors.

However, in section 2.2 we discussed why good support for persistence is a requirement for next-generation agent-based applications. In this section we will concentrate on existing agent systems that have addressed persistence to some extent. The objective is to show that none of these systems supports elaborated forms of persistence — as provided, for example, by PJava [5, 3].

Telescript [41] is one of the earliest commercial systems specifically aimed at building distributed applications based on mobile agents. Although access to implementation details is difficult, it is generally recognized that Telescript supports thread migration and some form of persistence for both data and code. However, it provides a (complicated) proprietary language and few (if any) development tools. These problems prevented Telescript from being widely accepted and used to build agent-based applications.

Java [1] and its applets have been claimed to support the agent paradigm. Applets are special Java classes that are compiled and written to a file on the Web server. Later on, the file that contains the applet can be copied to a browser like Netscape, linked to its address space dynamically, then instantiated and started. With JDBC, an applet can have access to (local or remote) relational databases, not taking into account security restrictions.

There are, however, several limitations with Java. First, an applet is just code; it does not include any data, apart from static variables that have the same initial value every time the applet is instantiated. Second, applets migrate by copy without the Java classes they refer, so they can only use libraries that are available everywhere. This either restricts applets to very simple programs (like moving pictures) or forces applets to contact the Web server for any interesting behaviour. (In alternative, the applet can take everything it needs but downloading time increases linearly to the amount of code being copied.) Third, applets can use relational databases via JDBC (when and if it becomes part of the standard Java release) but relational databases are not adequate to store complex data structures or applets themselves.

The Aglets Workbench [12] is a Java-based agent programming system with a particularity: integrated support for persistence. Aglets are small Java programs that can be sent between stand-alone Java applications and (unlike applets) return to their originating site. The workbench, a development tool to write distributed applications based on aglets, includes a database access library called JoDax. Even though JoDax is only syntactic sugar to access relational databases via ODBC [18], it does show interest for storing and retrieving data on agent-based applications.

More interestingly, when aglets migrate they carry data and their state — not only code like Java applets. Although there is very little information publicly available on implementation details, we have learnt [17] that Aglets use the standard Java run-time system and Sun's Java libraries. For example, aglets are linearized for migration by the object serialization mechanism [31, 35] that will probably be part of the next major release of Java.

We conclude that, although none of the existing agent systems supports elaborated forms of persistence, there is some interest and at least one project that has addressed this issue seriously.

4.2 Persistent Systems with Mobility

The persistent community has always been interested on distributed systems because many database applications are shared by a number of users in different computers. Distribution may also help with scalability, evolution and other aspects of persistence. Unfortunately, most of this effort has concentrated on closely-coupled (also called "transparent") distribution that has a number of limitations [40].

More recently, a number of projects on loosely-coupled distribution have started. A good example of this research area is the work based on Tycoon [19]. Tycoon is a persistent programming language with first-class procedures and threads, meaning that they are treated as any other object, e.g., created at run-time, put in the store, and reused later. It is now possible to migrate complex data, code and threads between autonomous Tycoon programs [20, 21, 22]. Although Tycoon runs on many computer platforms, it can be considered a proprietary language (for the purposes of this paper) because its syntax has no resemblance with Java.

One of the authors has also worked on similar issues with another persistent programming language called Napier88 [30, 29]. As a result, a number of models for communication between autonomous persistent programs have been designed and implemented [24, 28, 27, 25]. Like Tycoon, procedures and threads are first-class values in Napier88 and code can migrate between autonomous programs (but not threads). However, Napier88 can also be considered a proprietary language for the very same reasons.

PJava [5, 3] is a persistent version of Java that maintains the same syntax. Like Java, PJava is also object-oriented, type-safe, and has garbage collection (now extended to the database). Like Napier88, its predecessor, PJava implements orthogonal persistence (meaning that objects of any type can persist) and classes are stored in the database together with their objects.

The first prototype of PJava (PJava0) is now working on Sun machines with Solaris. PJava0 was built as a "proof of concept" only and as a result it still has a number of limitations such as: limited store size, simple garbage collection and no support for persistent threads. On the other hand, a number of applications based on PJava0 are being developed with promising results [13].

A second prototype (PJava1) is now being implemented that will solve the most important limitations of PJava0. As one of the Tycoon developers is now

#	Facility	*Mobile Agent Systems* Telescript	Java	Aglets	*Persistent Systems* Tycoon	PJava
1	*Migrate complex data*	+++	+++	++	+++	+++
2	*Migrate complex code*	+++	+	++	+++	+++
3	*Migrate together*	+++	—	++	+++	—
4	*Migrate threads*	++	—	—	+++	—
5	*Store complex data*	++	+	+	+++	+++
6	*Store complex code*	++	+	+	+++	+++
7	*Store together*	?	—	—	+++	+++
8	*Store threads*	?	—	—	+++	+++
9	*Same syntax as Java*	—	+++	+++	—	++
10	*JDK-compatible*	—	+++	+++	—	+

Table 1. List of Requirements Revisited

(+++: Excellent; ++: Good; +: Poor; —: No support)

part of the PJava team (Bernd Mathiske) we can also expect thread migration in the near future. It is also planned to port PJava to other popular operating systems.

4.3 Revisiting the List of Facilities

In this section we select three agent systems and two persistent systems to compare them based on the list of facilities presented in section 3. These systems were chosen for their *overall quality* and to cover the *widest diversity*, not because they support more or better facilities than others.

Table 1 at the top separates persistent from agent systems and groups the ten facilities in three categories: mobility, persistence and Java. The reader is remembered that support for all facilities is not required or even possible in a real system.

The first comment goes to Tycoon that receives the best marks overall. This is a consequence of persistence that addresses many of the same issues as mobility: migration of data and code, dynamic loading, type-safety, code portability, security restrictions, and so on. It is only natural that more than 10 years of research in persistent systems and their combination with distributed systems have produced a very good agent system. Napier88 and its communication models would rank similarly (except for thread migration). It should also be noted that PJava is represented here by its first prototype, future releases would probably receive even better marks than Tycoon (see section 4.2 and below).

Another curiosity is the lack of support for code mobility in Java. In fact, Java was intended to migrate code, but it migrates code in its simplest form: a byte array copied from a file. Although RMI [36] can be used to migrate data, there is no support to migrate code and data together, to store complex data or applets for future use, or send applets back to their originating site.

On the other hand, although Tycoon has a more impressive list of facilities, it is and will always be a proprietary environment. We conclude that, overall, the Aglets Workbench and PJava are closer to become a *Persistent Mobile Agent System* that will support the development of next-generation agent-based applications without requiring add-on packages for persistence and communication of complex data and code.

5 Summary and Future Work

In this paper we proposed a list of facilities for mobility and persistence that agent programming systems should offer to support the next-generation of agent-based applications. We then presented a survey of existing systems and compared them based on these facilities.

We conclude that, although there is no system yet that supports a good combination of facilities, the Aglets Workbench and PJava are closer to support them in the near future. This is good news for the software industry because it means that agent-based applications manipulating complex inter-related data will soon have an adequate development platform.

In order to validate the research work presented in this paper, we intend to implement a real-world agent-based application using either Aglets or PJava; or maybe both, since they should work well together. This plan follows naturally from our joint experience with: research on persistence and distribution [24, 28, 27, 25]; experience on Web application development [33, 32]; and the potential of existing persistent and agent programming systems.

References

1. K. Arnold and J. Gosling. *The Java Programming Language*. The Java Series. Addison Wesley, 1996. ISBN 0-201-63455-4.
2. M.P. Atkinson, P.J. Bailey, K.J. Chisholm, W.P. Cockshott, and R. Morrison. An approach to persistent programming. *The Computer Journal*, 26(4):360–365, November 1983.
3. M.P. Atkinson, L. Daynès, M. Jordan, T. Printezis, and S. Spence. An orthogonally persistent Java. *SIGMOD Record*, December 1996.
4. M.P. Atkinson and M. Jordan, editors. *Proceedings of the First International Workshop on Persistence and Java (Drymen, Scotland, September 1996)*, 1997. To be published as a Sun Technical Report.
5. M.P. Atkinson, M. Jordan, L. Daynès, and S. Spence. Design issues for persistent Java: A type-safe, object-oriented, orthogonally persistent system. In Atkinson et al. [6].
6. M.P. Atkinson, D. Maier, and V. Benzaken, editors. *Proceedings of the Seventh International Workshop on Persistent Object Systems (Cape May, New Jersey, USA, May 29-31, 1996)*. Morgan Kaufmann Publishers, 1996.
7. M.P. Atkinson and R. Morrison. Orthogonal persistent object systems. *VLDB Journal*, 4(3):319–401, 1995.

8. J. Baumann, C. Tschudin, and J. Vitek, editors. *Proceedings of the 2nd ECOOP Workshop on Mobile Object Systems (Linz, Austria, July 8-9, 1996)*. dpunkt, 1996.
9. K. Bharat and L. Cardelli. Distributed applications in a multimedia setting. In *Proceedings of the First International Workshop on Hypermedia Design (Montpelier, France, 1995)*, pages 185–192, 1995.
10. K. Bharat and L. Cardelli. Migratory applications. In *Proceedings of ACM Symposium on User Interface Software and Technology '95 (Pittsburgh, PA, Nov 1995)*, pages 133–142, 1995.
11. Borland International, Inc. *OPEN JBuilder*, 1996. http://www.borland.com/-openjbuilder/.
12. IBM Tokyo Research Lab. *Aglets Workbench: Programming Mobile Agents in Java*, 1996. http://www.trl.ibm.co.jp/aglets/.
13. M. Jordan. Early experiences with persistent Java. In Atkinson and Jordan [4]. To be published as a Sun Technical Report.
14. F. Knabe. *Language Support for Mobile Agents*. PhD thesis, Carnegie Mellon University, Pittsburgh, PA 15213, USA, December 1995.
15. K. Kono, T. Masuda, and K. Kato. An implementation method of migratable distributed objects using an RPC technique integrated with virtual memory management. In P. Cointe, editor, *Proceedings of the 10th European Conference on Object-Oriented Programming (ECOOP) (Linz, Austria, July 10-12, 1996)*, Lecture Notes in Computer Science, pages 295–315. Springer-Verlag, 1996.
16. C. Lamb, G. Landis, J. Orenstein, and D. Weinreb. ObjectStore. *Communications of the ACM*, 34(10):51–63, October 1991.
17. D.B. Lange. Private communication, 1996.
18. George Lawton. Agents to roam the Internet. Sunworld Online, 1996.
19. B. Mathiske, F. Matthes, and S. Mussig. The Tycoon system and library manual. Technical Report DBIS Tycoon Report 212-93, Computer Science Department, University of Hamburg, December 1993.
20. B. Mathiske, F. Matthes, and J.W. Schmidt. On migrating threads. In *Proceedings of the Second International Workshop on Next Generation Information Technologies and Systems (Naharia, Israel, June 1995)*, 1995.
21. B. Mathiske, F. Matthes, and J.W. Schmidt. Scaling database languages to higher-order distributed programming. In Paolo Atzeni and Val Tannen, editors, *Proceedings of the Fifth International Workshop on Database Programming Languages (Gubbio, Umbria, Italy, 6th-8th September 1995)*, Electronic Workshops in Computing. Springer-Verlag, 1996.
22. Bernd Mathiske. *Mobility in Persistent Object Systems*. PhD thesis, Computer Science Department, Hamburg University, Germany, May 1996. In German.
23. Microsoft Corp. *Microsoft Visual J++ Start Page*, 1996. http://www.microsoft.-com/visualj/.
24. M. Mira da Silva. Automating type-safe RPC. In O.A. Bukhres, M.T. Özsu, and M.C. Shan, editors, *Proceedings of The Fifth International Workshop on Research Issues on Data Engineering: Distributed Object Management (Taipei, Taiwan, 6th–7th March 1995)*, pages 100–107. IEEE Computer Society Press, 1995.
25. M. Mira da Silva. *Models of Higher-order, Type-safe, Distributed Computation over Autonomous Persistent Object Stores*. PhD thesis, Submitted to the University of Glasgow, 1996.
26. M. Mira da Silva and M. Atkinson. Combining mobile agents with persistent systems: Opportunities and challenges. In Baumann et al. [8].

27. M. Mira da Silva and M.P. Atkinson. Higher-order distributed computation over autonomous persistent stores. In Atkinson et al. [6].
28. M. Mira da Silva, M.P. Atkinson, and A. Black. Semantics for parameter passing in a type-complete persistent RPC. In *Proceedings of the 16th International Conference on Distributed Computing Systems (Hong-Kong, May, 1996)*. IEEE Computer Society Press, 1996.
29. R. Morrison, A.L. Brown, R.C.H. Connor, Q.I. Cutts, A. Dearle, G.N.C. Kirby, and D.S. Munro. The Napier88 reference manual release 2.0. Technical Report FIDE/94/104, ESPRIT Basic Research Action, Project Number 6309 — $FIDE_2$, 1994.
30. R. Morrison, A.L. Brown, R.C.H. Connor, and A. Dearle. The Napier88 reference manual. Technical Report PPRR-77-89, Universities of Glasgow and St Andrews, 1989.
31. R. Riggs, J. Waldo, and A. Wollrath. Pickling state in the Java system. In *Proceedings of the 2nd Conference on Object-Oriented Technologies and Systems (June 17-21, 1996, Toronto, Ontario, Canada)*, 1996.
32. A. Silva, G. Andrade, and J. Delgado. A multimedia database supporting a generic computer-based quality management system. In *Proceedings of the 9th ERCIM Database Research Group Workshop (Darmstadt, Germany, March 18-19, 1996)*, 1996.
33. A. Silva, J. Borbinha, and J. Delgado. Organizational management system in an heterogeneous environment - a WWW case study. In *Proceedings of the IFIP working conference on information systems development for decentralized organizations (Trondheim, Norway, August 1995)*, pages 84–99, 1995.
34. M. Strasser, J. Baumann, and F. Hohl. MOLE: A Java based mobile agent system. In Baumann et al. [8].
35. Sun Microsystems. *Object Serialization*, 1996. http://chatsubo.javasoft.com/-current/serial/index.html.
36. Sun Microsystems. *Remote Method Invocation*, 1996. http://chatsubo.javasoft.-com/current/rmi/index.html.
37. Sun Microsystems. *JavaSpaces*, 1997. http://chatsubo.javasoft.com/javaspaces/.
38. Sun Microsystems Inc. *JDBC: A Java SQL API*, 1996. http://splash.javasoft.-com/jdbc/.
39. Symantec Corporation. *Visual Café for Windows 95/NT*, 1996. http://cafe.-symantec.com/vcafe/vcpr1.html.
40. J. Waldo, G. Wyant, A. Wollrath, and S. Kendall. A note on distributed computing. Technical Report TR-94-29, Sun Microsystems Laboratories, 1994.
41. J.E. White. *Telescript Tecnhology: The Foundation for the Electronic Marketplace*. General Magic, 1994.

Open Resource Allocation for Mobile Code

Christian F. Tschudin <tschudin@ifi.unizh.ch>

Computer Science Department, University of Zurich, Switzerland and
International Computer Science Institute (ICSI), Berkeley, USA

Abstract. Mobile code technology leads to a new type of "open systems": instead of applying openness to a standardization process we now require the running systems to become open for foreign code. The question then is how far this technical openness can go for mobile code. The less constraints we impose on hosts running mobile code, the more can the benefits of mobile code be exploited. However, there must necessarily be basic constraints regarding the utilization of resources which are always finite and most of the time will be operated near the saturation point. In this paper we argue in favor of openness even at the level of resource allocation. We link this topic to (open) market models, describe the mechanisms we developed so far for communication messengers and show how they are used to allocate resources in an open way. Finally we present experimental results of validation runs which help us testing these mechanisms.

Keywords: **Mobile code, communication messengers, open resource allocation, market, computational ecosystems.**

1 Introduction

An important contribution of the computer network's standardization approach in the 80ies was the concept of *open systems*: open access to the standardization process and open decision procedures were the basis of acceptance, leading to communication systems where components from different vendors could be intermixed. This applied to interworking of "black boxes" like bridges or routers, but also to software components inside a host where application programmer interfaces laid the ground for portable software (e.g., POSIX). The technical solutions involved in these open systems, however, are themselves not open i.e., leaving little choice on how a given service is to be implemented. This is different with open distributed systems based on mobile code where users can program the network and influence the way a service is provided. Technically spoken this means that the implementation of the network's element now become open: hosts have to accept virtually arbitrary code coming from potentially unknown users.

Such technically open distributed systems have a special execution model: distributed applications are performed by multiple threads of execution, some of them being mobile i.e., started remotely and on demand. The latter point means that hosts may be faced with a large number of uncoordinated (and not coordinable) requests for executing mobile code, which always involve local computing resources. Imagine a global mobile code network consisting of a billion nodes serving some hundred millions of users each having ten to thousand mobile agents roaming around. In such a context it is virtually impossible to do resource authorization i.e., mapping from user to agent and further down to access rights. But even if this would be feasible, it would not solve the problem to arbitrate conflicting resource requests in situations of saturation, which we assume will be the normal mode of operation of such a system.

Thus, the challenge is twofold. First we want to find methods of doing resource allocation without relying on the impractical identity of mobile agents. And second, we want resource allocation to be *open*, that is, to let the resource allocation be steered *by* mobile agents *for* mobile agents instead of delegating this task to the hosts. We are investigating these goals with rather small mobile agents we call *communication messengers*.

1.1 The Messenger Approach

At the heart of messengers is the paradigm of instruction-based communications [11]. Based on a very simple communication model, namely the exchange of pure instructions and their mandatory detached execution, we obtain a universal communication environment in which classical communication protocols need not to be known and installed at a remote site. Using instructions it is perfectly possible to advice a remote host (also called execution platform) how to perform any protocol. Accidentally, this concept is also at the center of mobile software agents as it relies on the programming of remote computers. According to our definition a messenger is a thread of control which can trigger the transfer of arbitrary code to a remote computer such that: (i) this code has a chance to be executed remotely and independently, and (ii) the resulting remote thread may trigger another code transfer.

The messenger approach extends the instruction-based communication model with design guidelines that try to keep the resulting communication architecture as universal as possible. The most important design principle is strict locality in the sense that no host should provide a service that requires the cooperation of other hosts. Cross-platform services should be implemented by messengers themselves, leaving the messenger execution environment completely *protocol-neutral.* Another design decision is that messengers should be anonymous, considering that agent identity (and related concepts like agent ownership etc.) is a cross-platform service which must be handled above the platform level.

The challenge with this approach is to design and build a working environment which has nice "global" properties. Because there may not be any coordination work done by the execution environments, the well-behavior of a messenger-based network fully relies on the decentralized decisions taken by independent messengers. The good global behavior thus has to "emerge" from local behavior and cannot be imposed in any way although it can be influenced by defining the border conditions that messengers have to obey. The believes underlying our research is that a set of instructions, local services and platform behaviors can be designed such that good global behavior becomes possible. Section 2 introduces and discusses the concept of *open* resource allocation. Section 3 describes the mobile code environment `MØ` and emphasizes on the aspects of memory and money for messengers. How openness is achieved in this environment is explained in section 4, which also reports on experimental results obtained. Related work is briefly discussed in section 5, just before the concluding summary.

2 Open Resource Allocation

Messengers are quite small and minimalistic mobile agents, wherefore we found it more appropriate to look at resource allocation at a very fine granularity. But even if larger units are considered, a mobile code system must provide mechanisms to allocate its resources to the roaming agents. We first elaborate on the "openness" in resource allocation and link it with the concept of markets from micro-economics. Then we sketch – what we think will be – the typical scenario for which resource allocation has to work.

2.1 Major Types of Lowlevel Resources

CPU time, memory and bandwidth are the most important resources that are relevant to mobile software agents. There are, of course, a lot of other local resources like files, data base access, windowing system etc., but which we do not consider here because they regard high-level agreements or conventions between users and the hosts.

CPU: The most simple allocation strategy here is to devalue the CPU resource by simply admitting more and more mobile agents. This is easy and leads to devaluation which already is an open allocation strategy. Another approach is a reservation system were agents obtain single processing time slots, thus a processing time guarantee. 'Open' in this context would mean that *every* mobile agent that tries to acquire a timeslot has *a chance* to obtain it, thus that there are no discriminatory elements favoring messengers based on provenance, task or destination.

Memory cannot be diluted like the CPU resource – it resembles more genuine "property". In this case an open resource allocation has to be based on "urging" memory owners to release the resource as soon as possible. The pressure to do so comes from other agents that state their memory needs.

Bandwidth is similar to processing time in the sense that communication requests can be queued or dropped (resource dilution). The other possibility is that fixed parts of the bandwidth are assigned.

2.2 Resource Markets

The most important element of open resource allocation is the non-discriminating choice process, for which money provides a perfect basis. Money is anonymous and not resource specific: it is open in yet another sense in that even service resources provided by mobile agents can be allocated too although the underlying system does not need to know these services in advance. Open thus means non-discrimination also with respect to the services which may be provided either by the executing system itself or by mobile agents.

Introducing money as a mean for exchanging electronic commodities and services creates a market place where these different goods can be traded. This market in fact does the resource allocation by mediating offers and demand and resolving conflicting interests. The price is used for expressing the interest (purchaser) and signals the scarcity of a good (supplier). In fact, we adopt a purely microeconomic point of view.

The absolute price of a good is – in this market view – irrelevant, thus there has not to be a inherent relation between prime costs and the price paid for a good (which in fact depends on the good's utility for the purchaser). However, prices have to be grounded somewhere. In our mobile code environment it will be the runtime systems which assigns local prices to the resources and services it offers. It can do that in a non-profit way in order to provide just the signaling aspect, making scarce resources more expensive than when running under light load. The execution platforms thus implement a "virtual nature" and charge each individual inside this world for its resource consumption. Mobile agents are then free to trade resources they have at any price they want. For example, the price for memory defined by the system may at some moment in time be rather high: a mobile agent could sell its own memory resources at a lower price (thus would be preferred over the system) and, if memory was acquired at times were prices were low, may even make some benefit. The whole system consisting of execution platforms and mobile agents together with the market mechanisms becomes a computational ecosystem [2].

2.3 Working model

Before we look in more detail at the practical implication of a market model for our communication messengers, we will sketch a picture about what we think will be the normal mode of operation. Firstly we assume a network of execution platforms with no access restrictions, thus a messenger is free to go where it likes, to create new threads and acquire as much memory and CPU time as possible. In fact we can think of this world of being populated by useless resource eating messengers similar as there is a (seemingly) useless idle thread in each UNIX system. Thus, the base is a saturated system where each resource is occupied. What we would like to have is that when *useful* messengers are injected into that world, they get a fair amount of these resources. Whether they can acquire more resources than the average of the useless messengers depends on the amount of extra money they bring into the network. In a first approximation we can think of the workstation owner and author of the messenger that he or she can create money and can feed it to the useful messengers. Thus, human users express their preferences in terms of money too and indirectly steer this way the utilization of resources.

Based on the differentiation between the useless messengers and the ones that have extra money it is possible to create messenger populations that do not depend directly from a user. Such populations implement a distributed service (e.g. routing, or locating nodes with low prices) which they sell to the useful messengers, enabling them to finance the extra effort necessary to provide the service. Thus, the picture we want to draw is that of a flat world of equally entitled messengers. Distributed applications and services are implement by messengers which work as "cliques" and which form super organisms that are able to reach far beyond than what could be achieved by a single messenger. These messenger families work in parallel (and under competition), where their relative strength and size is ruled by the usefulness to the messengers with the extra money.

3 A Messenger Environment

MØ (m-zero) is an almost literal implementation of the messenger paradigm. MØ is at the same time: (i) a programming language for messengers, (ii) a format for representing messengers "on the wire", and (iii) the name of an execution environment that is able to interpret the language. In this section we give an overview of the concepts behind MØ and report on the corresponding software.

3.1 Execution Model

The aim of the messenger environment MØ is simplicity and minimality [9]: only what we think is essential for mobile code was included (see figure 1). The core of MØ is the execution platform where incoming messengers are turned into concurrent threads. These threads are anonymous and can therefore not directly communicate with each other. Data exchange has to be done via a shared memory area, synchronization is supported by simple thread queues. The submission and reception of mobile code is not restricted by security protocols as we follow an *open security model* for mobile code [10].

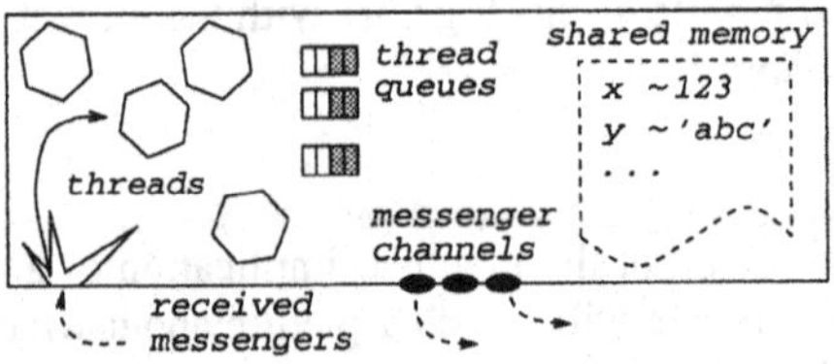

Fig. 1. The logical view of a messenger execution platform.

Communication channels link neighboring platforms by a simple and unreliable datagram service (garbled messengers are silently dropped). Because most channels impose limits on the admissible datagram length, messengers must provide their own fragmentation and reassembly logic. In fact, messengers have full control on the external representation sent along the channels (they could send arbitrary byte strings).

Anonymous threads: In MØ there are no "handles" or thread identifiers that could be used to address or act on a thread. If the thread was not programmed to cooperate in some way, it remains invisible to other threads (except for its side effects, of course). A remote thread is created by sending a messenger (datagram). It is also possible to create a new concurrent and coresident messenger thread which will be anonymous too.

Shared memory area: There are several public "dictionaries" in a MØ platform that can be used by the threads to persistently store arbitrary data under self-chosen names. Most of the time these names are created at run-time in a random fashion in order to avoid name clashes. One such dictionary – `globaldict` – is readable and writable but cannot be browsed which gives a simple form of data isolation.

Thread queues: Threads can decide to queue up in a thread queue. Queued threads which are not at the queue's head become blocked until they advance or a self-chosen timeout occurs. Thread queues are created on demand and can be put into a stopped state, allowing to control the progress of the queued threads.

These frugal interaction means are sufficient to implement the classical inter-process communication primitives like read/write or full rendez-vous (see e.g., the appendix in [11]).

3.2 Data model

The MØ language resembles very much POSTSCRIPT. Thus, it is a stackbased, high-level (i.e., pointerfree) and not object-oriented language. There are "simple" data instances and "composite" ones. Simple data objects (`int`, `time`, `name` etc.) fully fit into a slot of the so called element table while composite objects (`array`, `dict` etc.) are represented by references – the composite object's content is placed in a special heap area (called *virtual memory* in POSTSCRIPT). The difference between simple and composite objects becomes clear when we look at the effect of duplifying the stack's top element: after the `dup`, there will be two copies of the simple objects. For a composite object, only the reference is duplified such that changes applied to one reference are also visible through the other reference.

Creating composite objects automatically implies the allocation of some memory in the heap area. Unlike many object-oriented environments of today (like JAVA or OBERON), MØ uses explicit reference counting instead of periodic garbage collection runs: a composite object be removed from memory as soon as its reference counter drops to zero. This may be slower, but the reference counts are important for memory accounting purposes (we have always a true picture of memory occupation) and because they allow to debit memory costs according to the share factor expressed by the reference count.

3.3 Memory model

The default mode of operation is that each messenger thread works within its own private memory area. If data should be shared between threads, they have to reside in the shared memory area which has its own heap. The transfer from the private to the shared memory area is semi-transparent: putting a composite entry into one of the predefined shared dictionaries or arrays automatically creates a copy of the private variable. If the thread wishes to keep a handle on the now shareable copy, it has to explicitly fetch it from the shared data structure afterwards[1]. The MØ interpreter keeps track of variables for being sharable or private: putting a private value into a sharable instance automatically involves a copy, so that there are never references from the shared memory area back into some private memory area (see the left part of figure 2).

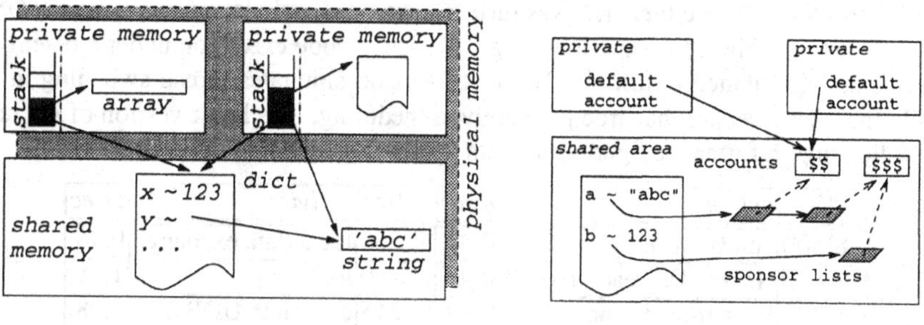

Fig. 2. Private and shared memory area / The sponsoring of shared dictionary entries.

Messengers can acquire (i.e., buy) memory resources "in advance" by specifying the amount of memory that should be put aside right now. The platform will make a reservation and implicitly will satisfy subsequent memory requests from this pool: a messenger can thus avoid failures due to memory shortages (or learn about them at reservation time). Once this pool becomes empty, memory has to be acquired "at the spot market". Private memory that is freed during an operation is returned to the pool. Messengers can also adjust the pool size in the other direction: lowering it means that reserved memory is given back to the system and the messenger is reimbursed.

3.4 Money model

The MØ platform provides a special data type called `account`. Accounts store a certain amount of money in units of fictitious "conchs". Each messenger thread has a default

[1] Note that in MØ the access to shared memory is always via the MØ data types, which is different from "shared memory" found in UNIX systems.

account to which consumption of system resources is charged. Account variables are sharable data objects and can in fact be shared by coresident messenger threads even as their default account. This enables division of labor: one thread concentrates on the distributed algorithm it implements while another or even several other messengers are responsible for "fund raising".

There are no operators for direct account–to–account operations: instead money has first to be withdrawn, resulting in a *check*. Checks are 64-bit strings that can be freely passed between threads and then be cashed on another account. Detecting double-spending is easy because checks have local validity only. Thus, each platform has its own local currency[2]. The local currency is used in MØ as a tool for linking local resource demand and offer inside a given platform but also across multiple messenger platforms. Checks enable messengers to go to a remote platform and sell (but not cash) the check, obtaining a countervalue in the remote platform's currency. The potential purchaser of such a check at the remote site would be a messenger that needs some resources at the seller's origin. Exchange between a remote check and local currency will usually not be on a one–to–one basis but will reflect the ratio of available resources between platforms. We envisage specialized "arbitrage messengers" that try to exploit (i.e., benefit from) asymmetries in exchange rates, leading to accurate exchange rates.

3.5 The MØ Implementation

A first implementation of MØ was published in 1994 [12] for UNIX platforms and is written in ANSI-C. Since then, MØ was further developed and also ported to bare ("OS-less") i386 machines for experimenting with native code execution under messenger control i.e., distributed LINUX [5]. The UNIX version simulates thread switching in C while the i386 version has true preemptive scheduling. The latest version of MØ has the following performance figures on a Sun Sparc10/model 40:

#/sec	activity	msec	#/sec	activity	msec
58'800	empty MØ loop	0.02	2'800	local data exchange	0.36
11'600	shared dict read or write	0.09	740	local hop	1.35
5'300	inter-thread sync	0.19	245	complete UDP hop	4.08

The MØ source code also includes cryptographic routines like des and md5, drivers for the datagram channels (UDP, ethernet and serial line) and miscellaneous utilities (MØ code preprocessor, messenger formatter, interactive command interpreter etc.).

4 Resource Management in MØ

In this section we present the solutions we adopted so far for making MØ an open resource allocation environment. The first resource that we managed in MØ was the CPU.

[2] In fact, a global currency would be a crossplatform service that has to be implemented with messengers. Building a global currency into the platforms would not scale well and would be difficult to operate (detection of double spending, fraudulent money creation). However, note that our model with strictly local currencies does not exclude a global currency: it even supports several of them. In fact, it may be more economic for messengers to agree on one currency they trust in instead of having to change their means each time they want to make a hop. But with the messenger approach mobile agents are free to trade exchange overhead against security and trust. Again, arbitrage and money exchange messengers will adjust the rates between local and global currency, also reflecting the trustworthiness of a global currency.

Currently we are working on the memory resources while channel bandwidth was not considered yet. The main task is to design the dynamic pricing of a platform's resources and to devise a set of additional programming primitives enabeling messengers to behave "resource–aware". What we have to test is that resources are allocated according to the (relative) amount of money messengers invests in order to obtain them.

4.1 Lottery Scheduling

Lottery scheduling [14] is a very simple but effective form of letting messengers choose themselves the intensity at which they want to proceed. Each messenger thread indicates a number of tickets that should participate in a CPU time lottery. A drawing is organized at the end of each timeslice: the thread that owns the winning ticket obtains the CPU for the next time slot.

This system has the advantage over a round robin scheduling or priority based schemes that threads can adjust their relative execution speed at will. Furthermore, it is simple to implement and achieves a statistically fair allocation of the CPU according to the self-chosen rate. Adding more threads to the system just "dilutes" performance and penalizes the threads on an equal basis. One problem with giving control over priorization to messengers is that all messenger could set their number of tickets to the maximum. The incentive not to do that is again money i.e., messengers are charged according to the effective timeslots used and the number of tickets invested in the lottery.

4.2 Memory Accounting and Data Sponsoring

The goal of doing accounting of (and charging for) memory is to create an automatic "drainage" mechanism that removes data for which there is not sufficient interest, thus to have a mechanism which works beyond simple reference counting. In contrast to ageing we allow messengers to control the expiration process by investing more or less money in the memory resources. There are two limited memory resources in MØ that have to be considered: plain (physical) memory and entries in the element table. Plain memory is used for the thread's private memory, which also includes the private element table that can grow if required. So charges for private data only account for the physical memory used (including the memory pool mentioned in 3.3).

In the persistent shared memory area, however, we have no data owners as entries should persist even if the creating messenger terminates. To which entity should therefore shared memory occupation and the utilization of element table entries be charged? The solution we adopted is *data sponsoring*. A one–time charge is applied when a messenger thread puts something into the shared memory area. In this case we charge for the memory needed to create a copy. From then on, we have no owner anymore: the trick is to associate anonymous accounts to the *links* that keep the copy's reference count bigger than 0. Periodically (once in a second), the platform scans all shared element entries, computes a price for each of them and charges it to the sponsoring accounts. Links for which there are is no sponsor money left are removed which means e.g., for shared dictionaries, that we undefined an entry, or for shared arrays that we replace an entry by a `null` value. The right part of figure 2 shows the relation between accounts and entries in shared data structures.

When computing the price for a shared data item, we keep track of memory and element table usage. Because the size of the shared memory area's element table is static, we have to add a component to the plain memory price that reflects the scarcity of free table entries. For both types of limited memory resources we use the same formula to compute the prices in the next debit round:

$$price_{n+1} = (price_n + \frac{10100}{101 - load_n} - 99)/2$$

where $load$ is the utilization ratio in percents (0...100). This formula gives a minimal price of 1 for an empty machine which can rise drastically (up to 10'000) the more we approach a 100 percent load.

The graph to the left of figure 3 shows the effect of "memory drainage". There were two threads in the system. One thread slowly filled in 600 entries and sponsored each of them with a fixed amount of money (150 conchs). The other thread polled every 0.5 seconds the number of entries that were defined in `globaldict` (shown as impulses). During the first 12 seconds, the number of entries increments linearly. At this time the first entries run out of sponsors such that the number drops. Eventually, an equilibrium establishes until the filling thread terminates and the number of entries decreases. The diagram also shows the price curve for a single element table entry that attains a peak of 13 conchs (this information is usually not available to messengers). From the diagram is clearly visible that prices have a slight delay which is due to the smoothing and the inductive price computation.

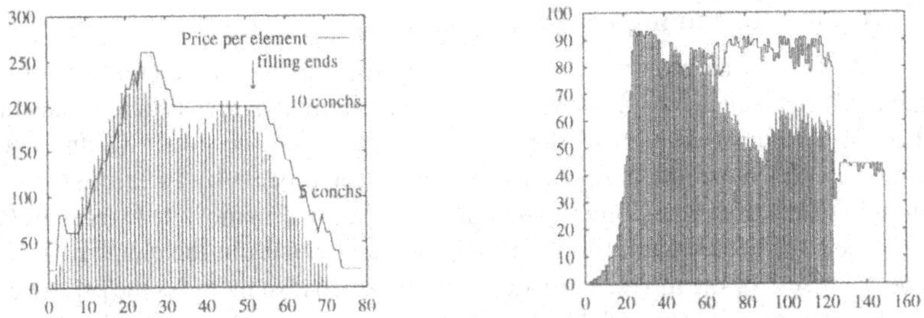

Fig. 3. The effect of memory drainage / Forking threads competing for memory.

4.3 Memory (Re)cycling in Saturation Situations

For testing the allocation of memory resources we cannot copy lottery scheduling: Once a messenger occupies memory, we can not partially or temporarily revoke it. In order to look at memory allocation in saturation situations, we "dynamize" memory usage i.e., we examine how families of messengers behave in terms of assigned memory when each messenger has a limited lifetime and new messengers are created as soon as possible. We made experiments with forking messengers that create two identical coresident threads (with some waiting before and after) and then terminate. Depending on the waiting time, this first leads to an exponential growth before an equilibrium is found. Of course, limited memory and finite money resources may cut the growth quite below the equilibrium.

Two forking messengers were started, leading to two messenger families which compete for the scarce memory resource. What was to be shown is that the amount of memory obtained and consequently the size of the families depend on the money feed received by the two messenger families: one family received 1 mega–conchs per second, the other family only half that amount.

The exponential growth is nicely documented in the right diagram of figure 3 where we have an exponential increase at the beginning (impulses are for messenger family one, the white space below the step curve for the second family). The system was configured such that there is not more memory available than for a little less than 90 coresident messengers, so an upper limit of 90 threads is observable. When we start the second messenger family (at tick 60), it quickly establishes a population of about 30 threads and pushes the first messenger family back to 60 messengers (ratio 1:2 as expected according to the money feed ratio). At tick 120 we cut off the money feed for the high memory priority threads: the number of remaining messengers raises to 45 which is the equilibrium for a 500 k–conch/sec funding. This means that without memory saturation the total 1.5 M–conch/sec money feed could support some 130 concurrent messengers.

This experiment shows that open resource allocation can be built for non-preemptible resources like memory *if* there is enough pressure on the resource owners to release all or parts of them. In our test case we programmed a limited lifetime, but in future versions we will use a money mechanism to force thread termination. The net result is that we transformed the static resource allocation problem into a money distribution problem.

4.4 Discussion and Outlook

At this experimental stage it is too early to assess that a mobile code system with open resource allocation can be operated at large scale. However, as we argued in the introduction, we think that there is no other choice because a global coordination of all resource utilization is not feasible. Mainly the problem of not being able to predict the global behavior of a fully decentralized resource allocation scheme remains unsatisfactory. In fact, we are share this situation with designers of large scale routing or other widely deployed protocols where even pushed simulations are of limited value for predicting the protocol's behavior in reality. With open resource management we have even less possibilities to influence the overall system's behavior: finally it boils down to adjusting price curves inside each platform, either arriving at a set of static price formulae or to find adaptive pricing schemes that lead to a workable environment for a large set of platforms. The other adjustable elements are the mobile code programs that actively participate in the resource market and which, should some defects should be found in a platform's correct pricing, may be used for work arounds.

One of the next experiments will be with messengers that do idle hoping between two execution platforms, which of course requires that we can assign prices to communication channels. We note here that the concept of "busy-looping-does-not-harm-if-the-machine-is-empty" has only limited validity when it comes to shared networks like an Ethernet. Here we have to find solutions to measure a network's load as well as "true communication costs" and to reflect them back into the messenger platform. A related topic is the question of exchange of local and global currencies that we already mentioned in section 3.4 as well as linking money creation to the human user's preferences.

Another task is the development of smart resource management and trading routines for messengers. Currently we have little knowhow about doing price computations with input values that may drastically differ from one machine to the other and even inside one machine. Also, the resource trading strategies of messengers will become an important element for the overall system's stability. Here we count on the advantage of mobile code i.e., if more robust money handling becomes available, it can be immediately deployed. Also, the small size of messengers encourages the deployment of a large number of messengers which in turn means that the volatility in the local resource markets will be high, which is an important condition for a market's efficiency.

5 Related Work

There are a lot of cross-connects between the approach we described here and partly quite old research in several domains. However, distributed low level computer resource allocation is seldom treated in an integrated fashion. This is true even for precursory work like remote evaluation that has very similar resource allocation problems as mobile software agents have but where this problem is only briefly mentioned in the section on server security [7]. (In the following we omit general references to work on mobile agents).

Mobile software agents and money: Well known is the teleclick concept of GeneralMagic. Also, the concept of "energy" can be found that would limit the radius of action and the potential harm a mobile agent could do. However, we are not aware of papers on how teleclicks or other accounting units are used to arbiter in case of overload and how prices are fixed, nor where such a mechanism was put in place for doing resource allocation.

Ecosystems: Markets for processing time were already proposed in 1968 [8]. We already mentioned lottery scheduling, which in fact belongs to the domain of operating systems research [14] but which stems from more general research on the dynamics of computation and experiments on computational economies [13]. One prominent reference for this concept is [2] from 1988, a more recent paper can be found under [3]. Note that most of the time, centralized markets are considered and mobile code is not taken into account at all. Furthermore, experiments concentrate on processing time and disregard non-preemptible resources. Applying microeconomics to problems in the area of networks is also not a new idea [1, 6], to cite just a few, although this too was not applied to mobile code yet (but this may change: watch Yemeni's Web page on the announced "netscript").

Distributed systems: Distributed control in general is an old topic, also the question of stability in such a setting. Just for two arbitrary examples we mention AMOEBA's bullet file server where files which were not referenced by the directory server for some time are automatically removed (touching a file, however, seems to be free). The other example is Jacobson's changes to the TCP/IP retransmission mechanisms [4], thus a modification of local rules that lead to better global performance (congestion avoidance).

6 Summary

We presented a novel approach of combining mobile code systems with microeconomics in order to do open resource allocation. Open resource allocation means that resources are granted on a non-discriminatory basis. Resource utilization is handled by mobile software agents which moreover are forced to manage their proper resource consumption. Open resource allocation furthermore means that the set of goods that can be traded is not restricted by the system. Communication messengers lend themselves very well for such an approach. They are small and aim at doing resource allocation at a rather low level. We reported on our prototype and how we do the underlying resource accounting necessary for grounding the resource market. Our system enables us to run several hundreds of concurrent messengers and to do first experiments with a microeconomy for local resources. The next steps will be the distributed setting and the development and programming of trading strategies. We firmly believe that resource management for mobile software agents at large cannot be based on an authorization system or concepts which rely on administred global services.

References

1. D. F. Ferguson, C. Nikolaou, and Y. Yemini. An economy for flow control in computer networks. In *Proceedings of the IEEE Infocom-89*, pages 110–118, 1989.
2. B. A. Huberman, editor. *The Ecology of Computation*. Elsevier, 1988.
3. Bernardo A. Hubermann. Computation as economics. Presentation at the Second International Conference in Economics and Finance. URL: http://www.unige.ch/ce/ce96/ps/huberman.eps, June 1996.
4. V. Jacobson. Congestion avoidance and control. In *SIGCOMM'88 Conference on Communications Architectures & Protocols*, pages 314–329, August 1988.
5. Guy Neuschwander. Exécution du code natif dans l'environnement MOS. Diploma thesis, University of Geneva, November 1996.
6. J. Sairamesh, D. F. Ferguson, and Y. Yemini. An approach to pricing, optimal allocation and quality of service provisioning in high-speed packet networks. In *Proceedings of the IEEE Infocom'95*, pages 1111–1119, 1995.
7. J. W. Stamos and D. K. Gifford. Remote Evaluation. *ACMTPLS*, 12(4), 1990, pages 537–565.
8. I. E. Sutherland. A futures market in computer time. *CACM*, 11(6), 1968.
9. Chr. F. Tschudin. Minimality as the Leitmotiv for mobile code. Presentation at the 2nd German Workshop on Mobile Agents (DeMAT-II). http://www.ifi.unizh.ch/groups/bauknecht/tschudin/research/demat96-eng.ps.gz, September 1996.
10. Chr. F. Tschudin, G. Di Marzo, M. Murhimanya, and J. Harms. Welche Sicherheit für mobilen Code? In K. Bauknecht, D. Karangiannis, and S. Teufel, editors, *Proceedings der Fachtagung SIS'96 Sicherheit in Informationssystemen*, pages 291–307, Vienna, March 1996. English abstract: http://www.ifi.unizh.ch/groups/bauknecht/tschudin/research/sis96-abstract.html.
11. Christian F. Tschudin. *On the Structuring of Computer Communications*. PhD thesis, Université de Genève, 1993. Thèse No 2632. ftp://cui.unige.ch/pub/tschudin/phd-{123}.ps.Z.
12. Christian F. Tschudin. *M0 - a messenger execution environment*. Usenet newsgroup `comp.sources.unix`, Vol 28, Issue 51–62, June 1994. ftp://cui.unige.ch/pub/m0/m0-manual.ps.Z
13. C. A. Waldspurger, T. Hogg, B. A. Hubermann, J. O. Kephart, and W. S. Stornetta. Spawn: a distributed computational economy. *IEEE Transactions on Software Engineering*, 18(2):103–117, February 1992.
14. Carl. A. Waldspurger and William E. Weihl. Lottery scheduling: Flexible proportional–share resource management. In *First Symposium on Operating System Design and Implementation (OSDI), USENIX Association*, pages 1–11, 1994.

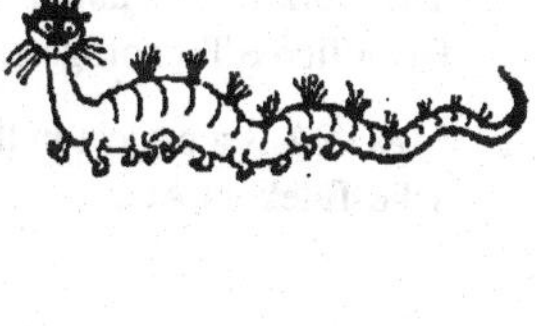

A Distributed Transaction Model Based on Mobile Agents

Flávio Morais de Assis Silva[1], Sven Krause
Technical University of Berlin/GMD Fokus
Hardenbergplatz 2, 10623 Berlin, Germany
Phone: +49-30-25499160, Fax: +49-30-25499202
Email: [flavio,krause]@fokus.gmd.de

Abstract. This paper describes a model of agent-based transactions, i.e., distributed transactions which are realized with the use of *mobile agents*, for an environment of heterogeneous and autonomous systems. Combining an asynchronous operation mode (provided by agent mobility) with the enforcement of complex control flows with transactional semantics, agent-based transactions represent an adequate base concept for reliable processing in future distributed systems, like virtual enterprises and electronic markets. Among other properties, agent-based transactions provide a very suitable support for transaction processing in massively distributed environments; support high adaptivity to dynamically changing environments; and are adequate to support processing requirements of mobile devices. In this paper we consider only transactions which are implemented by a single mobile agent. The presented transaction model is being developed in the context of the MAGNA[2] mobile agent project, under development at GMD Fokus and Technical University of Berlin.

Keywords: Distributed Transaction Processing, Mobile Agents, Mobile Agent Platforms, Workflows, Extended Transaction Models

1. Introduction

A *mobile agent* (or simply *agent*) is a self-contained software element responsible for executing a programmatic process, which is capable of *autonomously migrating* through a network between logical "places" called *agencies*. When an agent migrates, its execution is suspended in the original agency, the agent is transported (i.e. program code, data, and execution state) to another agency in the network, where it resumes execution.

Mobile agents enable a new form of interaction between *clients* and *servers* called *Remote Programming*. In remote programming, a mobile agent representing a client program can transport itself to a remote agency in order to interact with servers residing at that agency. An agency typically corresponds either to one host or to a set of hosts connected by a local area network. Inside an agency a mobile agent can interact with servers at a high quality of service level, compared to remote communication through low quality networks.

In this paper we describe a transaction model for supporting correct and reliable execu-

---

1 The work of this author is partially supported by Conselho Nacional de Desenvolvimento Científico e Tecnológico (CNPq), Brazil

2 MAGNA is a project in the R&D programme of DeTeBerkom GmbH, a subsidiary of Deutsche Telekom AG.

tions of agent-based activities in a distributed environment composed of *heterogeneous* and *autonomous systems* (*multi-system environment*). In this model, a mobile agent is used to represent a transaction which *migrates* through the network *asynchronously*. Within this paper, such activities are referred to as *agent-based transactions*. Agent-based transactions support mobility while enforcing complex control flows with transactional semantics. The flexibility achieved with agent-based transactions makes it a concept, which, among others:

- *is very suitable for supporting transaction processing in massively distributed environments*: communication via RPC may introduce delays and excessive retransmissions when communicating peers are too far away from each other and connected through low-quality links. Remote programming improves the quality (in terms of performance and reliability) of transactions by bringing the clients (agents implementing a transaction) closer to servers;
- *is very suitable for supporting activities in dynamically changing environments*: distributed systems are constantly subject to changes, such as the addition and removal of information sources and servers without a formal global control and registration, and failures. Due to its *asynchronous* operation mode, an agent-based transaction executes progressively, without depending, in general, on the availability of agencies it previously touched, allowing agencies to go up and down without affecting the further processing of the transaction. By supporting the specification of complex control flows, agents allow the specification of code that can be highly adaptive to failure situations and changing environments;
- *provides an adequate support for mobile devices:* such components are only intermittently connected to the network. When they are connected, the connections are commonly expensive, unreliable and provide low bandwidth. After being launched from mobile devices, agent-based transactions (due to *asynchronism)* allow the original device to be disconnected or turned off and only reconnected again later, in order to receive the results of the transaction;
- *fulfills coordination requirements of different types of applications*: by providing concepts for the flexible specification of complex control flows and different transactional semantics, agent-based transactions can satisfy coordination and synchronization requirements according to application needs. Agent-based transactions may also implement mobile versions of some extended transaction models and workflows, what adds the flexibility of mobility to the properties of such models.

The items above reflect some of the typical requirements of emerging distributed systems, like electronic markets and virtual enterprises. Agent-based transactions provide enhanced flexibility compared with traditional transaction concepts for coordinating activities in such environments.

This paper is structured as follows. Section 2 presents an example of an agent-based transaction, which demonstrates some of the main characteristics of this type of transactions. Section 3 presents the agent-based transaction model, describing firstly the requirements it should fulfill and afterwards the general structure of agent-based transactions. Section 4 describes the support for agent-based transactions which needs to be provided on servers and in a mobile agent platform. Section 5 discusses the presented transaction model in terms of related works and concludes the paper.

2. An Example of an Agent-based Transaction

A specification of a transaction gives rise to one mobile agent. Figure 1 illustrates an example of an agent-based transaction (inspired by the example given in [4]). The execution of an agent is represented by a set of *tasks*, each one executed at a certain agency.

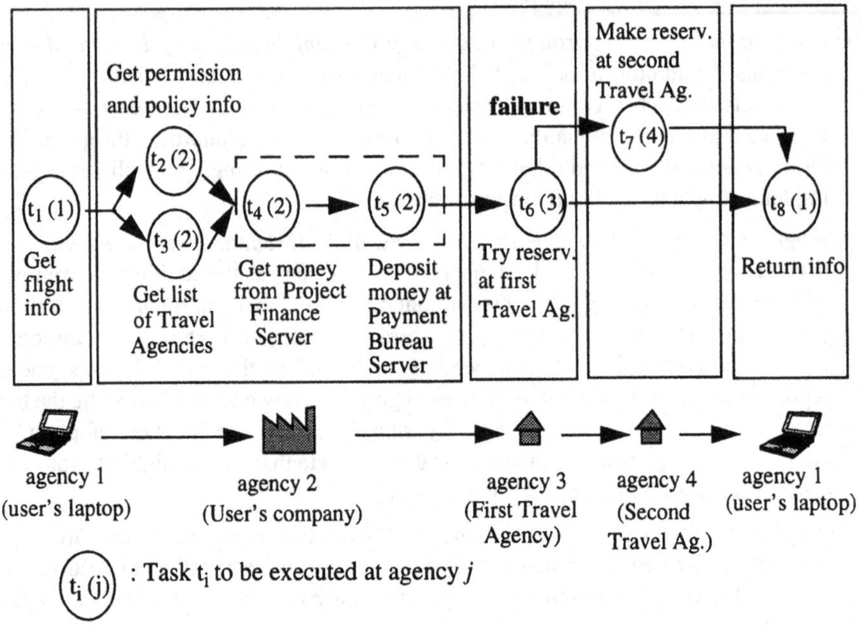

Fig. 1. Example of agent-based transaction

An employer of a company needs to make a flight reservation. He has a portable computer, which is able to access his company's LAN via a public network. This user interacts with an application running on his own computer which starts an agent-based transaction to make the flight reservation. Firstly, the agent interacts with the user to obtain the information about the flight request (task t_1, fig. 1). The company has a travel policy and a number of preferred Travel Agencies, so the agent initially travels from the laptop to the employer's company. The mobile user then disconnects his computer from the network. At the company, the agent engages in a dialogue with the company's Business Policy Server in which the agent communicates its task, that is to perform a transaction to obtain an airline seat (task t_2, fig.1). The Business Policy Server performs some internal verifications to approve the employer's travel and to obtain additional information, like the maximum ticket price allowed. The agent also interacts with the company's Service Providers Database in order to obtain a list of Travel Agencies which can be visited (task t_3, fig.1) in order of preference. The interactions with the Business Policy Server and with the Service Providers database can be performed in parallel. Afterwards, the agent must check for funds with the Project Finance Server and, if there is enough funding, transfer a sufficient amount of money to the company's Payment Bureau Server (tasks t_4 and t_5, fig. 1). This Bureau will effectively perform the payment later on, after it receives a request from the contacted Travel Agency (the payment is not part of the transaction). Tasks t_4 and t_5 should be performed in isolation from other transactions carried out at the agency. Otherwise, other transactions may produce inconsistent information about the amount of money available in the company (for example, a transaction which makes a general report on the amount of money available in the company).

The agent then travels to the first Travel Agency to be visited. There the agent performs a dialogue with the on-line reservation system, which processes the reservation request (task t_6, fig.1). However, in the given scenario the Travel Agency cannot provide a flight according to the request.

The agent then goes to the next Travel Agency in the list. There, the request is made again. This time the Travel Agency returns a number of candidate seats. According to the information obtained from the user and the Business Policy Server, the agent selects a preferred candidate and requests the reservation (task t_7, fig. 1). Afterwards the agent returns to the user with the necessary information about the reservation. Since the user has disconnected from the network, the agent is held at a gateway. When the user reconnects, the agent presents the information (task t_8, fig. 1).

3. Agent-based Transaction Model

3.1. Requirements

Mobile agents operate in an environment of *heterogeneous* and *autonomous* systems. Many different types of servers can be accessed. Heterogeneous servers may provide different transactional management support at their interfaces. Some servers may provide only a set of service primitives at their interface, with no transaction management primitives (for example, for beginning and ending transactions). These servers handle each service invocation as a complete transaction, controlled in its entirety by the server. Other servers may provide transaction management primitives, some providing also a *visible prepared to commit state*[1].

Agents may have to interact with different servers using *different languages*. For example, to access a SQL database, the agents invoke queries in SQL. To access a network managed system, the agent invokes CMISE (or SNMP) requests. The existence of standardized interfaces for services and transaction management (as defined, for example, in the OMG OMA and by X/Open) as well as the use of knowledge representation languages, like KQML (*Knowledge Query Manipulation Language*) and EDI (*Electronic Data Interchange*), play a very important role.

Agent-based transactions execute in an *extremely dynamic environment*, where servers

---

1 A server provides a *visible prepared to commit state* when, at the end of a transaction, it can maintain the data blocked waiting for a commitment decision (commitment or rollback) from the transaction user.

are added and removed from the system with no formal control. The exact execution flow of an agent-based transaction might only be determined at runtime. For example, consider an agent that should find the best price for some product. Firstly, the agent must interact with some information provider (for example, a trader [7]) to get a list of existing suppliers of the product and then visit each of them. The specific servers and also the *number* of servers to interact may only be known at runtime. This example shows also that agents should have access to *information suppliers,* like a Trader facility and a Directory [12].

Agent-based transactions should support *very complex applications.* Mobile agents may be used, for example, as a mechanism to transport a very complex workflow to be executed at a certain agency.

An agent-based transaction *must terminate in a certain finite time period,* when the user should know the results of the transaction. Mobile agents *cannot* be lost or stay indefinitely blocked due to some crash. That may make the environment stay in an inconsistent state, since only part of the agent-based transaction may have been executed.

Due to the autonomy of servers or due to the own nature of a service requested by the agent (for example, a service that implies movement of some physical component), agent-based transactions are typically *long-living.* Parts of the transaction should then be allowed to commit before the whole transaction commits and the occurrence of a failure during the processing of the agent-based transaction should not, in general, result in the cancelation of the parts of the transaction already executed. The agent should be able to recover from the failure and continue executing the transaction, in order not to lose the executed work done until the failure point. Therefore, agent-based transactions should support the notions of *alternative tasks* and *compensation.* An alternative task substitutes *functionally* a failed task. A compensating task cancels the effects of a committed task *semantically.* However, not every task can be compensated. Consider, for example, a task that makes a hole in a board. Support for such tasks should also be supplied.

In order to fulfill synchronization requirements of different types of applications, agent-based transactions should also consider the existence of *data dependency* spanning more than one system. The maintenance of such dependencies requires a form of *global synchronization,* i.e., the synchronization of accesses made by more than one agent over a set of servers.

The *movement pattern* of an agent to execute a transaction should be determined not only for the normal execution flow of the agent, but also for the *compensation process.* It can be expected that most of the times a compensation for a task will be done at the same agency where the compensated-for task was executed. But more flexibility would be achieved without this assumption.

3.2. Agent-based Transaction Structure

Tasks and Internal Data

In the concept presented in this text a transaction is executed by only *one* mobile agent. The transaction implemented by an agent represents a *global transaction* to be performed over the whole network. This global transaction is a combination of a set of *tasks* (or *subtransactions* of the global transaction) according to some defined control and data flow.

While executing the transaction, the agent collects information obtained by the interactions with servers. These data are referred to as *agent internal data.* These data are kept persistent while the agent executes.

Values of the agent internal data may be assigned to tasks *input parameters* and tasks may also produce new values for the agent internal data as *output parameters.*

Internally each task has a set of *execution states.* Transitions between task states are affected and externally observed by a set of *events* associated with the task. Each task corresponds to the execution of a *local transaction* using primitives of the interface of a server. Local transactions execute with the ACID (*Atomicity, Consistency, Isolation, Durability*) properties. The abstract external structure of a task is shown in Figure 2.

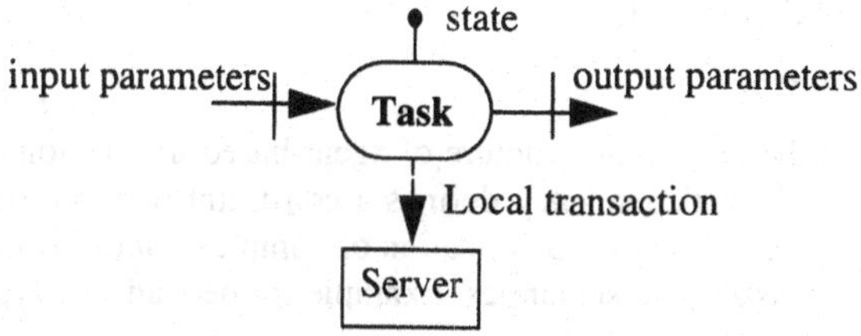

Fig. 2. General structure of a task

Tasks are classified as *abc* or *abpc*[1] tasks. This classification reflects the structure of the task in terms of states and events. An abstract representation of the internal structure of tasks is presented in Figure 3. Both types of tasks have an *initial state* (inactive state), an *executing* state and two types of final states: *committed,* which represents a successful completion of the task, and *aborted,* which represents a failed termination of the task. Abpc tasks have an aditional state, the *prepared to commit state* (Figure 3b). The prepare to commit state represents a state from which the task can always either be committed or rolled back. This state allows the execution of a commitment protocol (*Two-Phase Commit*) involving that task.

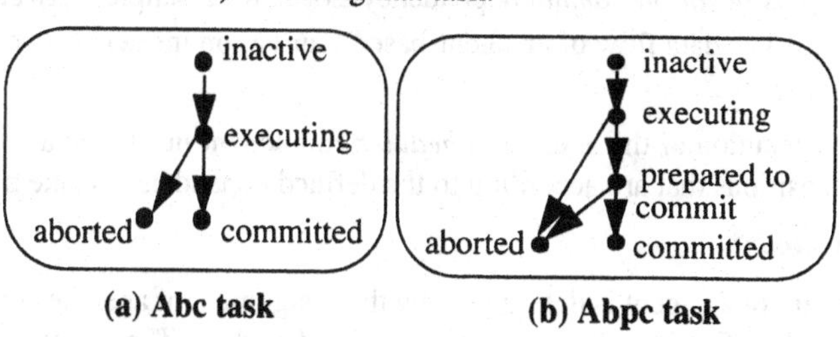

Fig. 3. Internal structures of tasks

These types of tasks reflect different autonomy degrees that a server may have in rela-

1 The acronyms *abc* and *abpc* are related to the events associated with tasks of such types: *abc (abort(ed), begin, committed)* and *abpc (abort(ed), begin, prepared_to_commit, commit).*

tion to the agent. Servers which provide a prepared to commit state exhibit less autonomy. Servers with more autonomy provide their services as a set of primitive methods.

Tasks are also classified as compensatable and non-compensatable. For each compensatable task there is a corresponding compensating task. A compensatable task can commit (and then reveal its results) before the whole agent-based transaction commits and, in case the effects of a compensatable task must be cancelled after its commitment, the corresponding compensating task is executed. Compensating tasks compensate only semantically, i.e., the effects of the compensated task are cancelled according to application semantics. The state of the data accessed by the task may not be exactly the same as it was before the compensated task was executed. Non-compensatable tasks represent tasks to which there is no way of compensating. These tasks commit only when the whole transaction commits. A compensatable task may be either an abc or an abpc task. A non-compensatable task must be an abpc task.

A task may also be specified as being *vital*. If a vital task aborts, the whole agent-based transaction must be cancelled.

Definition of Control Flow

The definition of the execution structure of agent-based transactions is done with the use of *dependencies*. A dependency defines a constraint over the occurrence of task events. Dependencies allow the specification of complex control flows and the definition of different transactional semantics. Examples of dependency types are:

- *Begin-on-Commit Dependency* (t_j BCD t_i): the execution of task t_j is triggered when task t_i commits;
- *Begin-on-Abort Dependency* (t_j BAD t_i): the execution of task t_j is triggered when task t_i aborts;
- *Weak-Begin-on-Condition Dependency* (t WBCondD c): the task t can only execute if condition c is true (the condition c can represent, for example, if some value returned by a previous task has a certain value).

In the example in section 2, there is a *begin-on-abort* dependency between tasks t_6 and t_7 (t_7 *BAD* t_6). A *begin-on-commit* dependency exists, for example, between task t_6 and t_8 (t_8 BCD t_6). The data flow of an agent-based transaction influences the definition of the control flow.

During the execution of the agent, a *scheduler* component inside the agent guarantees that only transitions that are according to the defined dependencies take place.

Agent Movement

The movement of an agent is determined by the assignment of agencies to tasks. Every task has an identification of an agency associated with it. The agent must be in the specified agency to execute the task[1]. If, during the execution of an agent-based transaction, a task triggered for execution is associated with an agency different from the

---

1 Observe that the model does not exclude agents at an agency from accessing servers at other agencies

agency where the agent is currently located, the agent moves to the specified agency.

A mobile agent cannot move at any point during its execution. In a well-formed agent-based transaction specification, the agent only moves when each task is inactive (it did not run), its execution has already finished or it is in the prepared to commit state (for Abpc tasks). At runtime, the agent scheduler guarantees this property by setting appropriate dependencies among tasks dynamically.

The specification of the agency where a task instance must be executed may be only determined at runtime. For example, as the result of a query to the Trading Service.

Isolated Execution

To fulfil the requirement for isolated execution of some of the agent tasks (to maintain data dependency among servers), tasks of an agent-based transaction may be grouped into *ACID groups*. In the example of section 2, tasks t_4 and t_5 are specified to be run in an ACID group. ACID groups contain only abpc tasks. An ACID group executes isolated from tasks in the same or in other agents. Tasks in an ACID group do not have to be executed all at the same agency.

Concurrency Control

Since agents may concurrently access common sets of servers, some global synchronization criterion must be used to guarantee correctness of the overall system.

For servers that do not provide a visible prepared to commit state, only *local consistency* is achieved, i.e., the synchronization of agents accesses is done by each server independently. This global synchronization criterion is reasonable for an environment of autonomous systems, where it is not expected that data dependencies exist among systems. Our concept assumes that each local server provides local serializable schedules. Therefore local consistency is trivially enforced by the server schedulers. Global consistency in this case is achieved through the enforcement of transactions control flow (transaction dependencies) and on the compensatability of tasks.

With servers that provide a visible prepared to commit state, an agent can perform a commitment protocol. In this case it is further assumed that the local concurrency control algorithm of each server is rigorous[1]. That guarantees that global serializability can be achieved with a commitment protocol[2] [3]. This allows the execution of a set of tasks in an isolated way, what supports data dependency between systems.

Recovery

When an agency recovers from a failure, new copies of the agents that were active at the agency at the time of the failure are created. Each of these agents then performs *forward recovery*, i.e., the agent recovers its state (internal data state and state of the tasks) and continues executing the agent-based transaction from where it was inter-

---

1 A scheduler is *rigorous* if no data item may be read or written until the transaction that previously wrote it either commits or aborts and no data item may be written until the transaction which previously read it either commits or aborts [3]

2 If the scheduler is not rigorous, the decentralized concurrency control algorithm provided in [2] can be used for achieving global serializability.

rupted. *Backward recovery*, i.e., the cancellation of the effects of the agent-based transaction, however, may also occur. Backward recovery is performed:

a) when a vital task aborts; or

b) upon an agent user request, when, for some reason, the user wants to interrupt the execution of the transaction.

When the agent performs backward recovery it terminates all unfinished tasks, rolling back all active and non-compensatable tasks that are in the prepared to commit state. This is done from the agency where the agent currently is, i.e., for tasks in remote agencies in the prepared to commit state, the agent and the corresponding servers communicate remotely. Afterwards, the compensatable tasks are compensated by the agent in the reverse order in which the compensated-for tasks executed. The agent, however, moves to the corresponding agencies to execute the compensating tasks. Parameters of compensating tasks are defined by the application (agent) when the compensated-for task is committed, including the definition of the agency where the compensating task must be executed[1]. Compensation tasks for tasks which belong to an ACID group are also executed with ACID properties.

Agent-based transactions enforce *semantic atomicity*, where either the transaction is executed successfully or the effects of the transaction are reversed from a *semantical point of view*[2].

Agent-based Transaction Termination

If no backward recovery occurs, an agent-based transaction executes until the goal of the transaction is achieved, i.e., the transaction achieves an *acceptable state*. The agent-based transaction is then committed (successfully executed). During commitment, the agent commits all non-compensating tasks that are in the prepared to commit state. The commitment is performed from the agency where the agent currently is.

4. An Architecture for Supporting Agent-based Transactions

The functional components that support the execution of agent-based transactions are represented in Figure 4.

An agency comprises servers accessed by applications (travel agencies, banks, etc.) and supporting DAE and DPE services. The DAE represents basic services for supporting mobile agents executions (agent code interpreters, a security service, agent mobility service, among others) [8] and also specific services for supporting agent-based transactions. In Figure 4 the transaction support specific services are represented by the *Agent Transaction Service* component, while the other services are represented

1 In general the compensating task will be executed in the same agency where the task to be compensated executed. However, our model is flexible and allows that another agency may be specified.

2 The recovery process described above represents the *general* recovery concept. For coping with agents being unavailable for long periods of time the recovery process must be described in more detail, what was not addressed in this paper.

by the *General Agent Execution Support Services* component. The services provided by the DAE are based on the services provided by the DPE. The DPE provides for transparent RPC interactions between clients and servers and a set of generic services which support distributed applications, like *naming service, persistency service,* among others.

Each server has its own *scheduler* which controls concurrent accesses to the server and makes local recovery. Servers are encapsulated in *wrapper objects*. A wrapper object transforms specific ways of interacting with a server to a common form of access known by mobile agents. Wrapper objects may provide, for example, IDL interfaces with standard transaction management primitives such as the ones defined by OMG. Furthermore, the interfaces provided by the wrapper objects must be *reliable*. Failures may not prevent an agent from knowing the result of a local transaction executed at a server. The result of a service request done by an agent at an unreliable server´s interface with no explicit transaction management primitives may be simply lost if some failure occurs after the service was executed, but before the agent received the result.

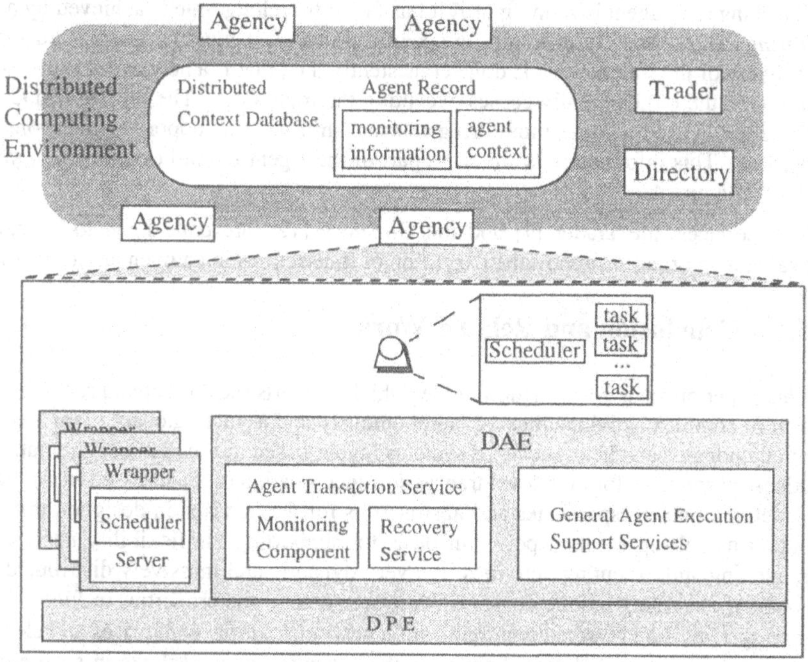

Fig. 4. Functional components that support agent-based transaction executions

The agent control flow is enforced by a *scheduler* inside the agent. The scheduling may be based on a representation of the transaction specification in terms of models like *predicate transition nets* or *rules*. The scheduler also controls the execution of a commitment protocol with servers, in order to support ACID groups (see section 3).

The *Recovery Service* component of the Agent Transaction Service is responsible for recovering agents that were executing at the agency when a failure occurs. When an agency recovers from a failure, this component controls the reactivation of the agents and sends a signal to each of them to order recovery of their activities.

Each agent performs its own recovery using information stored during its execution. Each agent stores and retrieves recovery information using the *Distributed Context Database*. Recovery information comprehends values of the agent internal data and information about the agent execution state.

Recovery information should be highly available. An agency crash, for example, may make an agent inactive and not reachable for a long time. The transaction being executed by that agent, however, should not be blocked. In this case a new agent can be created which tries to recover the activity. Towards this end, the new agent accesses the recovery information of the original agent at the context database. Therefore, recovery information is stored and made accessible in a distributed way. The information about each agent is stored in its *Agent Record*. The recovery information of an agent (represented in Figure 4 by the *agent context*) can be accessed by the new agent, by providing it with the necessary security information. The Distributed Context Database must support replication of agent records, to improve availability of recovery information, and movement of objects, to accompany the movement of the agent.

Checking if an agent is running or if it has failed for a long time is achieved by a *monitoring component*. By executing a specific protocol, it must be guaranteed that the recovery of the transactions is done consistently, i.e., that if a new agent starts executing, then the old one really ceases executing the transaction. The Distributed Context Database is used to store monitoring relevant information supporting the monitoring protocol. This information is stored as part of the Agent Record (*monitoring information,* in Figure 4).

Two services, the Trader [7] and the Directory [12], are considered to be globally available in order to support the execution of transactions in an open environment.

5. Conclusion and Related Work

This paper presents a transaction model which supports the correct and reliable execution of complex activities that can autonomously and asynchronously roam a network of autonomous and heterogeneous systems (agent-based transactions). Associated with adequate concepts for high level transaction specification (not addressed in this paper), which provide transparencies and abstractions for the transaction designer, this transaction model represents a powerful basis for supporting the flexibility necessary on modelling and executing activities in a very dynamic and massively distributed environment, including mobile devices. These are some of the properties of future distributed systems, like personal communication networks, virtual enterprises and electronic markets. The presented model supports the execution of workflows in such environments, with the advantage over traditional concepts that the workflow can move.

The transaction model presented in this text relates to many research activities. The specification of dependencies and their enforcement at runtime was considered as a basic concept for a series of research activities on providing support environments for extended transaction models and workflow systems [1][5][6]. An agent-based transaction represents a recoverable activity which should be able to continue execution irrespective of failures (forward recovery). Such ideas were considered in [9] and [11].

Our model supports local consistency maintenance, as used in S-transactions as an adequate concept for supporting transactions in an environment of autonomous systems [10]. Differently from S-transactions, our approach assumes that different servers can provide different autonomy degrees, and enforces data dependency between systems as well, with ACID groups.

This model is being developed at Technical University Berlin/GMD Fokus, in the context of the MAGNA project, funded by DeTeBerkom, a subsidiary of Deutsche Telekom AG. This project develops a mobile agent platform based on the OMG OMA and Java, as the agent programming language. The presented work may be extended in different directions, for example, by supporting for task nesting and for the execution of one transaction with *multiple* agents.

References

1. Attie, P.C., Singh, M.P., Sheth, A., Rusinkiewicz, M. Specifying and Enforcing Intertask Dependencies. *Proceedings of the 19th VLDB*. Dublin, Ireland. 1993
2. Batra, R.K., Rusinkiewicz, M. A Decentralized Deadlock-free Concurrency Control Method for Multidatabase Transactions. *Proceedings of the 12th International Conference on Distributed Computing Systems*. June, 1992.
3. Breitbart, Y., Georgakopoulos, D., Rusinkiewicz, M., Silberschatz, A. On Rigorous Transaction Scheduling. *IEEE Transactions on Software Engineering*. 1991
4. Chess, D., Grosof, B., Harrison, C., Levine, D., Parris, C., Tsudik, G. *Itinerant Agents for Mobile Computing*. Technical Report RC 20010, IBM T.J.Watson Research Center. October 17, 1995.
5. Chrysanthis, P.K., Ramamritham, K. ACTA: The SAGA Continues. In *Database Transaction Models for Advanced Applications*. A.K. Elmagarmid (editor). Morgan-Kaufmann Publishers. San Mateo, USA. 1992
6. Georgakopoulos, D, Hornick, M.F., Krychniak, P. An Environment for the Specification and Management of Extended Transactions in DOMS. *Proceedings of the 3rd International Workshop on Research Issues on Data Engineering: Interoperability in Multidatabase Systems*. April, 1993
7. ISO/IEC. *Information Technology - Open Distributed Processing - ODP Trading Function - Part 1: Specification - ISO/IEC 2nd DIS 13235-1*. June, 1996
8. Krause, S., Morais de Assis Silva, F., Magedanz, T., Popescu-Zeletin, R., Mina Falsarella, O., Arias Méndez, C.R. MAGNA - A DPE-based Platform for Mobile Agents in Electronic Service Markets. *Proceedings of ISADS'97*. Berlin. 1997
9. Pitoura, E., Bhargava, B. A Framework for Providing Consistent and Recoverable Agent-Based Access to Heterogeneous Mobile Databases. *SIGMOD Record*. Vol. 24, No. 3. September, 1995.
10. Veijalainen, J., Eliassen, F., Holtkamp, B. The S-Transaction Model. In *Database Transaction Models for Advanced Applications*. A.K. Elmagarmid (editor). Morgan-Kaufmann Publishers. San Mateo, USA. 1992
11. Wächter, H., Reuter, A. The ConTract Model. *Database Transaction Models for Advanced Applications*. A.K.Elmagarmid (editor). Morgan Kaufmann Publishers, San Mateo, USA. 1992. pp. 219-263
12. ITU-T/ISO/IEC. *Information Technology - Open Systems Interconnection - The Directory: Overview of Concepts, Models and Services (X.500)*. 1993

A Toolset for Architecture Independent, Reconfigurable, Multi-Agent Systems

Marcus J Williams and A T Bendiab

Computer Supported Concurrent Engineering Research Group, Dept of Mechanical Engineering, Design and Manufacture, Manchester Metropolitan University,
http://www.csce.mmu.ac.uk/
m.j.williams@mmu.ac.uk, a.t.bendiab@mmu.ac.uk

Abstract. Large computer systems are expected to have long lifetime. For this reason, a system should evolve as user and system demands change. Attempts have been made at this in the field of distributed systems where configuration languages have been developed for just this purpose. Multi-agent systems provide a better solution to this problem but lack the development environments that are available for traditional software. This paper presents a generic agent shell and two agent system languages, ADLe (definition language) and ARCLe (reconfiguration language) for use with this shell. It is proposed that they will provide the basis for an environment that fills this gap.
Keywords: re-configuration, multi-agent systems, agent programming.

1 Introduction

The toolset in this paper is built upon a model of agents as intelligent service providers. An agent provides services for other agents to use and for internal use to further its own goals. The services in this model are considered to be separate from the behaviour of the agent itself, so agents providing the same services are essentially equivalent until you look at their respective behaviours. This model provides a powerful architecture to build mobile agents as it allows us to abstract away from the language centred mobility of most mobile agent systems today.

As we have said, support for mobile agents currently tends to be language centred (ie languages offer migration facilities) although there are notable exceptions to this rule. Examples of this tendency can be found in Java [6], AgentTcl [7], Obliq [2] and in many other agent programming languages. This limits the languages that can be used for mobile agents. The toolset described in this paper approaches the problem from a different direction. By offering migration as a service we can program our agents/services in almost any language that can be run on the target machines.

Agent development toolsets are few and far between. Again they tend to be language centred (Telescript [19], Sumatra [1]) and so are really just development environments for that language. A few toolsets have been developed recently including the Knowbot operating system (KOS) [9] and Tacoma [11]. KOS provides a run time environment similar to the generic shell described in this paper and allows a user to submit Knowbot Programs for running on a server, reporting progress back to the user. The user programs run in a safe language that runs in a 'padded cell' environment. It is proposed that the generic toolset in this paper allows agent development (using the model of agents as intelligent service providers) that is not dependent on the language in use.

1.1 Motivation for Configuration Toolset and Agent Systems

Large computer systems are expected to have a long lifetime [15]. In the life of a computer system the services it is expected to perform will evolve as the users need evolves (and new technology is introduced). This means that a large system cannot be assumed to remain static for it operational lifetime. In a distributed system, evolutionary change is not the only change a system needs to be able to cope with. Operational changes, such as physical/logical location, component degradation, system redimensioning etc., also need to be catered for. Thus, a system must exhibit the flexibility to adapt. Sloman classifies the flexibility requirements for distributed systems as: Functional flexibility or the ability to modify the system to perform new functions; Implementation flexibility or re-implementation without change in function; Topology flexibility (physical and logical hardware and software mappings); and Time-domain flexibility which gives an indication of when a system can be changed - ie. does it need to be shutdown (static) or can changes be made on-the-fly (dynamic).

Multi-agent systems, when viewed as software components in a distributed system, can be seen to provide this flexibility: Functions within the agency can be changed by adding or altering agent's services or even agents themselves; Reimplementation of an agent or service is equally as easy as the new agent is brought on-line to activate the new services; Physical and logical topology issues are solved relatively easily due to the nature of mobile agent systems (mobile agents are aware of some logical topology and are able to react to changes within it). However, problems arise within the functional, the topological-mapping and time-domain flexibility of agencies, and these have yet to be addressed in current multi-agent systems.

An important aspect of functional flexibility within a system is that one must be able to identify the implications of a change on the system. Currently, many multi-agent systems are built using rapid prototyping methods. In a large system these methods do not allow for this sort of flexibility. A development environment and methodology of some sort would ease this problem. Mapping flexibility is needed for the mappings of agents and data onto a physical topology. In an agent environment the processors they run on are typically heterogeneous and as such this mapping is limited unless an interpreted language is used such as Java [6] or Python [18]. Migration gives this mapping a very dynamic aspect in mobile agents and control of this mapping is done at an agent level[1]. Time-domain flexibility in an agent system is good but currently there is no

[1] Global control is provided in the toolset as this is useful for debugging while developing agents - it may also prove to be useful when agents are on-line

provision for control over it. As agents migrate, systems change and so their time-domain flexibility changes. This introduces problems of reversibility and may present problems of security and robustness. By providing an environment where authorised, dynamic changes can be made and are logged automatically, we overcome these problems.

1.2 Motivation for Reconfiguration within Agent Systems

In large distributed systems, there are a wide variety of resources which require management that are often bound to a machine and/or process, eg. buffer space, processor, devices, communication channels, etc [15]. The aim of resource management is to provide allocation on demand with low delay and high throughput. Allocating and scheduling resources is usually based on hard-coded, local decisions at a machine as this makes it more autonomous.

In our model of agents, that of intelligent service providers, the services themselves are also resources. However, as resource controllers, agents are both intelligent and autonomous and as such can learn resource management strategies dynamically. Couple this with the ability to reconfigure themselves (and their resources) and you gain the ability to optimise your resource allocation how and when the demand arises. Optimal solutions can be stored and brought in to deal with the same situation at a later date. Some forms of resource bottle necks may also be solved by passing control of a resource to another process or by passing knowledge of how a resource can be provided to another component. This sort of reconfiguration demands the use of mobile agent systems.

2 Configuration

To provide flexibility, the programming of individual system components and the building of the systems from instances of these components needs to be separated. This configuration approach allows the programmer to pick up (and prevent) a lot more errors at compile time that occur in large and complex systems.

The CONIC software architecture was designed to be used for the production of large, distributed systems [13]. It reflects the need for a separation of component programming and system configuration by having a separate language for each. The CONIC programming language is based on Pascal, which has been extended to support modularity and message-passing primitives. A component in a CONIC system is an instance of a module defined in this language. Communication is done via ports.

The configuration language is used to specify both the initial system and the subsequent changes to that system. In doing so it provides for dynamic reconfiguration allowing incremental changes on a system without stopping the unaffected components. A module hierarchy can also be defined at this level to create complex module types (modules containing other modules). The configuration script sets out which modules it uses, creates instances of them on the machines they are to run on and links the communication ports together. The modules specified in the component language are "plugged" together at these ports to build the system with the required behaviour.

The Darwin [12] structuring language, a derivative of CONIC's configuration language, generalises CONIC's approach by being largely independent of the language used to program processes. Primarily, the main advantage over CONIC that Darwin has is its ability to express dynamically changing (evolving) process structures (hence its name).

To ensure portability, processes that are structured using Darwin are written in a subset of a traditional language such as C, Modula-2/3 or Pascal. This subset is extended to include message passing capabilities. The Darwin language itself is kept independent of the precise semantics of the communication facilities.

3 Overview

Coupled with a solution that provides the flexibility required in large systems (described above), these ideas would provide a powerful development environment for agent-based systems. In order to this we must be able to:

1. specify the atomically executable tasks (that solve particular subproblems);
2. specify services in terms of their components tasks;
3. specify agents in terms of the services they provide and their specific behaviour;
4. describe an agency in terms of the agents that make it up;
5. describe a system in terms of the agencies contained within it;
6. provide a generic shell to execute these descriptions within;
7. provide a means to interoperate with legacy systems (ones that do not normally interact with one another).

To this end, we are investigating a agent-based solution to the problem of developing flexible, robust multi-agent systems. Currently, the toolset provides:

- *Generic Agent Shell* - This module provides the base operations an agent (in this system) can provide. They include: an extended contract-net negotiation protocol, a simple communications language, a service executor/scheduler, a configuration language, an internal monitor process, a security module, and a reasoner. The shell also allows any module to be replaced so that other reasoning paradigms/scheduling methods can be used at a later date.
- *Agent Definition Language (ADLe)* - Agents are viewed as intelligent service providers. Using ADLe we define agents in terms of the services they provide. These services are then defined in terms of the atomically executable tasks that make them up. These tasks are described in an interpreted language.
- *Agent (Re-)Configuration Language (ARCLe)* - This script based language instantiates agents defined in ADLe earlier with a behaviour and binds them to their respective machines/resources. This configuration is performed at runtime, meaning that agents can reconfigure themselves on demand. The

configuration language also provides a means to update tasks, services and agent configurations interactively at run-time (both programmatically and interactively). A generic shell is wrapped around the instantiation providing the agent with negotiation and communication skills.
- *Communication wrappers* - The agent shell (and therefore agent itself) is unaware of the communication method it is using. Currently wrappers have been developed that allow the agent to communicate using sockets, CORBA [8] or via WWW Servers. It is up to the developer to choose which one is used by their agent. The CORBA based wrapper is implemented on top of Prism Technology's OpenBase [17], a CORBA compliant distributed object platform.

This paper introduces the toolset and then goes on to describe example applications that are under development using the shell.

4 Agent Definition Language (ADLe)

At the definition level, agents are viewed as service providers and/or consumers. Agents are therefore defined in terms of the services they provide (see EBNF below). The services, in turn, are defined in terms of the tasks or services required to perform them. If a service uses a task then it will be local to that agent; if it uses a service then it will tend to be a service provided by another agent.

```
<agent-definition> ::=
   "agent" <agent-defn-name> "{"
      [ "provides"
           { <service-description> ";" }* ]
      [ "uses"
           { <service-description> ";" }* ]
      [ "requires"
           { <resource-description> ";" }* ]
   "}"
<service-description> ::=
   "service" [ "(" ["NONNEGOTIABLE"]
                   ["PUBLIC"|"PRIVATE"]
                   ["ONE"|"MANY"] ")"] <service-name>
```

Thus, an agent is defined by listing the services it will potentially *provide* or *use* and by listing all resources it *requires*. Services are listed in the form of their headers (much like C functions are in a header file). Literals following the 'service' keyword define the behaviour of the service. NONNEGOTIABLE means that an agent will provide this service at all times (ie it is not negotiable). The PUBLIC and PRIVATE attributes tell the service executor whether the service is a local service for internal use. ONE and MANY defines whether the service can be executed concurrently with other services. The service definition defaults to being negotiable, public and non-concurrent.

The description language is similar to that of ADEPT's [10] service definition language. Services are described as a set of tasks the agent has to perform in order to satisfy the request. A task is atomically executable from the point of view of the agent executing it.

```
<service-definition> ::=
   <service-description> "{"
      <execution-model> "(" <task-list> [ "," <task-list> ]
      ")" ";" "}"
<task-list> ::=
   { <execution-model> "(" <task-list> [ "," <task-list> ] ")" }
   | <task-name>
<execution-model> ::=
   "PAR" | "SEQ" | "TRY"
```

The service definition is interpreted by the service executor when a request for that service comes in (if it is agreed upon). It is executed as a transaction that fails if any of the tasks within it fail. Within the service there are multiple levels of transactions allowing the SEQ, PAR and TRY statements to also be transactional. Nested PAR, SEQ and TRY commands allow a degree of control over how the tasks will be executed. PAR executes a set of tasks in parallel and SEQ does it in sequence. The TRY statement tries each task in turn until one succeeds at which point it exits successfully. If all the tasks within the statement fail then the whole TRY fails and so the transaction/service itself fails.

Roll-back of transactions relies on the persistency model employed by the service executor. First, a local copy of the agents knowledge base (KB) is made. This is passed to the service executor. All global variables for a service are stored in this copy. If a service succeeds this knowledge base is then committed to the main store of the agent. Further local copies of the KB are made for each task so that as a task succeeds in executing, so its KB can be committed to the overall local copy. Currently a simple truth maintenance system is employed to maintain the consistency of the KB.

Tasks are currently defined in Python, an object-oriented, interpreted language. An interface between Python and the C++ shell is provided by the use of the Python API, embedding the Python executor in the shell.

5 Agent (Re-)Configuration Language (ARCLe)

After the definition level, we have a set of agent 'classes' available to instantiate. The reasoning behind this is that agents that provide the same services should have the same agent definition. It is only upon instantiation, when they are given a behaviour that they will differ. This is not enforced by the toolset which allows equivalent classes to coexist provided they have different names. It is the authors opinion, however, that this serves only to confuse in large systems.

There are two different ways the user can configure the system, at compile time or at run time. At compile time the initial system configuration is placed in a script that starts the system up. At run time the user connects to a local configuration manager and types configuration commands interactively. At run time, agents are also given the ability to configure themselves. This allows them to be much more adaptable to their environment.

The commands available to the user are:

- *inst* - This creates an instantiation of an agent class at a particular machine (that has to be running a configuration manager as well). It also tells the configuration manager what file it should pick up the behavioural description from.
- *form group* - This groups a set of agents. This forms a secure group that only accepts reconfiguration commands from within itself.
- *form composite* - This also groups a set of agents. However, where it differs from the *form group* command is that externally, the group appears to be a single agent.
- *update* - This allows a service/task/behaviour on an agent to be updated 'on-the-fly'. The update occurs immediately, but any outstanding contracts using the previous service/task will be honoured using the old version.
- *merge* - This command merges two agents. Currently this is implemented using a version of the *form composite* command.
- *migrate* - The specified agent is moved to a new machine (ie. 'jumps' to a different position)
- *pass* - This allows knowledge or service/task definitions to be passed between agents. An argument specifies whether the information is to be removed or not from the source. When the user is controlling the configuration process it allows the addition of new services to agents.
- *authorise* - This command provides access to the authorisation database within an agent.
- *set* - This command gives access to various debugging controls on agents in the system (not described here).

The behaviour of an agent is described within the reasoner module of the agent. Currently this is implemented in a language based on OPS5 [5]. This can, for instance, give an agent goals that it must pursue or could simply kick a set of services into action.

6 Generic Agent Shell (GAS)

The main considerations when designing the shell were that it:

- was both simple and extensible;
- was independent of the platform it was running on;
- provided a means to execute requests for services defined;
- behaved in the manner described by the behaviour definition;
- offered a minimum set of agent 'modules' that an instantiation could use;

- the module interface would be well defined so that extension modules were easy to introduce.

Further more, agents should not have to be aware of the physical location of other agents or services (although should be able to access this information if it becomes important). This means agents communicate via aliases which reduces the local dependencies of both agents and their services. Agents 'jump' to a logical address where services/resources exist that they wish to use locally[2].

The shell contains seven modules dedicated to communication, services, reasoning, negotiation, internal monitoring, security and debugging. These modules execute concurrently as threads. A message comes in to the communication module and if it is recognised as a module command, is forwarded to the relevant module. If not, it is assumed to be a service request and is sent to the service module. This is how a user extends the set of commands an agent can process. If the user wants an agent to understand KQML [4] all they have to do is implement the KQML performatives as non-negotiable services provided by the agent (see service module section).

The following modules are fully implemented:

- *Communication Module* - Provides the method by which an agent can send a message to another agent. It also provides commands to forward a message to a specified agent and map an agents alias to a physical location. When sending a message, if the alias is known, the module can deal with it itself. However, if it is unknown, it forwards the message to a name server to deal with it. The name server will notify the agent of the alias/location mapping after it has sent the message on its behalf. Wrappers are provided for CORBA, Web and socket-based agents. An agent is unaware of the wrapper it is using. This means socket or Web based agents that migrate onto a CORBA architecture will become CORBA based agents (and vice versa). The wrapper deals with any complications that arise in the transfer. Thus, a programmer no longer has to worry about the communication issues.
- *Service Module* - This module is made up of three separate components. Firstly, an executor which controls the execution of services as they are needed. Secondly, a scheduler that works out what order to execute services in and thirdly a timer facility that signals the scheduler if services need to be performed. Associated with this module are a definition repository, where the agents service and task description are kept, and a contract database that keeps track of outstanding contracts. This module offers commands to set up contracts and subscriptions for services. It uses the security module to work out authorisation details when it is executing a service. We can extend the command set offered by the agent through the use of services defined in the service repository.
- *Reasoning Module* - This module currently contains an OPS5 style (symbolic) reasoning engine to provide the run time behaviour of the agent. The

[2] In this system the logical address corresponds to the name of the agent providing the migration service.

OPS5 language has been extended to support execution of services, message sending and fairly complex computations (using Python). To reduce conflicts within the ruleset and increase efficiency, context switching has also been introduced. A special context reserved for initialisation exists to perform start-up routines.

- *Negotiation Module* - The negotiation facilities provided in this module extend upon the contract net protocol (CNP) [16]. The CNP is essentially a one-shot protocol executing the offer, bid, accept stages once only. Extensions [14, 3] that include making the protocol an incremental cycle have increased the CNP's usefulness. An agent sends out an offer to which multiple agents reply with their bids. Some are rejected out right but the rest are refined using the offer/bid process again and again until a contract has been settled. The extensions proposed in this module allow an agent to reject and accept bids with qualifications. These qualification provide hints to the bidder of what it would need to change for the bid to be accepted. The bidder can then bid again taking these into account. Also some temporal constraints have been introduced so that the agents can limit how long the negotiation process takes. The negotiation uses generic factors such as time, cost and quality within the bidding process. If a user wishes to change this, a facility to introduce a 'service distance function' is provided that must return a score for a bid (higher scores winning).

The following modules are under development:

- *Internal Monitor Module* - As the agent is running, the monitor process builds a profile of service, task and knowledge use. When this profile becomes stable the agent will make decisions based on heuristics on whether or not to 'palm-off' services/knowledge to other agents so that it becomes less loaded (and so more efficient). Options that are available to it include duplication of services/knowledge onto another agent (which can be on another machine), starting up another agent that only provides those services and physically passing the services to another agent. An agency can therefore load balance itself upon demand using this module. Currently this module does not attempt any pre-emtive action. However it is planned that the agent should store previous profiles so that decisions based on these, and the current profile can be made before over-loading occurs.
- *Authorisation Module* - The module uses public key methods to provide each agent with a unique signature that it uses to identify itself. This signature is very unlikely to be forged and so is used to verify an agents authorisation to access services on another agent. This module maintains a security database containing every agent that it deals with. Each agent has an associated clearance/trust level that defines what it can do. The agent can have as many levels of trust as it wants and allows for as fine or course granularity of access definition as it needs (down to a command by command level). This is useful when an agent has been given a task/service from another that it does not trust. Malicious hosts are dealt with in a similar manner. This is because in order to migrate to a host machine, an agent has to trust the

migratory service provider (which is an agent). Because of this a host has a trust level that is equal to that of the service providing agent.

– *Debugging Module* - This module allows the agent to log its actions. Each agent has a trace level that determines what actions will be logged. The debugging commands allow the trace level to be set and messages to be sent to the trace files. The module also provides status commands so that another agent can query its status (these tend only to be used by the configuration manager).

7 Implementation of Configuration Manager

At first the configuration manager was to be implemented as a program separate to the generic shell. However, it was soon realised that by implementing it on top of the shell itself (as an agent) we would gain a much more flexible manager. Essentially, the configuration commands can be seen as services the manager agent provides. We then have full control over what agents are allowed to (re-)configure. Equally we can stop certain agents jumping (migrating) onto or off certain machines. Other interesting facilities include the ability of agents to subscribe to configuration services and for an agent to negotiate for these facilities. Subscription can work for an agent in two ways: firstly we can control periods over which certain agents are (or are not) allowed access to configuration commands; secondly, agents that subscribe to an update service (for instance) can all be updated at the same time when a single configuration command is executed. Negotiation allows an agent to 'buy' its way onto a machine and hence have access to its resources.

By implementing this on top of the shell, we only have to define the configuration services. Everything else is inherited from the shell. The manager also takes advantage of the behavioural facility of the shell. It watches over the agents on its machine so that if one goes down it can bring it back up again (this is relatively simple using the persistency model that is employed in the agents). Its goals are simply to keep agents in its charge running.

8 Implementation of Name Server

Any agent can run as a name server as the facilities a name server would provide are simply registration services. The generic shell provides this and also the facility for forwarding of messages. For this reason, any agent within an agency can be designated a name server. However, it sometimes makes it easier to have a separate name server as we can then extend the services it provides. To implement one, a user just starts a stub shell up (ie one with no services/behaviour). It is then a dedicated name server.

The registry information is stored in a hash indexed list so there are few overheads even for large lists. The name server will not become a bottle neck in large systems because of the way the name lookup service is implemented. If an agent,

A, wants to send a message to agent, B, then if A knows where B is located (ie. it is in agent A's name database) it transmits the message itself using whatever communication wrapper it is provided with. If, however the name lookup returns a null, then agent A forwards the message via a nominated name server. This name server forwards the message and returns the lookup information for agent B to agent A. Gradually, each agent builds up a name database of agents that it uses frequently and the name server is used less frequently.

9 Conclusions

As was said in the introduction, mobility tends to be supported within an agent language in current mobile agent systems. The toolset described attempts to remove this dependence by viewing agents as service providers and migration as a service. The toolset still needs work in this area. At the moment it assumes that the agent and its services are going to be written in Python. However, there is no reason why it cant be extended to any interpreted language. This would be relatively easy as the service definition language has been kept language independent and there is a well defined interface to the services themselves.

The generic agent shell provides a minimal set of modules for implementing an agent. By using this shell an agent programmer can concentrate on programming his or her agent rather than being tied down to problems of communication/negotiation etc. This is not to say that they do not have control over these issues, but that they do not have to worry about them if it is not necessary for the implementation. Agent characteristics, such as mobility, negotiation etc are inherited from the shell and so do not have to be programmed by the user. The shell is very easily extended via the use of services and the behavioural language.

The power behind the toolset described in this paper, is in the dynamic configuration. Both agents and users can re-configure the system to as fine a granularity as they want (or are authorised to). The system as a whole becomes extremely adaptable to change. Where the shell differs from KOS and other toolsets is that it offers this reconfigurable environment. Everything from the services, tasks and knowledge it provides, to the 'padding' on the cell is reconfigurable *dynamically*.

10 Acknowledgements

This work is financed by the EPSRC in collaboration with Prism Technologies Ltd, Gateshead.

References

1. A. Acharya, M. Ranganathan, and J. Saltz. Distributed resource monitors for mobile objects. In *Fifth IEEE International Workshop on Object Orientation in Operating Systems*, Oct 1996.

2. L. Cardelli. Obliq: A language with distributed scope. Technical Report 122, Digital Equipment Corporation, Systems Research Center, 1994.
3. S.E. Conry, K. Kuwabara, V.R. Lesser, and R.A. Meyer. Multistage negotiation in distributed constraint satisfaction. *IEEE Transactions on Systems, Man, and Cybernetics*, Dec 1991.
4. T. Finin, J. Weber, G. Wiederhold, and M. Genesereth. Draft specification of the kqml agent-communication language. Technical report, DARPA Knowledge Sharing Initiative External Interfaces Working Group, June 1993.
5. C.L. Forgy. Ops5 user manual. Technical report, Carnegie Mellon University, Pittsburgh, July 1981. CMU-CS-81-135.
6. J. Gosling and H. McGilton. The java language environment: A white paper. Sun Microsystems, 1995.
7. R.S. Gray. Agent tcl: A transportable agent system. In J. Mayfield and T. Finin, editors, *CIKM Workshop on Intelligent Information Agents, Fourth International Conference on Information and Knowledge Management*, Baltimore, Maryland, Dec 1995.
8. Object Management Group. The common object request broker: Architecture and specification revision 2.0. Technical report, July 1995.
9. J. Hylton, K. Manheimer, F.L. Drake Jr, B. Warsaw, R. Masse, and G. van Rossum. Knowbot programming: System support for mobile agents. In *Fifth IEEE International Workshop on Object Orientation in Operating Systems*, Oct 1996.
10. N. R. Jennings, P. Faratin, M. J. Johnson, P. O'Brien, and M. E. Wiegand. Using intelligent agents to manage business processes. In *First International Conference on The Practical Application of Intelligent Agents and Multi-Agent Technology*, London, UK, 1996.
11. D. Johansen, R. van Renesse, and F.B. Schneider. Operating system support for mobile agents. In *Fifth IEEE Workshop on Hot Topics in Operating Systems*, May 1994.
12. J. Kramer, J. Magee, M. Sloman, and N. Dulay. Configuring object-based distributed programs in rex. *IEE Software Engineering Journal*, 7(2):139–149, Mar 1992.
13. J. Magee, J. Kramer, and M. Sloman. Constructing distributed systems in conic. *IEEE Transactions on Software Engineering*, 15(6), 1989.
14. T. Sandholm and V. Lesser. Issues in automated negotiation and electronic commerce: Extending the contract net framework. In *First International Conference on Multiagent Systems*, pages 328–335, San Fransisco, 1995.
15. M. Sloman and J. Kramer. *Distributed Systems and Computer Networks*. Prentice Hall International, London, 1987.
16. R.G. Smith. The contract net protocol:high-level communication and control in a distributed problem solver. *IEEE Transactions on Computing*, 12(29):1104–1113, 1980.
17. Prism Technologies. Openbase technical overview, 1996.
18. G. van Rossum. Python tutorial. Technical report, Centrum voor Wiskunde en Informatica, Amsterdam, May 1995. Technical Report CS R9526.
19. J.E. White. Telescript technology:mobile agents. General Magic. Whitepaper 4.

Author Index

Lecture Notes in Computer Science

For information about Vols. 1–1141

please contact your bookseller or Springer-Verlag

Vol. 1142: R.W. Hartenstein, M. Glesner (Eds.), Field-Programmable Logic. Proceedings, 1996. X, 432 pages. 1996.

Vol. 1143: T.C. Fogarty (Ed.), Evolutionary Computing. Proceedings, 1996. VIII, 305 pages. 1996.

Vol. 1144: J. Ponce, A. Zisserman, M. Hebert (Eds.), Object Representation in Computer Vision. Proceedings, 1996. VIII, 403 pages. 1996.

Vol. 1145: R. Cousot, D.A. Schmidt (Eds.), Static Analysis. Proceedings, 1996. IX, 389 pages. 1996.

Vol. 1146: E. Bertino, H. Kurth, G. Martella, E. Montolivo (Eds.), Computer Security – ESORICS 96. Proceedings, 1996. X, 365 pages. 1996.

Vol. 1147: L. Miclet, C. de la Higuera (Eds.), Grammatical Inference: Learning Syntax from Sentences. Proceedings, 1996. VIII, 327 pages. 1996. (Subseries LNAI).

Vol. 1148: M.C. Lin, D. Manocha (Eds.), Applied Computational Geometry. Proceedings, 1996. VIII, 223 pages. 1996.

Vol. 1149: C. Montangero (Ed.), Software Process Technology. Proceedings, 1996. IX, 291 pages. 1996.

Vol. 1150: A. Hlawiczka, J.G. Silva, L. Simoncini (Eds.), Dependable Computing – EDCC-2. Proceedings, 1996. XVI, 440 pages. 1996.

Vol. 1151: Ö. Babaoğlu, K. Marzullo (Eds.), Distributed Algorithms. Proceedings, 1996. VIII, 381 pages. 1996.

Vol. 1152: T. Furuhashi, Y. Uchikawa (Eds.), Fuzzy Logic, Neural Networks, and Evolutionary Computation. Proceedings, 1995. VIII, 243 pages. 1996. (Subseries LNAI).

Vol. 1153: E. Burke, P. Ross (Eds.), Practice and Theory of Automated Timetabling. Proceedings, 1995. XIII, 381 pages. 1996.

Vol. 1154: D. Pedreschi, C. Zaniolo (Eds.), Logic in Databases. Proceedings, 1996. X, 497 pages. 1996.

Vol. 1155: J. Roberts, U. Mocci, J. Virtamo (Eds.), Broadbank Network Teletraffic. XXII, 584 pages. 1996.

Vol. 1156: A. Bode, J. Dongarra, T. Ludwig, V. Sunderam (Eds.), Parallel Virtual Machine – EuroPVM '96. Proceedings, 1996. XIV, 362 pages. 1996.

Vol. 1157: B. Thalheim (Ed.), Conceptual Modeling – ER '96. Proceedings, 1996. XII, 489 pages. 1996.

Vol. 1158: S. Berardi, M. Coppo (Eds.), Types for Proofs and Programs. Proceedings, 1995. X, 296 pages. 1996.

Vol. 1159: D.L. Borges, C.A.A. Kaestner (Eds.), Advances in Artificial Intelligence. Proceedings, 1996. XI, 243 pages. (Subseries LNAI).

Vol. 1160: S. Arikawa, A.K. Sharma (Eds.), Algorithmic Learning Theory. Proceedings, 1996. XVII, 337 pages. 1996. (Subseries LNAI).

Vol. 1161: O. Spaniol, C. Linnhoff-Popien, B. Meyer (Eds.), Trends in Distributed Systems. Proceedings, 1996. VIII, 289 pages. 1996.

Vol. 1162: D.G. Feitelson, L. Rudolph (Eds.), Job Scheduling Strategies for Parallel Processing. Proceedings, 1996. VIII, 291 pages. 1996.

Vol. 1163: K. Kim, T. Matsumoto (Eds.), Advances in Cryptology – ASIACRYPT '96. Proceedings, 1996. XII, 395 pages. 1996.

Vol. 1164: K. Berquist, A. Berquist (Eds.), Managing Information Highways. XIV, 417 pages. 1996.

Vol. 1165: J.-R. Abrial, E. Börger, H. Langmaack (Eds.), Formal Methods for Industrial Applications. VIII, 511 pages. 1996.

Vol. 1166: M. Srivas, A. Camilleri (Eds.), Formal Methods in Computer-Aided Design. Proceedings, 1996. IX, 470 pages. 1996.

Vol. 1167: I. Sommerville (Ed.), Software Configuration Management. VII, 291 pages. 1996.

Vol. 1168: I. Smith, B. Faltings (Eds.), Advances in Case-Based Reasoning. Proceedings, 1996. IX, 531 pages. 1996. (Subseries LNAI).

Vol. 1169: M. Broy, S. Merz, K. Spies (Eds.), Formal Systems Specification. XXIII, 541 pages. 1996.

Vol. 1170: M. Nagl (Ed.), Building Tightly Integrated Software Development Environments: The IPSEN Approach. IX, 709 pages. 1996.

Vol. 1171: A. Franz, Automatic Ambiguity Resolution in Natural Language Processing. XIX, 155 pages. 1996. (Subseries LNAI).

Vol. 1172: J. Pieprzyk, J. Seberry (Eds.), Information Security and Privacy. Proceedings, 1996. IX, 333 pages. 1996.

Vol. 1173: W. Rucklidge, Efficient Visual Recognition Using the Hausdorff Distance. XIII, 178 pages. 1996.

Vol. 1174: R. Anderson (Ed.), Information Hiding. Proceedings, 1996. VIII, 351 pages. 1996.

Vol. 1175: K.G. Jeffery, J. Král, M. Bartošek (Eds.), SOFSEM'96: Theory and Practice of Informatics. Proceedings, 1996. XII, 491 pages. 1996.

Vol. 1176: S. Miguet, A. Montanvert, S. Ubéda (Eds.), Discrete Geometry for Computer Imagery. Proceedings, 1996. XI, 349 pages. 1996.

Vol. 1177: J.P. Müller, The Design of Intelligent Agents. XV, 227 pages. 1996. (Subseries LNAI).

Vol. 1178: T. Asano, Y. Igarashi, H. Nagamochi, S. Miyano, S. Suri (Eds.), Algorithms and Computation. Proceedings, 1996. X, 448 pages. 1996.

Vol. 1179: J. Jaffar, R.H.C. Yap (Eds.), Concurrency and Parallelism, Programming, Networking, and Security. Proceedings, 1996. XIII, 394 pages. 1996.

Vol. 1180: V. Chandru, V. Vinay (Eds.), Foundations of Software Technology and Theoretical Computer Science. Proceedings, 1996. XI, 387 pages. 1996.

Vol. 1181: D. Bjørner, M. Broy, I.V. Pottosin (Eds.), Perspectives of System Informatics. Proceedings, 1996. XVII, 447 pages. 1996.

Vol. 1182: W. Hasan, Optimization of SQL Queries for Parallel Machines. XVIII, 133 pages. 1996.

Vol. 1183: A. Wierse, G.G. Grinstein, U. Lang (Eds.), Database Issues for Data Visualization. Proceedings, 1995. XIV, 219 pages. 1996.

Vol. 1184: J. Waśniewski, J. Dongarra, K. Madsen, D. Olesen (Eds.), Applied Parallel Computing. Proceedings, 1996. XIII, 722 pages. 1996.

Vol. 1185: G. Ventre, J. Domingo-Pascual, A. Danthine (Eds.), Multimedia Telecommunications and Applications. Proceedings, 1996. XII, 267 pages. 1996.

Vol. 1186: F. Afrati, P. Kolaitis (Eds.), Database Theory - ICDT'97. Proceedings, 1997. XIII, 477 pages. 1997.

Vol. 1187: K. Schlechta, Nonmonotonic Logics. IX, 243 pages. 1997. (Subseries LNAI).

Vol. 1188: T. Martin, A.L. Ralescu (Eds.), Fuzzy Logic in Artificial Intelligence. Proceedings, 1995. VIII, 272 pages. 1997. (Subseries LNAI).

Vol. 1189: M. Lomas (Ed.), Security Protocols. Proceedings, 1996. VIII, 203 pages. 1997.

Vol. 1190: S. North (Ed.), Graph Drawing. Proceedings, 1996. XI, 409 pages. 1997.

Vol. 1191: V. Gaede, A. Brodsky, O. Günther, D. Srivastava, V. Vianu, M. Wallace (Eds.), Constraint Databases and Applications. Proceedings, 1996. X, 345 pages. 1996.

Vol. 1192: M. Dam (Ed.), Analysis and Verification of Multiple-Agent Languages. Proceedings, 1996. VIII, 435 pages. 1997.

Vol. 1193: J.P. Müller, M.J. Wooldridge, N.R. Jennings (Eds.), Intelligent Agents III. XV, 401 pages. 1997. (Subseries LNAI).

Vol. 1194: M. Sipper, Evolution of Parallel Cellular Machines. XIII, 199 pages. 1997.

Vol. 1195: R. Trappl, P. Petta (Eds.), Creating Personalities for Synthetic Actors. VII, 251 pages. 1997. (Subseries LNAI).

Vol. 1196: L. Vulkov, J. Waśniewski, P. Yalamov (Eds.), Numerical Analysis and Its Applications. Proceedings, 1996. XIII, 608 pages. 1997.

Vol. 1197: F. d'Amore, P.G. Franciosa, A. Marchetti-Spaccamela (Eds.), Graph-Theoretic Concepts in Computer Science. Proceedings, 1996. XI, 410 pages. 1997.

Vol. 1198: H.S. Nwana, N. Azarmi (Eds.), Software Agents and Soft Computing: Towards Enhancing Machine Intelligence. XIV, 298 pages. 1997. (Subseries LNAI).

Vol. 1199: D.K. Panda, C.B. Stunkel (Eds.), Communication and Architectural Support for Network-Based Parallel Computing. Proceedings, 1997. X, 269 pages. 1997.

Vol. 1200: R. Reischuk, M. Morvan (Eds.), STACS 97. Proceedings, 1997. XIII, 614 pages. 1997.

Vol. 1201: O. Maler (Ed.), Hybrid and Real-Time Systems. Proceedings, 1997. IX, 417 pages. 1997.

Vol. 1202: P. Kandzia, M. Klusch (Eds.), Cooperative Information Agents. Proceedings, 1997. IX, 287 pages. 1997. (Subseries LNAI).

Vol. 1203: G. Bongiovanni, D.P. Bovet, G. Di Battista (Eds.), Algorithms and Complexity. Proceedings, 1997. VIII, 311 pages. 1997.

Vol. 1204: H. Mössenböck (Ed.), Modular Programming Languages. Proceedings, 1997. X, 379 pages. 1997.

Vol. 1205: J. Troccaz, E. Grimson, R. Mösges (Eds.), CVRMed-MRCAS'97. Proceedings, 1997. XIX, 834 pages. 1997.

Vol. 1206: J. Bigün, G. Chollet, G. Borgefors (Eds.), Audio- and Video-based Biometric Person Authentication. Proceedings, 1997. XII, 450 pages. 1997.

Vol. 1207: J. Gallagher (Ed.), Logic Program Synthesis and Transformation. Proceedings, 1996. VII, 325 pages. 1997.

Vol. 1208: S. Ben-David (Ed.), Computational Learning Theory. Proceedings, 1997. VIII, 331 pages. 1997. (Subseries LNAI).

Vol. 1209: L. Cavedon, A. Rao, W. Wobcke (Eds.), Intelligent Agent Systems. Proceedings, 1996. IX, 188 pages. 1997. (Subseries LNAI).

Vol. 1210: P. de Groote, J.R. Hindley (Eds.), Typed Lambda Calculi and Applications. Proceedings, 1997. VIII, 405 pages. 1997.

Vol. 1211: E. Keravnou, C. Garbay, R. Baud, J. Wyatt (Eds.), Artificial Intelligence in Medicine. Proceedings, 1997. XIII, 526 pages. 1997. (Subseries LNAI).

Vol. 1212: J. P. Bowen, M.G. Hinchey, D. Till (Eds.), ZUM '97: The Z Formal Specification Notation. Proceedings, 1997. X, 435 pages. 1997.

Vol. 1213: P. J. Angeline, R. G. Reynolds, J. R. McDonnell, R. Eberhart (Eds.), Evolutionary Programming. Proceedings, 1997. X, 457 pages. 1997.

Vol. 1214: M. Bidoit, M. Dauchet (Eds.), TAPSOFT '97: Theory and Practice of Software Development. Proceedings, 1997. XV, 884 pages. 1997.

Vol. 1215: J. M. L. M. Palma, J. Dongarra (Eds.), Vector and Parallel Processing – VECPAR'96. Proceedings, 1996. XI, 471 pages. 1997.

Vol. 1216: J. Dix, L. Moniz Pereira, T.C. Przymusinski (Eds.), Non-Monotonic Extensions of Logic Programming. Proceedings, 1996. XI, 224 pages. 1997. (Subseries LNAI).

Vol. 1217: E. Brinksma (Ed.), Tools and Algorithms for the Construction and Analysis of Systems. Proceedings, 1997. X, 433 pages. 1997.

Vol. 1218: G. Păun, A. Salomaa (Eds.), New Trends in Formal Languages. IX, 465 pages. 1997.

Vol. 1219: K. Rothermel, R. Popescu-Zeletin (Eds.), Mobile Agents. Proceedings, 1997. VIII, 223 pages. 1997.

Vol. 1220: P. Brezany, Input/Output Intensive Massively Parallel Computing. XIV, 288 pages. 1997.